Mike Ross is a faithful pastor, ~~a~~ a dear friend. I am delighted to commend this guidebook through the Psalms, having already benefitted from its ministry. The Reformers not only thought we ought to sing the Psalms, they thought that we ought to have the Psalms as the very core of a well-rounded spiritual experience. Sadly, in the church today, at least here in the west, the Psalms have been largely lost, and, until we recover them, we will be imbalanced, undernourished and unprepared for the fight of faith. The Psalms give us the divine expression of Christian experience of life in a fallen world, on the way to the age to come. Read, drink deeply and grow.

J. Ligon Duncan III
Senior Minister, First Presbyterian Church, Jackson, Mississippi
President, Alliance of Confessing Evangelicals
Chairman, Council on Biblical Manhood and Womanhood

The Psalms, Calvin said, are an anatomy of all the parts of the soul. Christians who want to grow in grace and maturity can't get enough of them. They are as needful as food and drink. Without them, Christians develop distorted views on the nature of what they can expect as pilgrims on their way to heaven. Mike Ross, a friend and colleague, provides the sure touch of a seasoned pastor, an insightful biblical scholar and a watchful shepherd as he takes us through these songs of Zion. And doxology is what you can expect to give as you read these pages. Get ready to burst into song!

Derek Thomas
John E. Richards Professor of Systematic and Practical Theology,
Reformed Theological Seminary, Jackson, Mississippi

Over the past fourteen years it has been my privilege to hear Mike Ross preach hundreds of sermons, including many on the Psalms. As I have learned, and as this book testifies, he is a faithful servant of God, and a trustworthy expositor of Holy Scripture. Choice selections from the work of others enrich his studies. He consistently imparts the Word to the depths of the heart (see Ps. 119:10-11): that is, his preaching informs the mind, stirs the emotions, and moves the will. I believe that reading this book will have this threefold effect on you; and that you will have cause to grow in praise and love for the Holy Trinity celebrated here.

Knox Chamblin
Professor of New Testament, Emeritus,
Reformed Theological Seminary, Jackson, Mississippi

Most Christians today would echo the early Disciples request to Jesus, 'Lord, teach us to pray'. What better way for us to learn than to use the prayer and praise book of the Bible, the book of Psalms, the book that Jesus himself used? Mike Ross, an experienced Presbyterian pastor, helps us use the psalms in our daily prayer and praise. He points us to a balanced, biblical spirituality which will help us draw closer to Christ. Excellent.

David A. Robertson
Minister, St Peter's Free Church, Dundee, Scotland

# THE
# LIGHT
# OF THE
# PSALMS

*Deepening your faith with every Psalm*

Michael F. Ross

**CHRISTIAN FOCUS**

## Dedication

Archie Parrish

Pastor, Evangelist, Revival Man, Prayer Warrior, Churchman, Mentor, Friend, Lover of the Psalms and of Christ.

*"Mark the blameless and behold the upright,*
*for there is a future for the man of peace"* (Ps. 37:37).

Unless otherwise noted all scripture quotations from The Holy Bible, English Standard Version Copyright © 2001 by Crossway Bibles, a division of Good News Publishers. Used by permission. All Rights Reserved.

© Michael F. Ross, 2006

ISBN 1-84550-150-0
ISBN 978-1-84550-150-1

10 9 8 7 6 5 4 3 2 1

Published in 2006
by
Christian Focus Publications Ltd.,
Geanies House, Fearn, Tain,
Ross-shire, IV20 1TW, Scotland
www.christianfocus.com

Cover design by Moose77.com

Printed and bound by J. H. Haynes & Co. Ltd., Sparkford

# Contents

# ACKNOWLEDGMENTS

This book began back in 2001 when Archie Parrish and I discussed the possibility of forty days of prayer for the Presbyterian Church in America, prior to our annual general assembly. With Archie's encouragement and influence, Jim Bland of Mission to North America and Charles Dunahoo of Christian Education and Publications, both of the PCA, approved and funded the project. The plan soon became fifty days of prayer, beginning each year on America's National Day of Prayer (first Thursday in May) and ending at the close of the general assembly.

In 2002, 2003, and 2004, we published the Psalter devotions; fifty psalms per year. Thanks to Archie, Jim, and Charles, and to their wonderful staff at MNA and CEP in publishing these prayer guides.

My gratitude goes to Fred Marsh of MNA. Fred has patiently been my principal editor. Fred's sensitivity to various cultures and groups, his breadth of vision for the Church, and his extremely calm demeanor have served this project and me well. I also want to thank my intern, Brent Sadler, who has prepared the final edit for publication – and this in the midst of having a first child, graduating from seminary, and preparing for a new ministry in Texas!

I am indebted to Phil Ryken of the Tenth Presbyterian Church in Philadelphia and J. Ligon Duncan of the First Presbyterian Church in Jackson. These two friends, brothers, and colleagues, have been gracious enough to offer publishing advice and to provide both forward and epilogue, respectively, for the book. Busy as these two PCA leaders are, they made time in their schedule and room in their lives for me and this book.

I am forever indebted to Steve Lanier. It was he who first contacted Willie Mackenzie at Christian Focus Publishers and suggested they publish both my dissertation on preaching (*Preaching for Revitalization*: Christian Focus, 2005) and these Psalm devotions. Steve has been a great encourager and a "can do" influence in my life and ministry.

Most of all, I am indebted to my wife, Jane, who had typed, edited, and retyped every one of these devotions for the past five years (in 2005: The Parables; in 2006: Biblical Texts on Revival). Jane has burned a lot of midnight oil to meet deadlines for both the PCA and Christian Focus Publishers. What a gracious helper and partner! Her life of prayer and praise has been a source of grace and joy to me for twenty-eight years.

It is the prayer of both author and publisher that these Psalms and devotions bless your soul as much as they have enriched us who have prepared them. *"I will sing to the Lord, because He has dealt bountifully with me"* (Ps. 13:6).

# FOREWORD

"There is no other book in which we are more perfectly taught the right manner of praising God, or in which we are more powerfully stirred up to the performance of this religious exercise." Thus wrote John Calvin. The book that he had in mind, of course, was the Book of Psalms – the praise book of the people of God.

According to Calvin, the psalms teach us to rejoice by declaring what God has done for us. He has showered us with many generous blessings. He has performed mighty deeds of salvation. He has cared for us with a father's tender love. For these and all his other gifts he deserves our everlasting praise. As Calvin explained in the preface to his commentary on the Psalms:

> There is no other book in which there is to be found more express and magnificent commendations, both of the unparalleled liberality of God towards his Church, and of all his works; there is no other book in which there is recorded so many deliverances, nor one in which the evidences and experiences of the fatherly providence and solicitude which God exercises towards us, are celebrated with such splendour of diction, and yet with the strictest adherence to truth; in short, there is no other book in which we are more perfectly taught the right manner of praising God, or in which we are more powerfully stirred up the performance of this religious exercise.

Calvin's words provide a fitting introduction to this devotional guide because they focus on God's praise, which is the theme of all the psalms. The guide itself was written by my friend and colleague Mike Ross, who serves as senior minister of Christ Covenant Presbyterian Church in Charlotte, North Carolina. It is organized thematically rather than canonically. It is also divided into three parts, each of which gives special honor to one of the Three Persons in the Godhead.

"God Our Refuge" focuses on psalms that prove God the Father's protective care in times of danger and distress. "God Our Redeemer" is a celebration of God the Son for his redemptive work and headship over the church. "God Our Rejoicing" worships God for his being and work in the Holy Spirit. The psalms in this section include the famous "Songs of Ascent" (Pss. 120–134) that pilgrims used to sing on their way up to the temple in Jerusalem, as well as the very last psalms in the Bible – the triumphant hymns that close the Psalter with a crescendo of praise. Pastor Ross thus ends his series of devotionals the way the Psalms end, and the way our lives will end: with high praise to the Triune God for his glory and grace.

These studies in the psalms have been a great help to my soul, and I pray that they will also be a blessing to you. Although the devotionals are short enough to fit into even the busiest schedule, they are rich in their biblical, theological, and practical content. Each chapter explains the context and structure of a biblical psalm. Often there are historical illustrations or contemporary connections that help explain what the psalm means. Along the way, Pastor Ross also shows how each psalm relates to Christ and the Christian life. Many of his devotionals have a personal quality that reflects the spiritual experience of their author. So as you read this booklet, you will come under the warm spiritual care of an experienced pastor.

The best way to use this book for daily devotions is to begin by praying for the Holy Spirit to help you understand the Scriptures and to have fellowship with Jesus Christ through prayer. Then read the psalm itself. As helpful as these devotions are, the greatest blessing comes from God's own Word. When you are finished reading the psalm and studying the devotional, take time to pray for the kingdom of God, for your local church, for the people you love, and for your own personal concerns.

This book has been prepared as a stimulus for prayer, so be sure to pray! And in your prayers, do not forget to give high praise to God. One good way to do this is to pray through each psalm. As you pray over the words of Scripture, the Holy Spirit will make them the song of your heart, and God himself — who is your Refuge and your Redeemer — will become your Rejoicing.

Philip Graham Ryken
Senior Minister, Tenth Presbyterian Church,
Philadelphia, Pennsylvania

These Psalms for devotion, meditation and prayer are in three sections, and were originally used for three years during the Presbyterian Church in America's fifty days of prayer, beginning on the American National Day of Prayer and following through its General Assembly. The sections gather and group the Psalms by themes and collections within the Psalter itself and focus them on the three Divine Persons of the Trinity. They are now published for wider use by the Christian church in many denominations.

Part One is entitled *God Our Refuge: Celebrating God the Father — Jehovah,* and focuses on the First Person of the Trinity. The Psalms that make up our devotional guide for this section include the Songs of Zion, the Enthronement Psalms, the Imprecatory Psalms, the Wisdom Psalms, the Royal Psalms, the Seven Penitential Psalms and the Psalms of Restoration and Revival. These Psalms and devotions called us to repentance, surrender and rest in God, our Father in Heaven.

Part Two is entitled *God Our Redeemer: Celebrating God the Son — Jesus Christ,* and focuses on the Second Person of the Trinity. These devotions help us to pray through the truths surrounding Christ's redemptive work and headship over the Church. These Psalms include the Prayers for the Sick, the Golden Chain of Trust (Pss. 3–10), the Fugitive Psalms, the Psalms of Trust, a collection entitled "Psalms for a Nation in Decline" (Pss. 77, 78, 88, 42 and 43, 44, 50 and 74), the Psalms of Petition, Prayers of Lament and Five Psalms of Thanksgiving.

Part Three is entitled *God Our Rejoicing: Celebrating God the Holy Spirit — The Paraclete.* These fifty Psalms call us to worship, work and witness in the power of the Spirit. These fifty devotions are divided into seven collections: Three Songs for the Nation Under God, Psalms of Revelation, the Pilgrim Psalms (the Songs of Ascents), the Hallel Psalms, Psalms for Times of Trouble, Seven Songs of Wonderment and the Psalms of Pure Praise (Pss. 145–150).

As we work our way through these Psalms of the Spirit let us not forget that we pray them and sing them not alone. We join with those throughout the world who are using this book as a guide to the psalms, or who are meditating on the psalms in other ways. We pray these Psalms "surrounded by a great cloud of witnesses," on earth and in heaven, who have used and still use the Psalter as, in the words of Dietrich Bonhoeffer, "the prayer book of the Bible." Finally we follow the lead of Jesus Christ our Lord who "always lives to make intercession for us," and who, no doubt, prays the Word of God to God for us. St. Augustine reminded us that "Christ Himself is the singer of the Psalms." Therefore, in a very real sense, these hymns to God, sung by Christ and composed by the Spirit are a privileged look into the intimate conversation of the Trinity concerning the kingdom of God – God our Refuge, God our Redeemer and God our Rejoicing – praying for us, preaching the Gospel and praising one another for their great works of grace and glory. So let us rejoice in God our Rejoicing! And let us do what the Spirit commands us to do: "Let everything that has breath praise the LORD!" (Ps. 150:6, the last verse of the Psalter).

# Part I:

# God Our Refuge:
# Celebrating God the Father – Jehovah

*It is better to take refuge in the LORD
than to trust in man.
It is better to take refuge in the LORD
than to trust in princes.*

*Psalm 118:8, 9*

## DAY 1 THE CITY OF GOD

# Read Psalm 118

*"It is better to take refuge in the LORD than to trust in man.*
*It is better to take refuge in the LORD than to trust in princes."*

Psalm 118:8, 9

Today you begin a prayer effort to pray for the church of Christ worldwide and for reformation and revival in all her ministries and congregations. Our prayer theme for this section is Psalm 118:8, 9 – "God our refuge."

This Psalm was the favorite of the great reformer, Martin Luther. Of this Psalm 118 Luther wrote, "This is my psalm, my chosen psalm. I love them all; I love all the Holy Scripture, which is my consolation and my life. But this psalm is nearest my heart, and I have a familiar right to call it mine. It has saved me from many a pressing danger from which neither emperor, nor kings, nor sages, nor saints could have saved me. It is my dear friend, dearer to me than all the honors and power of the earth." May this dear psalm, and those which follow it in this prayer guide, encourage, refresh and redirect us.

We will follow themes of prayer, using a set of psalms that apply to that theme. Each day you will be asked to read a psalm, read a short devotion on that psalm and pray for the reformation and revival of the church. For this first week we will read and pray through the Psalms of Zion, psalms about the "City of God" (Pss. 46, 48, 76, 84, 87 and 122). As we do so, we will focus our prayers on our mission to our own nation and our efforts to bring to the cities of men this "City of God" known as The church.

In AD 426, after Rome fell to Alaric the Visigoth in 410, and when many feared that "Christendom" might come to an end, St. Aurelius Augustine, the Bishop of Hippo (in North Africa) wrote a masterpiece entitled *The City of God*. Augustine reminded us that kingdoms come and go, world-class cities rise and fall, but "The City of God" – the church of Christ – perseveres and prevails. In God's sovereign plan the cities of man are conquered with Gospel love and truth by "The City of God."

Augustine drew this vision of reformation and revival from Psalm 48, one of the Psalms of Zion. He saw in *De Civitate Dei* ("The City of God") the hope of every nation: "God is in the midst of her; she will not be moved; God will help her when morning dawns" (Ps. 46:5). Let us pray together that God's morning of reformation and revival will dawn upon our church and our nation, and that the church in our cities will lead to the hope of which we sing: "Thine alabaster cities gleam, undimmed by human fears."

## DAY 2 THE RIVER THAT MAKES GLAD

### Read Psalm 46

*"There is a river whose streams make glad the city of God."*
Psalm 46:4

Psalm 46 may certainly be considered the battle-hymn of the Reformation. This psalm inspired Martin Luther's famous hymn, *Ein' Feste Burg* (A Mighty Fortress), drawn from the repeated refrain of this psalm: "The LORD of hosts is with us; the God of Jacob is our fortress." Rowland E. Prothero comments upon this psalm's influence on Luther: "There were moments when even he felt something akin to despair, and he asked with the Psalmist, 'Why art thou cast down, O my soul?' In such hours he would say to Melancthon, 'Come, Philip, let us sing the 46th Psalm;' and the two friends sang it in Luther's version, 'Ein' feste Burg ist unser Gott.' The version is characteristic of the man."

As we go forward into the cities of our nation in order to establish the City of God, we ought to sing this psalm and focus on its confident truth. In particular, verse four reminds us, "There is a river whose streams make glad the city of God." That river with streams is, of course, the presence of Christ and the rivulets of His Gospel. This little river, with its tiny streams, seems insignificant to the world. And yet it makes glad the church of God. Bishop George Horne of Norwich (1730–1792) comments, "Such is the ground on which the church erects her confidence. Instead of those waters which overwhelm the world, she has within herself the fountain of consolation, sending forth rivers of spiritual joy

15

and pleasure; and in the place of secular instability, she is possessed of a city and hill, which stand fast for ever, being the residence of the Eternal." H. C. Leupold adds this clarification: "Trivial as it seems in contrast with the mighty Euphrates or Tigris, it may, nevertheless, in its own way well symbolize the insignificant appearance of the kingdom of God in the eyes of the world. What the world despises makes glad the people of God."

Just as these rivulets irrigate the fields of Jerusalem and refresh her people, so the local churches in our great cities flow in multiple streams into the river of life in our metropolitan wastelands, bringing spiritual joy and soul-quenching grace to lives saddened with sin and parched by dead religion. These local churches look so insignificant to the world but, in reality, they offer the "rivers of living water" Jesus promised to those who trust in Him (John 7:37-39).

The life of Christ in His people makes glad the City of God. The streams of Gospel grace flowing from those congregations are the only hope the city of man has for new life and true joy.

## DAY 3 GOD IN HER CITADELS

### Read Psalm 48

> *His holy mountain, beautiful in elevation, is the joy of all the earth, Mount Zion in the far north, the city of the great King. Within her citadels God has made himself known as a fortress.*
>
> Psalm 48:1-3

Psalm 48 is the second of the Songs of Zion (Pss. 46, 48, 76, 84, 87 and 122), psalms about "The City of God," the church. This particular song of the City of God celebrates the wonder and beauty of Zion as a type of the heavenly New Jerusalem yet to come. The sons of Korah mention a key truth about God's City: God is "within her citadels." The picture is one of God, manning the ramparts of the city wall, to defend His church. One of the pilgrim psalms reinforces this truth: "Unless the LORD builds the house, those who build it labor in vain. Unless the Lord watches over the city, the watchman keeps awake in vain" (Ps. 127:1).

We need to remember this truth in the planting and building of our churches in the cities and towns of our nation. We often think, "If only some influential people would join us. If only we had more wealthy families. If only the prominent people would come to church here. Then we could really have an impact on this city!" But such is worldly thinking. God builds His Church (Matt. 16:18) and most often with the "little people" of the city, not the privileged or powerful. God is glorified in doing special things through common folk, more than in doing "big" things through big spenders. The City of God conquered the City of Rome and the Roman Empire, not by winning senators and generals to Christ but by capturing peasants, merchants and foot soldiers with the Gospel.

David Dickson (1583–1662) puts this truth in perspective for us: "The church is the joy of the whole earth, by holding out to all the light of saving doctrine, and showing the authority, power, wisdom, and grace of Christ; who is her great King, and who beautifieth her, for the illumination of the blind, dark world."

What we need to pray for are spiritual riches, spiritual power and spiritual influence in the cities in which we live. God is protecting His church and He has given to us His Spirit to enrich and empower us in our mission to our nation. (John Wesley was right when he said, "The greatest thing of all is that God is with us.") Don't worry about the "pretty people" helping to build the Church. The Beautiful One, Jesus Christ is already with us. This is our confidence.

## Day 4 God is known in Zion

### Read Psalm 76

*In Judah God is known; his name is great in Israel. His abode has been established in Salem, his dwelling place in Zion.*

Psalm 76:1, 2

Modern Western cities are the sanctuaries of pluralism. Multiple races, manifestations of ethnic diversity and a multitude of competing religions turn city life into a spiritual mosaic. As a result ecumenical tolerance that attempts to blend all religions into one is the spiritual rule of the day. In America, for instance, national prayer meetings and religion in the public square confirm this fact. Consequently, Christians are often intimidated about sharing their faith and preachers are often shamed into silence. Christianity in America has retreated into the cocoon of privatized religion.

Psalm 76 is one of the Psalms of Zion, psalms about the City of God (the church). Its opening verses make a politically incorrect statement that is nevertheless true: " In Judah God is known.... His dwelling place [is] in Zion" (vv. 1, 2). In other words, only in the church of Jesus Christ can God be known and God be found. Joseph A. Alexander of Princeton (1809–1860) correctly notes: "It was only in the ancient church that his name was fully known, his perfection clearly manifested."

We may often feel shamed to silence. We may grow tired of the postmodern refrain: "Who are you to force your religion upon other people?" And we will certainly be hurt by the secular portrayal of evangelical and reformed Christianity as a right-wing, narrow-minded, mean-spirited movement. But the fact remains: There is no other way to know God except through Jesus Christ (John 14:6), and Jesus can only be known in His church.

If we love our neighbors we will invite them to our church that they might find God through discovering the real Christ. Dr. Billy Graham has often said that the vast majority of people who come to know Christ do so after a friend or relative invites them to church. As old-fashioned as it may seem, bringing people to church is still the best way to evangelize the unconverted. The combination of the preached Word, the prayers of the people and the fellowship of the brethren remain a powerful force for evangelism, even in our big, post-modern cities (See Acts 2:42-47).

The way to bring people together is not by muddling all religions into one, but by clearly and kindly setting forth the uniqueness of Christ and Christianity, and uniting men through faith in Jesus. This is really what the city of man needs: "And this is eternal life, that they may know you the only true God, and Jesus Christ whom you have sent" (John 17:3).

## DAY 5 THE HIGHWAYS TO ZION

### Read Psalm 84

*How blessed are those whose strength is in you, in whose heart are the highways to Zion."*

Psalm 84:5

Psalm 84 is one of the Songs of Zion which speaks of the loveliness and preciousness of the church of God. These psalms about the City of God remind us of a Biblical truth moderns have forgotten: Those who love God also love His church. One of the church fathers, Cyprian, correctly wrote: "If any man would have God as his Father he must also have the Church as his mother." Oh, that we in our age would rediscover the privileges and joys of the local church!

In the city people are busy, in fact too busy, with commuting, entertainment, dining out, recreation and the complexities of metropolitan life. In the squeeze for time the church is often pinched out. Church, for many Christians, has become optional, even peripheral, to their spiritual life. But the psalmist, in love with God, also feels a great affection for the church: "Blessed are those whose strength is in you, in whose heart are the highways to Zion." In other words, to have in our hearts the "highways to Zion" is to desire the joy and pleasures that are found only by those whose spiritual pilgrimage leads them to Christ and His church.

It is a sad but true fact that Americans are "herd animals" drawn to two things irresistibly: the latest fad and large crowds. This is the main reason large churches become "mega" churches; attending such churches "catches on" and going to church there becomes a movement of sorts. How God might use our modern love for crowds and trendiness! What would happen if those in our own denomination became genuinely enthusiastic about involvement in their church? Think of what would happen in our cities if, in our churches, joy replaced duty, praise replaced criticism and a welcoming spirit replaced a censorious one!

We must, once again, realize that the best tool for planting a church, for growing a church or for building up a ministry is the genuine joy of members enthusiastically bringing others to the church. When we once again get excited about our local church the City of God will grow. As John Brown of Haddington wrote of this psalm in 1775: "So let my heart cry out for God, the living God. So let me covet earnestly intimate fellowship with him in his ordinances. So let me praise his name, and hold on in his way, till I arrive at the Zion above. So let God be my friend, my protector, my supplier, my store, and the everlasting rock of my rest." What a joy to be, by God's grace, one "in whose heart are the highways to Zion."

## DAY 6 THIS ONE WAS BORN IN ZION

### Read Psalm 87

> "Among those who know Me I mention Rahab and Babylon; Behold, Philistia and Tyre, with Cush – "This one was born there," they say. And of Zion it shall be said, "This one and that one were born in her"; For the Most High himself will establish her"

Psalm 87:4, 5

Psalm 87 is a moving psalm, a song about Zion, the City of God, in which Jehovah takes a census and lists where the people of the earth were born. When He comes to His elect, He proudly says, "And of Zion it shall be said, 'This one and that one were born in her,'" that is, in the City of God. Matthew Henry writes, "Zion is here compared with other places, and preferred before them; the church of Christ is more glorious and excellent than the nations of the earth. It is owned that other places have their glories…. 'Here and there one famous man, eminent for knowledge and virtue, may be produced, that was a native of these countries; here and there one that becomes a proselyte and worshipper of the true God.' …The worthies of the church far exceed those of heathen nations, and their names will shine brighter than in perpetual records." In Western cultures folk heroes and roll models are entertainers, athletes and politicians, but few men and women of the church are esteemed as such. But then, again, we must ask ourselves, "Who is counting?"

God takes note of His "worthies," his saints whose lives, prayers, witness and work make an eternal difference in the cities of man. God sees not as man sees. The Lord's values are different from man's. The Christians of our culture need not feel inferior or think of themselves as those who "don't count." What we are doing in and through our churches is the most important thing going on in our nation on any given day, in any given week.

The Lord takes note of us, "this one was born there," in the City of God, born from above for a heavenly purpose. And His recognition is all we need. John Newton wrote a famous hymn based upon this psalm: "Glorious things of Thee are spoken, Zion, city of our God." In that hymn Newton also speaks of the glorious blessing given to God's elect: "Savior, if of Zion's city I, through grace, a member am, let the world deride or pity, I will glory in Thy name: fading is the worldling's pleasure, all his boasted pomp and show; solid joys and lasting treasure none but Zion's children know." Let the men of the city think what they will of the church; those of the City of God know better.

## DAY 7 PRAY FOR THE PEACE OF THE CHURCH

### Read Psalm 122

*For my brothers and companion's sake I will say, "Peace be within you!"*
*For the sake of the house of the LORD our God I will seek your good.*

Psalm 122:8, 9

As the church goes so goes the city; our weakened churches have led to secular cities. The best thing that could happen to our nation is the revival of the church of Christ. And so the best thing we can do is to pray for the prosperity of the church.

Psalm 122 is a "double psalm," both a song of Zion (City of God) and a Song of Ascents (Pilgrimage Song). It sings of Zion, the City of God, and prays for her welfare. When the psalmist tells us to "pray for the peace of Jerusalem," he does so for a very strategic purpose. Let John Calvin explain: "In this verse he adds a second reason why he cared for the Church – that he did so, because the worship of God so far from remaining entire would go to ruin unless Jerusalem continued standing ... for if she is 'the pillar and foundation of truth,' the inevitable consequence of her destruction must be the extinction of true piety."

The psalmist is concerned over the evangelization and spiritual state of his neighbors, those who dwell in the City of Man but who need to live in the City of God (vv. 8,9). Is it not always a challenge to "play it safe," to cluster with people who are similar to us, to move out into the suburbs for "security" purposes, to send our kids to private academies or to home-school them in order to avoid the "unclean" people of the world? Jack Miller was once confronted with this challenge: "If we divide people culturally into the 'washed' and the 'unwashed,' my group usually went after the washed. The problem with this ... was that the vast majority of the people in the world are 'unwashed.'" But it is these very unclean folks, these "dangerous" souls who need Christ and His church the most. Tim Keller is correct: "Christians are not to live where it is safe, but where we are most useful to both the city that is and the City to Come. You can't go to places with the greatest spiritual and physical hunger – the greatest material and spiritual need – and not also go toward an overall more dangerous place. It is hard to see how we reveal the beauty of God's coming city to the world if we only live in the safe places where there are no needs or even opportunities to reach out to people who are different. Think of the incarnation."

The revival of true religion in our land depends upon the reformation of your church denomination, the revitalization of your local church, and the renewal of your faith and life! Now, is it not important for you to "pray for the peace of Jerusalem"? Remember: As it goes for the City of God so it goes for our nation. And it's tough to pray for the peace of a place in which you won't even live!

## DAY 8 THE KINGDOM OF GOD

### Read Psalm 47

*For the LORD, the Most High, is to be feared, a great king over all the earth.*

Psalm 47:2

The Kingdom of God can rightly be considered the main theme of the Bible. God, through His Son, Jesus Christ, is reclaiming His world and reestablishing His rule over His rebellious, sin-infested creation. The Bible climaxes with this wonderful statement: "The kingdom of the world has become the kingdom of our Lord and of his Christ, and he shall reign forever and ever" (Rev. 11:15). The mission of Jesus in this world was to bring the Kingdom of God to consummation. The opening words of Christ's public ministry made that clear: "'The time is fulfilled, and the kingdom of God is at hand; repent and believe in the gospel'" (Mark 1:15). The apostles carried on this kingdom-centered ministry and left to us a kingdom-centered mission, just as Christ commissioned: "'And this gospel of the kingdom will be proclaimed throughout the whole world as a testimony to all nations, and then the end will come'" (Matt. 24:14).

In the Psalter there is a collection of seven psalms, known as the Enthronement Psalms, that celebrates the universal lordship of Christ and the Kingdom of God. As we focus our prayers on world evangelization and our own mission to the world, we shall read, meditate upon and pray through these Enthronement Psalms. Each of these seven hymns is very similar in both format and content, and yet each differs in the picture it presents of Christ the King. The first of these seven Enthronement Psalms is Psalm 47.

This beautiful psalm paints a picture of the world clapping and cheering as the king returns from His last and final victory over the kingdom of men. It proclaims with great joy, "The shields of the earth belong to God; he is highly exalted" (v. 9). The image is of Christ's heavenly throne room with its walls covered with the shields of every nation conquered by the gospel. In this psalm Christ the King is referred to as "the pride of Jacob" whom God loves (v. 4).

23

Where I attended college 104,000 people filled the football stadium each Saturday afternoon. The pageantry and passion burst forth when the announcer shouted over the loud speakers, "Ladies and gentlemen, the Pride of the Buckeyes!" and out marched the Ohio State University Band. What few people understood was that the "Pride of the Buckeyes" was really concentrated in one man: the drum major. As he strutted down the field to the sound of "The Buckeye Battlecry" he became the incarnation of all our pride, all our joy and all our hopes for victory.

Psalm 47 reminds us that the "Pride of the church" is found in the incarnation of God in Jesus Christ. All our hopes, all our prayers and all our longings for the victory of God are realized in Jesus Christ. As He marches through history, the peoples of the earth clap their hands and "shout to God with loud songs of joy" (v. 1). The Pride of Jacob has come and victory is now certain. Christ will conquer the nations for God!

## DAY 9 THE ETERNAL THRONE OF GOD

## Read Psalm 93

*Your throne is established from of old; you are from everlasting.*

Psalm 93:2

In ancient times, when life was far less predictable and far more tenuous, men relished stability, control and routine. They wanted things to be the same, to go on according to the normal cycles and patterns of life. One bad crop year, one heavy rain, some political turmoil and life could end in disaster. Men liked the idea that God ruled the universe, and ruled it in a predictable manner.

Moderns feel the opposite. They thrive on change. Styles, new products, technology and medical care all float on new ideas, inventions and even novelty. "Keeping one's cutting edge" means more to people now than regularity and reliability. We are so smug about our scientific knowledge that we really believe that if it breaks we can fix it! But the reality is that life is more like the ancient world than the modern illusion.

Recent events in our culture – bombings, hijackings, anthrax mailings, and threats of jihad – have made us all realize, once again, how necessary it is for God to rule the world and give stability and safety to our lives. We may have trouble re-electing a president or prime minister for two successive terms, but we surely need God to "stay in office" a long time! "Change" may be a positive word in the postmodern West, but not when it comes to God and His administration.

Psalm 93 celebrates the eternal kingship of God and the eternal nature of His kingdom. The picture is one of God on His throne, resting from His divine labors of creation and containing "the floods" that threaten to break loose and sweep life away in a moment. We expect life to be "safe," predictable and stable, but we also realize that this is the same world in which Adam and Eve sinned and died, and in which the psalmist lived: a world quite dangerous and quite uncontrollable.

Deep down inside, modern men are as uncertain about the next day as the next man, and as the men of old in ancient times. We may run from this fact in our busyness and seek to eliminate this fear with dreams of "progress." But our modern minds know this ancient truth: Unless God rules over this dangerous planet, we don't have a prayer!

Children (and sometimes some adults) often ask me in these days, "Pastor, is this the end? Will the world be destroyed by a nuclear war?" The answer is that God will "end the world" by His own rod and not by our rockets. Life could get pretty rough in the wake of some nuclear holocaust. For many, life could become "a living hell." But life on earth will not turn into life in eternity until God, on the throne, makes it happen. Things could get "wild," but things will never be out of control. "The Lord reigns." His throne, and therefore His world, is "established." C. H. Spurgeon is correct: "Whatever opposition may arise, his throne is unmoved; he has reigned, does reign, and will reign for ever and ever. Whatever turmoil and rebellion there may be beneath the clouds, the eternal King sits above all in supreme serenity; and everywhere he is really Master, let his foes rage as they may."

And, incidentally, God is not up for re-election!

## DAY 10 THE GREAT KING ABOVE ALL GODS

# Read Psalm 95

*For the* LORD *is a great God, and a great King above all gods.*

Psalm 95:3

Psalm 95 may well be one of the most popular psalms in the Psalter. Historically known as the *Venite* (Latin for "Come!" the first word of the psalm), this psalm has been a part of both Catholic and Protestant daily prayers for over a thousand years. It is the first psalm sung or prayed at Vigils (midnight) that begins the day in the Divine Office of the monastery. It is the first psalm of the daily Morning Prayers of the Anglican Church. It is known as the *Invitatorium*, the "Invitatory Psalm" because of its two-fold invitation in verses 1 and 6.

John R. W. Stott comments on this psalm: "The *Venite* is essentially an invitation, and was formerly called the *Invitatorium* or 'Invitatory' Psalm. It contains an invitation in verses 1, 6 and 7: 'O come, let us sing, O come, let us worship,' and 'O that today you would hearken to his voice' (RSV). It is, in fact, a summons to the people of God, who know him as the 'rock' of their salvation (v. 1, literally), both to sing his praises and to hear his word. The *Venite* was recognised at least as early as the fourth century AD as being peculiarly appropriate at the beginning of public worship, and was sometimes sung while the worshippers were still assembling." The psalm is peculiarly suited to the worship of God and to the mission of the church.

It divides itself into two parts, each introduced by an invitation. "O Come, let us sing for joy to the LORD" introduces the first half of the psalm (vv. 1-5). These verses call us to worship God by communicating to Him, by singing, by expressing thanks and by praising Him with shouts of joy. The second half (vv. 6-10) begins similarly: "Oh, come, let us worship and bow down; let us kneel before the LORD, our Maker," but this invitation is a call to hear God, to listen to His Word and willingly submit to it in obedience (vv. 7-8). Those are the two sides to worship: praise and preaching, speaking to God and listening to Him. And those are the two sides to mission: bringing God's Word to the people of the earth so that they might worship God as He so designs. Stott summarizes this psalm: "Here, then, is the double invitation of this canticle. It is a summons to address God and to listen to God, to speak to him and him speak to us, to 'set forth his most worthy praise' and to 'hear his most holy word.' The balance is preserved throughout Morning and Evening Prayer: God speaks to man in the Scripture sentences, in the lessons and the sermon, while the congregation responds to him in psalms, canticles, prayers, hymns and the creed. This is the rhythm of worship, as the pendulum keeps swinging from God to man and from man to God." And this is the rhythm of world missions: God comes to men in mission that they might come to God in worship. God is "a great God, and a great King above all gods." All the worship offered to Allah, Krishna, ancestors and spirits belongs to God. In fact, the demons who live behind the masks of these gods "provoke the Lord to jealousy" (1 Cor. 10:19-22) and rob God of what is rightfully His.

These false gods created nothing. They are "spirits" but not the Spirit of life (John 6:63). These ancestors worshiped by men may be fathers to men but they are not the Father of us all (Acts 17:22-29). Krishna may be the lord of many deluded minds, but he is not the Lord of all creation (Col. 1:15-18). And Allah may be a god whose prophet is Muhammed, but he is not the Only, Living and True God, and he has no Son! This is the overriding truth of both worship and mission: "For He is our God, and we are the people of His pasture [i.e. world], and the sheep of his hand [i.e. church]." And for that reason we witness to men and worship unto God. And this Psalm 95 will someday give way to the "New Song": "Worthy are you to take the scroll and to open its seals, for you were slain, and by your blood you ransomed people for God from every tribe and language and people and nation, and you have made them a kingdom and priests to our God, and they will reign on the earth" (Rev. 5:9-10).

## DAY 11 A GOD TO BE FEARED

### Read Psalm 96

*Declare his glory among the nations, his marvelous works among all the peoples! For great is the LORD, and greatly to be praised;*
*he is to be feared above all gods. For all the gods of the peoples are worthless idols, but the LORD made the heavens.*

Psalm 96:3-5

Each of the seven Enthronement Psalms presents a unique picture of God as the king over all creation. These seven psalms (Pss. 47, 93 and 95–99) are hymns, following a standard format. In fact, they are descriptive hymns giving us reasons why we ought to praise God. And each follows a three-part outline: introduction (call to praise and worship), body (reasons why God is to be worshiped), and conclusion (a renewed call to worship with a final reason for praise). These seven Enthronement Psalms focus on God the creator and ruler of the world. W. H. Bellinger, Jr. informs us: "These psalms call upon the congregation to praise Yahweh with a new song because Yahweh rules over creation, over the earth, over the creatures upon the earth, and over the nations."

This psalm has three parts (strophes), each one revealing two reasons why God is to be feared by all the nations and adored by every person. In the first strophe (vv. 1-6) God is to be worshiped because of His historical record of great deeds and because of the beauty of His temple worship. When we present our God to the world we must preach Him from the historical books of the Bible and worship Him according to the regulative principle of His Word. Failure to do both will result in existential religion and consumer-oriented worship, neither of which yields to God the glory He is due.

The second strophe (vv. 7-10) yields to us two more reasons to worship God: the glory of His attributes and the righteousness of His judgments. Objective truth and sound theology are predicated upon true worship. Sound theology does not create proper worship; the reverse is true. John Calvin, in his masterful tract *The Necessity of Reforming the Church* sets forth the order of priority in true religion: "If it be inquired, then, by what things chiefly the Christian religion has a standing existence amongst us, and maintains its truth, it will be found that the following two not only occupy the principal place, but comprehend under them all the other parts, and consequently the whole substance of Christianity, viz., a knowledge, first, of the mode in which God is duly worshiped; and, secondly, of the source from which salvation is to be obtained. When these are kept out of view, though we may glory in the name of Christians, our profession is empty and vain. After these come the Sacraments and the Government of the Church." Reformed worship leads to a Reformed religion and a reformed life.

Finally, the third strophe (vv. 11-13) presents two final reasons for the worship of God: the glory of God's restoration of all creation and the perfections of His eternal government. These two truths give us the hope of a people who trust in Christ and worship the Triune God with eschatological vision. We are a people with hope that, in the end, God will make all things new.

Why do the nations need to know our God? Because He alone is worthy of the ascriptions of praise from the families of the earth. His eternal attributes, His past history, His present beauty in regulative worship, His righteous judgments, His future glory in the re-creation and His everlasting reign are all the reasons we need to "ascribe to the Lord the glory due His name." And they are motivations as well for the Great Commission.

## DAY 12 THE AWESOME GOD

## Read Psalm 97

*The LORD reigns, let the earth rejoice; let the many coastlands be glad!*
Psalm 97:1

We live in a silly age. And the reason why our age is so silly is that our religion – yea, even our God – is so cheap and "marketable." Years ago I was in a southern Californian seeker-driven church whose "introit" was an upbeat ditty entitled "We'll Do Our Best for You." You can now "get God" via an eight-minute sermonette at a drive-in church in Florida. Our God has evolved from clown ministry in the 60s to "skits" in the new millennium. He likes songs like "Jesus, We Just Want to Touch You," and is prone to "save the whales" while He lets us abort the babies. His "saints" are the likes of Princess Diana, His theologians are the likes of Oprah Winfrey and His prophets are the likes of Paul Harvey. And this is the God we want to export to the world? Pray tell there is more to God than this!

"Awesome" has also become a shallow, even silly, word. Cars, football defensive squads, a girl's youthful figure and the Grammy awards are now "awesome." But in fact, in truth, only God is awesome – worthy of our awe and our worship. Psalm 97 presents us with that reality. Psalm 97 tells us three facts about God that a silly culture and shallow age hate to hear: He is an impressive God (vv. 2-6); He is the only real, living God (vv. 7-9); and He is a holy God (vv. 10-12).

Our postmodern culture gags at these pronouncements, but the rest of the world does not! Believe it or not, the rest of the world appears relieved to discover these truths about God. That is exactly what the psalmist intimates: "Let the earth rejoice; let the many coastlands be glad!" (v. 1). And why should "primitive" people find attractive what "moderns" find reprehensible? Here's why....

For several millennia, the nations have worshiped gods they were afraid of but did not fear – they were terrified of their capricious evil but held no respect for them. Their gods were reactionary, arbitrary and even confusedly dangerous: none of them were truly sovereign. Their idols were perverted and mean: they wanted men's wives, demanded child sacrifice and put their devotees through the most sordid and sickening orgies imaginable. In short, the gods of the coastlands, the idols of the earth, are not respectable, real or righteous. The third world is ready for a first-rate God! More than we realize, they are tired of the old pantheon of perversion.

Interesting, isn't it, that in the Western world we've begun to experiment with a new god. He's an "open god" but not sovereign.

He's a trendy god, but not too concerned with holiness. He's a god who'd rather have a good laugh than a good life. He talks a lot about grace; he just doesn't understand what it is. People like him. The problem is, however, that you just can't worship him, because in the long-run men simply won't love and serve that which they don't respect, can't trust and wouldn't want to be like. Psalm 97 is reminding us that the Old God – the God of old – is good enough for all peoples. He alone will make the nations glad!

## DAY 13 THE VICTORY OF GOD

### Read Psalm 98

*Oh sing to the LORD a new song, for He has done marvelous things! His right hand and His holy arm have worked salvation for him.*

Psalm 98:1

Tremper Longman calls Psalm 98 "A Divine Warrior Victory Song." In fact, according to Longman, the phrase "new song" (v. 1) is a technical term for victory psalm. "These songs celebrate the new situation brought about by God's warring activity," states Longman. Psalm 98's three strophes reflect the three sides of God's warfare in the age-old, cosmic conflict: His past victories (vv. 1-3), His present kingship (vv. 4-6), and His future judgment (vv. 7-9). These three phases of warfare are historically and eschatologically logical: The king wins a victory, begins to rule His new vassals, and judges all His enemies and rebels. This is a short summary of redemptive history and a pattern for present mission activity.

The Gospel must captivate, win over and subdue a people; it must make God's enemies Christ's loyal subjects. The Holy Spirit must then establish God's kingdom rule over this newly-evangelized nation, "Christianizing" it over centuries. Finally, Christ must return to earth to consummate the kingdom, complete the mission and call all men before His throne for judgment.

This spiritual warfare must be stored in the front of our minds as we go about our ministry in this world and undertake our mission to this world. We are not building a business but establishing a kingdom. We are not managing God's affairs but fighting God's war. We are not looking for success but for victory!

We should know this truth already. The Apocalypse tells us: "And a great sign appeared in heaven: a woman clothed with the sun, and the moon under her feet, and on her head a crown of twelve stars. She was pregnant and was crying out in birth pangs and the agony of giving birth.... She gave birth to a male child, one who is to rule all the nations with a rod of iron, but her child was caught up to God and to His throne.... Now war arose in heaven, Michael and his angels fighting against the dragon. And the dragon and his angels fought back, but he was defeated and there was no longer a place for them in heaven. And the great dragon was thrown down, that ancient serpent, who is called the devil and Satan, the deceiver of the whole world – he was thrown down to the earth, and his angels were thrown down with him. ... Then the dragon became furious with the woman and went off to make war on the rest of her offspring, on those who keep the commandments of God and hold to the testimony of Jesus" (Rev. 12:1, 2, 5, 7-9, 17). And we should not be in doubt of the outcome, for the Revelation also informs us of a future "New Song," in the genre of Psalm 98: "And I heard a loud voice in heaven, saying, 'Now the salvation, and the power, and the kingdom of our God and the authority of His Christ have come, for the accuser of our brothers has been thrown down, who accuses them day and night before our God. And they have conquered him by the blood of the Lamb and by the word of their testimony, for they loved not their lives even unto death. Therefore, rejoice, O heavens and you who dwell in them!'" (Rev. 12:10-12). For this promise has been given to us about the victory of God in the consummation of His kingdom: "'The kingdom of the world has become the kingdom of our Lord and of His Christ, and he shall reign forever and ever'" (Rev. 11:15).

## DAY 14 HOLY IS THE LORD

### Read Psalm 99

*Exalt the LORD our God, and worship at His holy mountain;*
*for the LORD our God is holy!*

Psalm 99:9

Holiness is a "thing" with God. It really is. In fact, of all the adjectives describing God, "holy" is the most used. Jerry Bridges comments on this fact: "Certainly then, as one theologian has said, if it were proper to speak of one attribute of God as being more central and fundamental than another, the scriptural emphasis on the holiness of God would seem to justify its selection. Today we are inclined to emphasize the love of God, but we can never begin to appreciate His love as we should until we understand something of His holiness."

We thrust men, money and ministry into mission to the world because we love others around the world, and we desire to see them redeemed. But our love is informed by God's holiness and strengthened by our own sanctification. Sin deprecates God, destroys men and despoils the creation. R. C. Sproul masterfully summarizes the "exceeding sinfulness of sin" with these words: "When we sin we not only commit treason against God but we do violence to each other. Sin violates people. There is nothing abstract about it. By my sin I hurt human beings. I injure their person; I despoil their goods; I impair their reputation; I rob from them a precious quality of life; I crush their dreams and aspirations for happiness. When I dishonor God I dishonor all of mankind who bears His image. Wonder then that God takes sin so seriously?"

When Psalm 99 focuses on the holiness of God it zeros in on the primary motive of missions: "The LORD is great in Zion; He is exalted over all the peoples. Let them praise your great and awesome name! Holy is He! ... Exalt the LORD our God; worship at His footstool! Holy is He! ... Exalt the LORD our God, and worship at His holy mountain; for the LORD our God is holy" (Ps. 99:2, 3, 5, 9). There are two great religious evils in this life.

The first is atheism: to deny that there is a God at all or that mankind needs salvation from Him. The second great evil is even worse: to downplay or ignore the holiness of God and cause mankind to think that there could be salvation in some way other than through the imputed righteousness of Christ and the indwelling of the Holy Spirit. Puritan Stephen Charnock states: "Power is God's hand or arm, omniscience His eye, mercy His bowels, eternity His duration, but holiness His beauty." So then, the best message we have for a sin-sick and dying world is this: "The LORD is great in Zion; He is exalted over all the peoples. Let them praise your great and awesome name! Holy is He!" (Ps. 99:2,3).

## DAY 15 THE WARFARE OF GOD

### Read Psalm 35

*Contend, O LORD, with those who contend with me; fight against those who fight against me! Take hold of shield and buckler and rise up for my help!*

Psalm 35:1, 2

The earliest psalm recorded in the Bible is found in Exodus 15, a psalm written by Moses after Pharaoh's chariots were crushed in the Red Sea. In that psalm Moses writes: "The LORD is a man of war; the LORD is his name" (Exod. 15:3). That description is found throughout the Old Testament and is alluded to in the New Testament as well: God is a warrior. Tremper Longman has correctly stated: "One important and pervasive metaphor ... is the picture of God as a warrior, commonly referred to in secondary literature as the divine-warrior theme."

Within the 150 selections of God's inspired hymn-book are seven Imprecatory Psalms. They are known as such because the psalmist "imprecates" evil men; i.e. he curses and invokes evil or revenge upon the ungodly, in God's name. More precisely, he beseeches God to rise up and bring ruin upon evil men. We moderns are often uncomfortable with such prayers. But we should not feel this way because to love the good necessitates that we hate the evil. God is so: He upholds the righteous, but He, always and ultimately, destroys the wicked. Heaven and hell are proof of that fact.

*The Geneva Study Bible* instructs us in the nature of these imprecatory psalms: "Some psalms cry out not only for the righteous to be vindicated, but also for God to punish the wicked. Such prayers reflect the calling of Israel to holy war as God's instruments of judgment. With the coming of Christ to bear God's judgment, the warfare of God's people continues, directed now against 'spiritual hosts of wickedness in the heavenly places.'" That perspective should now dominate our church's ministry and our own witness in this world. We must "overcome evil with good" (Rom. 12:21). And this, of course, will embroil us in spiritual warfare alongside of God the Warrior.

Psalm 35 is the first of these seven Imprecatory Psalms. This psalm sets forth the reasons evil men should be punished by God, if they do not repent and change: these men hate the godly without cause (vv. 1-8), repay good with evil (vv. 9-16), wrongfully oppose the righteous (vv. 17-21), and delight in the church's distress (vv. 22-26). But it also sets forth the reasons for invoking God's judgment: to demonstrate God's righteousness, to establish God's authority over the ungodly, to lead the wicked to seek the Lord, and to cause the saints to praise God. Zeal for God, hatred of sin, love for the saints and concern for the lost world will cause us to enter into God's holy war. Emotionally we will imprecate the devil and his minions. Ecclesiastically we will combine resources and efforts to promote the Gospel in our world. Spiritually we will seek to keep this focus ever before us: "For though we walk in the flesh, we are not waging war according to the flesh. For the weapons of our warfare are not of the flesh but have divine power to destroy strongholds. We destroy arguments and every lofty opinion raised against the knowledge of God, and take every thought captive to obey Christ" (2 Cor. 10:3-5).

## DAY 16 THE UNGODLY IN GOVERNMENT

# Read Psalm 58

*Do you indeed decree what is right, you gods? Do you judge the children of man uprightly? No, in your hearts you devise wrongs; your hands deal out violence on earth.*

Psalm 58:1, 2

"There was a time in American political history when anyone reading Psalm 58 would have thought it somehow unreal, at least where the United States is concerned. Psalm 58 is about unjust rulers, and in those earlier halcyon days America was favored for the most part with leaders whose characters were upright and whose actions were above reproach. No longer. Today corruption is widespread even to the highest levels of political leadership, and Psalm 58 seems to be an apt prophetic description of our times." These are the opening words of the late James Montgomery Boice as he commented upon Psalm 58. As an Imprecatory Psalm, Psalm 58 calls down the judgment of God upon wicked rulers – corrupt government officials. John Calvin believes these men to be the officials of Saul's administration: "I rather incline to the opinion of those who conceive that he here gives (although only in courtesy) the usual title of honour to the counsellors of Saul, who met professedly to consult for the good of the nation, but in reality with no other intention than to accomplish his destruction."

The church of Jesus Christ in America suffers just such a situation at present. Its government, hiding behind the shibboleth of "separation of church and State", has sought to remove God from the public square. No one on the American religious scene is more opposed by its government than conservative, evangelical Protestants. American politics, even with a "born-again" president, is hostile to Biblical truth and ethics.

The task of reaching immoral leaders with the truth in high places, of changing the minds of pro-homosexual, pro-abortion and pro-liberal politicians, and of gaining a fair hearing with an antagonistic media seems impossible. Humanly speaking it is. America is so far gone down the road of postmodernity and secularity, that only the hand of God can rectify the problems. But that is exactly to whom the psalmist turns. God alone is our hope: "Mankind will say, 'Surely there is a reward for the righteous; surely there is a God who judges on earth'" (v. 11).

Perhaps God has judged us already! Maybe this government, and similar governments in other Western nations, is what we deserve! So as we pray for God to raise up God-fearing, Christ-honoring leaders, let us also pray for ourselves as citizens. John Brown put it this way: "While I sing, let me search out my corruptions, and bewail my obstinate refusals of Jesus Christ, and the counsels of His Word."

## DAY 17 THE SEVENFOLD PAYBACK

### Read Psalm 79

*Return sevenfold into the lap of our neighbors the taunts with which they have taunted you, O LORD!*

Psalm 79:12

The Imprecatory Psalms are difficult to accept, let alone to sing, pray or even preach. They seem so mean-spirited and even self-righteous. C. S. Lewis did not accept the Imprecatory Psalms as God's Word. He wrote, "The hatred is there – festering, gloating, undisguised – and also we should be wicked if we in any way condoned or approved it or (worse still) used it to justify similar passions in ourselves." Lewis went on to say of the Imprecatory Psalms, "They are indeed devilish."

Our doctrine of Scripture will not allow us to call theses psalms "wicked" or refer to them as "devilish" (2 Tim. 3:16,17). Rather, our love for God's Word forces us to wrestle with these psalms until we understand their meaning and embrace their ethos. James E. Adams has written a small book on the Imprecatory Psalms entitled, *War Psalms of the Prince of Peace: Lessons from the Imprecatory Psalms*. Adams says of himself, "My own experience with these prayers has brought me many times to sense God's very presence. As my understanding of them deepened through much study, comparing Scripture with Scripture, my prayer life has begun to enter into the very prayers of Jesus Christ. I've also been enabled to preach these psalms with great joy." We would do better to listen to Adams than to Lewis.

The problem we have with these psalms may well be the problem we have with sin: We no longer sense the "exceeding sinfulness of sin." As a result we no longer grieve over the affront corporate, cultural, "mass-produced" sin is to a Holy God. Because we no longer really live for the glory of God, but rather for the comfort of self, we no longer experience the emotion of the lost virtue called "righteous indignation."

We may have sensed a bit of it back on September 11, 2001 as the world watched the twin towers fall. But, in reality, we grieved for ourselves, not for a God dishonored by a secular state and a Muslim religion. The Psalmist is angry over the fact that God's will – not his own welfare – has been resisted. Thus he prays, "Return sevenfold into the lap of our neighbors the taunts with which they have taunted you, O Lord!" (v. 12). Oh that God would grant to us that kind of perspective and this kind of prayer!

## DAY 18 GOD TAKES HIS STAND

### Read Psalm 82

*God has taken his place in the divine council; in the midst of the gods he holds judgment.*

Psalm 82:1

In the post-exilic temple, the Levites chose seven psalms, known as the weekday psalms – one for each day of the week – to be sung at the morning and evening sacrifices.[1]

The psalm for Tuesday was Psalm 82, a psalm that celebrates the fact that God judges the rulers of this world. Asaph acknowledges

---

[1] These seven psalms were: Psalm 48 (Monday), Psalm 82 (Tuesday), Psalm 94 (Wednesday), Psalm 81 (Thursday), Psalm 93 (Friday), Psalm 92 entitled "A Psalm: A Song for the Sabbath" (Saturday) and Psalm 24 (Sunday). We know this information from both the Septuagint version of the Bible and the Hebrew Talmud.

that God "takes His stand" and brings the princes of this world to accountability. That is his earnest prayer: "Arise, O God, judge the earth" (v. 8).

We often feel that men in high places "get away with murder" – figuratively and literally: athletes who kill their spouses and get off due to a racially-weighted jury; presidents who sodomize aids and escape impeachment only through party politics; foreign leaders whose atrocities are not confronted because it would jeopardize a good economy. But Asaph informs us that God sees it all and will bring all to justice. Derek Kidner comments: "With its bold, dramatic form this judgment scene brings some clarity to a confused human situation. It takes us in a few words behind and beyond our present wrongs, to portray God's unbounded jurisdiction, His delegation of power, His diagnosis of our condition and His drastic intentions."

The saints cannot be discouraged by the irresponsible evil in high places. The world has always been this way, and more than likely will always be the same. We must "not grow weary of doing good, for in due time we shall reap, if we do not give up" (Gal. 6:9). In fact, by preaching bold and prophetic truth, even if attendance drops off; teaching our children God's ways, even if others think we are Neanderthals; by confronting sin with the inflexible truth of God's Word and the fluid grace of God's gospel – by these actions we give hope that a future generation of world rulers might walk uprightly and govern with righteousness. Pray for those in authority (1 Tim. 2:1-4) and live like men under authority (1 Pet. 2:13-17). And know that "God will bring every deed into judgment, with every secret thing, whether good or evil" (Eccles. 12:14). And that includes the high and mighty, for God does possess the nations ... and their rulers! (v. 8)

## DAY 19 WOULD GOD PLEASE SPEAK UP

### Read Psalm 83

*O God, do not keep silence; do not hold your peace and, do not be still O God.*

Psalm 83:1

Sometimes it seems as if God has lost His voice! The "uproar" of the godless (v. 2) is deafening, and the voice of God appears inaudible. Charles Colson wrote a book a few years back entitled *Who Speaks for God?* His answer was simply this: God speaks for Himself and speaks through His Word. This Imprecatory Psalm beseeches God to speak up and speak out, and in so doing to restrain evil and beat back God's enemies, the enemies of the church.

This psalm reflects a great confidence in God's Word – the living and abiding Word of Truth. It speaks as if God's Word alone can turn back evil, defeat satanic forces and set things aright. And, indeed it can. The power of God's voice, heard in His Word, is indeed awesome.

We have lost much of this confidence in God's Word. As a result we plan more and pray less; we look to politicians for answers and not to preachers; we build our churches more on business techniques than on biblical truth. We give more effort to "reshaping" the church for Generation-X than to passing on the truths of generations past. We've grown impatient.

In explaining this psalm H. C. Leupold wrote: "An address such as we find in this verse is spoken in the boldness of faith, which knows that it may speak freely to the Almighty. He seems so utterly unresponsive! Not a trace of interest and compassion has been noted. God often bides His time, and the children of men grow impatient until they cannot bear to keep silent any longer.... But the point is that God's people can bear His silence and inaction no longer." Herbert Carl Leupold was a Lutheran pastor and professor at the Evangelical Lutheran Seminary at Capitol University, in Columbus, Ohio, for forty-two years. He died in 1972. He wrote wonderful commentaries on Genesis, Isaiah, Daniel, Zechariah, Ecclesiastes and the Psalms. Last year

I visited Capitol University's library to see if I could find more of Leupold's writings. The sad fact was that no one I spoke to even knew who Leupold was. No one! Their greatest scholar … forgotten?

Is that not a parable for our times? One of the greatest evangelical Lutheran Old Testament scholars of our times, and our young people do not know who he was! Nevertheless, Biblical truth is invincible. Leupold's commentaries live on. You cannot silence the voice of the dead. And God's Word is ever living! You can never silence the voice of God. God will speak and speak for Himself, and when He does men will hear what He has to say and know who He is! His purpose is clearly set forth: "Be still, and know that I am God. I will be exalted among the nations, I will be exalted in the earth" (Ps. 46:10). God was known in Judah. May He be known once again in America and the West. His enemies may silence us, but they will never silence Him. For if you cannot silence the voice of the dead, then certainly you cannot silence the voice of the resurrected and living Christ!

## DAY 20 THE PEOPLE OF PRAYER

### Read Psalm 109

*But I give myself to prayer.*

Psalm 109:4

Psalm 109 is the longest and most detailed of the Imprecatory Psalms – the songs of God the Warrior. In this psalm David sets forth in great and passionate detail the accusations (vv. 1-5), the afflictions (vv. 6-13), and the animosity (vv. 14-20) of the ungodly toward the saints. Yet in the midst of his lament he says: "But I give myself to prayer…. My knees are weak from fasting" (vv. 4 and 24).

We sometimes suffer in the church and oftentimes go out into spiritual warfare, day by day, in a prayerless manner. Gone, it seems, are the days when pastors were expected to close their office doors in hours of prayer. Gone, it appears, are the days when General Assemblies called churches to days of fasting and prayer.

Gone, I'm afraid, is the spirit of spiritual warfare that unites the church, in fasting and prayer, in times of distress, disappointment or danger. If we really were a praying people we'd be a more victorious people. Can we deny this?

As we pray for those administering our denominations, let us pray that we would truly become "a praying people at worship, work, witness and warfare." God's design is for the church to conduct His business on her knees. Furious activity, growing bureaucracy, position papers, study commissions, committee meetings and increasing financial resources can never take the place of prevailing prayer.

It is offensive, to be sure, to be told that our denomination (and evangelical Christianity, for that matter) is not a praying church. Certainly we do pray, but we are not a praying church – a church in prayer (v. 4) and physically weak due to fasting (v. 24). Consequently, because we are not more in prayer our culture is more in trouble; because we are not weak with fasting we are not strong in spirit.

It may sound strange, but perhaps the first thing to pray for our denominations is that they would pray … really pray! For that is what a Christian should be: a man of prayer and fasting. Augustus Toplady (1740–1778) reminds us: "A Christian is all over prayer: he prays at rising, at lying down, and as he walks: like a prime favourite at court, who has the key to the privy stairs, and can wake his prince by night." What a beautiful thought: "Our denomination, a praying people at worship, work, witness and warfare!"

## DAY 21 DELIVER US FROM EVIL

### Read Psalm 140

> I know that the LORD will maintain the cause of the afflicted,
> and will execute justice for the needy."
>
> Psalm 140:12

When Jesus taught His apostles to pray, part of the pattern of prayer He set before them was to ask God to "deliver us from evil." Psalm 140, the seventh and last of the Imprecatory Psalms, teaches us what to specifically ask for in this deliverance from evil. The New American Standard Bible arranges Psalm 140 into five paragraphs. Each "strophe" is a prayer for deliverance from evil: a rescue from violence (vv. 1-3), a preservation from traps (vv. 4-5), an undoing of evil devices (vv. 6-8), a reversal of mischief (vv. 9-11), and the maintenance of a just cause (vv. 12, 13). Psalm 140 is prayer composed for the twenty-first century West.

This psalm is a treatise on human depravity, and as such makes up the majority of Romans 3:10-18. That which characterizes the unconverted soul, and dominates this psalm, is the issue of malicious intrigue. What may be difficult to face is this: These are times when even the converted act with malicious intrigue and cause pain to the other saints of God. David Dickson, a Scottish minister (1583–1662) explains that, "From the first request, learn, that most innocent and godly men, by the calumnies of the wicked, are sometimes cast into great dangers, whence they see no way of deliverance for clearing their name, or saving their life, except God find it out: and in this case God is and should be their refuge.... How wicked soever, how violent soever the enemies of God's children be, God can rescue his servants out of their hands."

We must face these facts in prayer and in penitent spirit, that we often see our churches infected with petty politics, wounded by gossip and slander, crippled by party strife and frequently made an uncomfortable place to worship and work because of personal animosity, jealousy and competition. Malicious intrigue is not just "out on the street," but can also be found in our administrative offices, our meetings and the hallways of our churches.

Perhaps our prayer, "deliver us from evil" ought to begin at home, with a long look into our own spirit. My denomination, the Presbyterian Church in America, each year ends its General Assembly by singing Psalm 133 – "Behold, how good and pleasant it is when brothers dwell in unity!" (Ps. 133:1). That psalm would mean much more to many more of us if God were to deliver us from our own malicious intrigues.

## DAY 22 THE TRUTH OF GOD

### Read Psalm 1

*But his delight is in the law of the LORD, and on His law he meditates day and night.*

Psalm 1:2

We live in an age of foolishness, when people are more interested in what is popular and trendy than in what is principled and true. For this reason the Bible's emphasis on wisdom is increasingly important for our times. The Psalter includes a dozen Wisdom Psalms – psalms that teach proverbial truth and lend guidance to the true worshiper of God. Psalm 1 is the most famous of these twelve Wisdom Psalms (Pss. 1, 14, 15, 36, 37, 49, 52, 53, 90, 111, 112, and 139).

It serves as a wonderful introduction to the whole Psalter, promising blessing for those who read, pray and meditate upon God's Word, and warning those who ignore the Scripture of their eternal loss. This psalm uses the Hebrew form of poetry known as parallelism to set before the reader a reinforced thought, stated in different words, but saying the same thing. In this case the singer is told to "walk … stand … sit …" as a wise man.

He is not to walk in the way of the wicked, displaying a lifestyle that loves what God hates. He should delight in God's law, God's will and God's ways. He is not to stand in the path of sinners, positioning himself in such a way as to be influenced by the world and its worldliness. He should dwell upon God's Word, renewing his mind in the counter-culture of the Holy Writ. He is not to sit in the seat of scoffers, snickering at biblical truth and pontificating upon that which is politically correct. He should plant himself in the Truth of God that is ever fresh and ever fruitful.

If there was ever a time when our churches needed confessional Christianity, expository preaching, biblically sound instruction, confidence in God's Word and a Scriptural worldview, it is in the dawning of the twenty-first century. Without solid curriculum, reformed literature, practical conferences, teacher training, leadership development, catechetical materials, and special attention devoted to the minds of our children and youth we will not know how to think and how to live for God.

One old prophet put it this way: "My people are destroyed for lack of knowledge.... So the people without understanding are ruined" (Hosea 4:6, 14). Such will be the case in America and the West as well unless the church rises up with a knowledge, understanding and bold message rooted in God's Word. In our age many say: "It doesn't really matter what you believe as long as you're sincere." The wise man knows better. "How blessed is the man" who walks in, stands in and sits in God's truth. And how "blessed is the nation whose God is the LORD" (Ps. 33:12) and who knows it! That is why Jesus prayed to His Father for us: "Sanctify them in the truth; your word is truth" (John 17:17). And we should pray the same for our church, our nation and our world.

## DAY 23 A LIFE OF INTEGRITY

### Read Psalm 15

*O LORD, who shall sojourn in your tent? Who shall dwell on your holy hill? He who walks blamelessly, and does what is right and speaks truth in his heart.*

Psalm 15:1, 2

Psalm 15 deals with the moral condition by which a man may dwell with God. Along with Psalm 24, this psalm was probably written to celebrate the bringing of the ark of the covenant up from the house of Obed-Edom to the City of David, Jerusalem, in 2 Samuel 6:12-19. "But the psalm has a wider application," John Stott rightly informs us. "It inquires into the terms on which any human being may dwell in God's presence, either in this life or in the life to come. The psalmist is clear that Jehovah is a holy God and that the sinner separates himself from God by his sin. 'Thou art not a God who delights in wickedness; evil may not sojourn with thee' (Ps. 5:4, RSV). Who, then may dwell with God?"

This Wisdom Psalm does not teach a salvation-by-works righteousness, but that a life of integrity verifies the fact that living faith animates the soul. James tells us that "faith without works is dead" (Jas. 2:17, 26) and Psalm 15 serves as a commentary on such living faith. The kind of man who lives with God, now and forever, is a person who loves his neighbor, keeps his word, uses his money compassionately and does not pervert justice. This sort of man is steadfast in both faith and works. "He who walks blamelessly and does what is right, and speaks truth in his heart" describes the life of a biblically informed and spiritually mature saint. "Walking ... working ... speaking," these are the goals of Christian education and of all Christian literature.

To walk blamelessly means that our lifestyle reflects a consistent application of both the doctrine and the ethics we profess to believe. We flesh out what we say we hold as our convictions. To do what is right means that we display an uncorrupted life where justice, mercy and humble religion (Micah 6:8) blend into a winsome whole, making us true salt and light. To speak truth in the heart means that there is a divine congruence between the values we really hold dear and the things we say to others. We practice what we preach. Bundle all this together and we're talking about integrity.

In the wake of Bill Clinton's American presidency, NCAA special investigations into sexual misconduct between coaches and students, compromised national security, marines breaking the honor code, and the general, postmodern deconstruction of language that makes truth elusive, there is a great need for and much talk about integrity.

Psalm 15 will not let us compartmentalize our religion – what we believe, how we live, and our manner of worship. John Stott states, "Psalm 15 is concerned with the conditions on which a man may dwell with God. It is specially noteworthy because it unites religion and morality in an indissoluble partnership.... That is, it concerns entirely our duty to our neighbour, since we cannot have a right relationship with God without a right relationship with men. We cannot expect to dwell in God's presence if we are not seeking our neighbour's good."

Ask yourself this question: What would my community be

like if all the evangelical Christians in the area really fleshed out what they sing in hymns, read in their Bibles and demand of their parents, politicians and pastors? At the very least, there would be a lot more people prepared to live with God ... forever!

## DAY 24 THE CALLING OF GOD

### Read Psalm 37

*Delight yourself in the LORD, and he will give you the desires of your heart. Commit your way to the LORD; trust in him, and He will act.*
Psalm 37:4, 5

The great pioneer missionary and explorer, David Livingstone, was a man permeated by the Scripture and especially the psalms. He grew up in a Christian home in Scotland, his mother a Highlander and his father a Lowland Covenanter. At age nine he won a Sunday-school prize of a New Testament with Psalms by reciting from memory all of Psalm 119. The day he sailed to Africa from Glasgow, he read to his parents and siblings Psalms 121 and 135 and then led in prayer. In Africa for thirty years, Livingstone toiled unceasingly to explore the continent, abolish slavery, bring medical aid to the diseased, evangelize the heathen and map out rivers, lakes and mountains. It was through the thirty-seventh psalm that he encouraged himself amidst fatigue, danger, extreme loneliness and lack of necessary supplies. The text that sustained him in what he called "this course in life in this country, and even in England," was Psalm 37:5, "Commit your way to the LORD, trust in Him, and He will act."

In fact, on his last expedition into the heart of present-day central Africa, Malawi and Tanzania, he died near Lake Tanganyika. He was found on May 1, 1873, dead on his knees, head in hands as in prayer, before a Bible opened to the Psalms. His life, from beginning to end, was shaped by the wisdom and worship of God in the Psalter.

A greater part of wisdom is knowing who you are in God's eyes and what God has called you to do with your life. There are hundreds of thousands (perhaps millions!) of evangelical

Christians who go through life without ever "delighting" in God or committing their way to Him; aimless lives with little more fruit than the heathen of darkest Africa or postmodern America. An entire generation of Christian young people is growing into adulthood without a sense of "calling" from God.

In 1993, John Stott was invited to give daily addresses to the Evangelical Fellowship of Anglican Churches, at a consultation in Canterbury, on the theme of "The Anglican Communion and Scripture." In his last address from Second Timothy Stott said to the young people, "I am naturally not expecting to live much longer. Any day now my summons may come. So I ask myself: 'Where are the Timothys of the end of the twentieth century, the young men and women who are determined to stand firm against the prevailing winds of fashion and refuse to compromise?' I pray that many may be found among you." Is this not a good question for the start of the twenty-first century?

Wisdom begins with the fear of the Lord, a healthy respect for and reverent devotion to God. And this must include two things. First, a person's primary delight must be in Jesus Christ and not in success, status or security in this life. Second, that our chief duty in life is to discern God's call on our lives and to commit ourselves to that calling, in Christ, wholeheartedly. Failure to fulfill either of these sacred responsibilities is to foolishly waste one's life. So, we ask again, "Where are the Timothys in our age, those young men and women, called by God into a life of sacred service?"

## DAY 25 THE WISDOM OF SIMPLICITY

### Read Psalm 49

*Man in his pomp yet without understanding, is like the beasts that perish.*

Psalm 49:20

Evangelical Christians have lost the spiritual discipline of simplicity and the grace of an uncluttered life. Proverbs 30:7-9 speaks of the joy and integrity of a life free from materialism and covetousness: "Two things I asked of you, deny them not to me before I die.

Remove far from me falsehood and lying, give me neither poverty nor riches; feed me with the food that is needful for me, lest I be full and deny you and say, 'who is the Lord?' or lest I be poor and steal and profane the name of my God." (ESV) Psalm 49, one of the Wisdom Psalms, also speaks in proverbial wisdom: "My mouth shall speak wisdom; the meditation of my heart shall be understanding. I will incline my ear to a proverb; I will solve my riddle to the music of the lyre." The sons of Korah go on to speak of a life not compromised and not cluttered by the "stuff of this world" (1 John 2:15-17).

Our drive for recognition in intellectual circles among churchmen, acceptance by power-brokers in the likes of Washington and Hollywood, and a comfortable suburban, middle-class religion will be the undoing of any denomination in the end. Many may disagree with this assessment, but permit me to illustrate my point. In 1974, two thousand five hundred Evangelicals from around the world gathered in Lausanne, Switzerland for the first International Congress on World Evangelization. At the end of the ICWE, the delegates forged out and signed the Lausanne Covenant. Part of that covenant read as follows: "Those of us who live in affluent circumstances accept our duty to develop a simple lifestyle in order to contribute more generously to both relief and evangelism." Surprisingly a number of American delegates refused to sign the covenant because the authors had chosen the word "simple" instead of "simpler." The wife of America's leading evangelical would not sign the covenant, saying, "You live in two rooms; I have a bigger home. You have no children; I have five. You say your life is simple and mine isn't!"

Yet the psalmist warns us in Psalm 49 that wisdom understands the folly of riches. Wealth cannot redeem immortal souls (vv. 7-9); it cannot prolong mortal life (vv. 10-12); and it cannot be taken into eternity (vv. 16-20). It is true: no hearse ever has a U-Haul trailer attached to it! It is "pomp" to pride oneself in and rely upon wealth, social standing and a life of "accomplishment and accumulation;" a most heinous form of spiritual pride. Psalm 49:13 warns, "This is the path of those who have foolish confidence; yet after them people approve of their boasts. *Selah*" (*Selah* — meaning, pause and think about that)!

Think about it. How much do you give to missions each year? Do you tithe — 10 percent of all that you accrue in one year? Do you regularly give to charities? Do you annually support institutions, fellowships or foundations? Have you made plans for your wealth once you're gone? Remember, to fail to do these things is to fail in life in the way of the fool! ""Man in his pomp yet without understanding, is like the beasts that perish." (vv. 12, 20). Your life and your legacy deserve a better ending than that! Work on a simpler lifestyle and plan for a richer legacy: Be wise with your wealth.

## DAY 26 LEARNING TO NUMBER OUR DAYS

### Read Psalm 90

> So teach us to number our days, that we may get a heart of wisdom.
> Psalm 90:12

Years ago a friend of mine gave me a book to read when I went on vacation to the beach. The book was entitled *Half Time: Changing Your Game Plan from Success to Significance* and was written by Bob Buford. Its premise was simple and yet profound: Once a person reaches the age of fifty he should plan for the last half of his life; planning to do what he always wanted to do in order to achieve a sense of significance in life. That plan may be to retire after thirty years of practicing surgery and spend the last few decades of life in short-term medical-mission work. Or perhaps the retired schoolteacher turns around to teach in the inner city — free of charge. The retired businessman becomes a church consultant. The ex-coach develops a sports ministry. The pastor-emeritus travels throughout the third world teaching in seminaries. You get the picture; the concept is rich.

Psalm 90 addresses itself to the wisdom of using the days of one's life to their fullest spiritual potential. As the oldest psalm in the Psalter — "A Prayer of Moses the Man of God" — it is predated only by Moses' psalm of Exodus 15. Psalm 90 reflects the mind, heart and wisdom of an aged Moses, perhaps written at Mount Nebo as he turns the mantle of leadership over to Joshua and offers Israel his last piece of inspired advice. Tested, tried and often frustrated by the ups and downs of leading the wilderness generation, Moses reflects on the great issues of life (Read 1 Cor. 10:1-13 for background). His "end of the matter (when) all has been heard" (Eccles. 12:13, ESV) is this: We are not responsible for what comes into our lives from God, but for how we used our lives in God's service.

Moses informs us that it takes the better part of a life – three score and ten – for most folks to gain wisdom: a wisdom about the terrible brevity of life (vv. 3-6), the folly of fallen humanity (vv. 7-10), the humiliation of our secret and besetting sins (v. 8), and the awesome predictability of God's indignant wrath over sin (v. 11). Surprisingly, the result of this wisdom is neither denial nor despair but a deliberate purpose to finish our lives in the work that is significant in God's eyes (vv. 12-17).

There is a great deal of concordance between Moses' psalm and Solomon's Ecclesiastes. Both expose to us the seven stages of life through which all God's saints must progress: the safety of childhood, the sensuality of puberty and young adulthood, the success we strive for in our thirties and forties, the security we pursue in our fifties, the satisfaction we seek in our retirement, the significance we long for before we die and the sanctification that has been our life's aim, only to be fully realized at death. Can we skip any stage? Probably not. Can we affect how long each stage takes? Probably so. That is why Moses prays, "So teach us to number our days that we may get a heart of wisdom."

The wise man plans in order to end his days doing something beyond success, security and satisfaction. He aims for a life of significance, and in so doing he caps off his life with a guarantee that his last days will lead to the glory of eternal holiness. We call that "finishing well." Moses would call that "a heart of wisdom."

## DAY 27 THE BLESSED MAN

# Read Psalm 112

*His righteousness endures forever.*

Psalm 112:3, 6, 9

Who does not want to be blessed? "Blessed is the man" appears as a formulary prayer and promise in repeated psalms (Pss. 1, 112, 119, 128 and elsewhere). The Old Testament wisdom literature promises "blessedness" where there is godliness. Psalm 112 is an acrostic, each of its twenty-two lines beginning with a successive letter of the Hebrew alphabet. This psalm provides for us a comprehensive description of "blessedness." It is a beautifully constructed psalm with an introduction (v. 1), a conclusion (v. 10) and three main points, each ending with the refrain: "His righteousness endures forever" (vv. 3, 9), or a variation, "the righteous ... will be remembered forever" (v. 6).

The first promise to the godly who live by God's Word and wisdom is for their prosperity (vv. 2,3). This prosperity comes in the form of descendants who are influential on the earth and use their wealth for compassionate purposes (vv. 2-4).

Second, in the order of "blessings" is vindication (vv. 4-6): His light shines in a dark world and enables the righteous man to "maintain his cause" – to prosecute his case for Christ and win both a hearing among men and a following for the Lord. His faith in God is vindicated before men and all can see it.

Third, the blessed man is guaranteed security. He does not fear "evil tidings" – stock-exchange downturns, war, layoffs at work or the latest Gallup polls. "His heart is firm, trusting in the LORD. His heart is steady; he will not be afraid." He has been a generous man toward the poor (v. 9) and a righteous man before God. Therefore "his horn is exalted in honor" (v. 9).

The result of all this is the vexation of the worldly man (v. 10). He simply cannot understand how such "dorks" get blessed and such "geeks" are held in high regard. They give instead of hoard, they are compassionate instead of assertive, they believe things nobody else does and live by standards everyone else repudiates, and yet they are blessed! But then, again, the world is foolish and never does understand the wisdom of God or the ways of godly men (1 Cor. 2:14-16).

Psalm 112 reminds us of an old virtue called "spirituality" and an old vice called "worldliness." We don't use that word much any more – "worldly" – but it's a good word and a legitimate label for postmodern life. In his wonderful book, *God in the Wasteland*, David F. Wells defines worldliness: "Worldliness is that system of values and beliefs, behaviors and expectations, in any given culture that have at their center the fallen human being and that relegate to their periphery any thought about God. Worldliness is what makes sin look normal in any age and righteousness seem odd. Modernity is worldliness, and it has concealed its values so adroitly in the abundance, the comfort, and the wizardry of our age that even those who call themselves the people of God seldom recognize them for what they are." That is worldliness. It is the antithesis of Psalm 112's wisdom.

How about it, are you "blessed"? I mean really blessed by the fruits of wisdom and not just fooled by the "abundance, comfort and wizardry of our age" (Wells). Can you discern the difference? Is your hope anchored in this refrain: "His righteousness endures forever"? Has Christ's righteousness been imputed to you and your righteousness imparted to succeeding generations? Remember: "The righteous will be remembered forever," but the worldly will be forgotten.

## Day 28 Search Me, O God!

### Read Psalm 139

*Search me, O God, and know my heart! Try me and know my thoughts! And see if there be any grievous way in me, and lead me in the way everlasting.*

Psalm 139:23, 24

J. J. Stewart Perowne has called Psalm 139 "the crown of all the psalms." Joseph Gelineau has entitled the psalm "The Hound of

Heaven." It is a psalm about the omniscient, omnipresent and omnipotent God keeping watch over His precious elect. Bishop G. A. Chase correctly observes: "The sense of the inescapable presence and all-seeing knowledge of God are a matter for joy, not terror."

We sometimes think that the idea of God always watching us is a tactic to be used in order to frighten little children into obedience. The thought of "the all-seeing eye of God" (Stott) is often neutralized for adults, as in Bette Midler's song, "*God Is Watching Us From a Distance*." But in Psalm 139 the watchful eye of God is put in proper perspective (a truth for assurance) and in proper relation (not from a distance but "close up and personal").

This Psalm presents the three attributes of God that are believed by all men and accepted as essential to His deity. First, God is omniscient: He knows all things (vv. 1-6). God knows everything and every thing about us. He knows us better than we know ourselves and understands the motives and the thoughts of our mind, even before they are formed! There is no fooling God and no impressing Him that we are anything other than what we are. The amazing truth in all of this is that in spite of what I really am – deep down inside where even I do not reach – God still loves me. There is no romantic idealism in God's love; He knows all about us and loves us relentlessly.

Second, God is omnipresent: He is everywhere and there is no place where He is not. He is in heaven (v. 8a), He is in hell (v. 8b), and He is in the remotest corner of the earth (v. 9). I may sometimes want to hide from the disconcerting gaze of God and His uncomfortable holy presence, but such is impossible. The mind-boggling truth is that wherever I go, and whatever I go through, God chooses to be with me. He is the friend who sticks closer than a brother at all times (Prov. 17:17).

Third, God is omnipotent: He is all-powerful (vv. 13-18). He is in complete control of my life from before my conception to my last breath. He made me like I am and guides me into what He wants me to become. There is no little detail, no fine print in my life not under the sovereign control of our loving God.

Add this all together and we arrive at the most precious truth of life: There has never been a time when God has not thought of us; there will never arise an event that will cause God to forsake us; and there is no power under creation to "separate us from the love of God which is in Christ Jesus our Lord" (Rom. 8:39). Therefore, I can confidently ask God to "search me" because He wants to save me from the "hurtful way" and take me home to heaven "everlasting."

On my office wall hangs a five-year-old's crayon scrawling of her first words – all run together – and her first theological foray into the world of God. My daughter gave it to me in 1984 after Sunday school one day. It's my favorite piece of art on my office wall and the deepest theological truth I have ever struggled to learn. In fact, I'm still learning it. It says simply this: "God will love you all the time." I often turn to gaze upon that picture and meditate on its truth. It's the essence of Psalm 139. And it's the consummate wisdom of a child of God.

## DAY 29 THE ANOINTED OF GOD

### Read Psalm 2

*Kiss the Son, lest He become angry, and you perish in the way.*
                                                      Psalm 2:12

Psalm 2 and its twin Psalm 110, are the two psalms most referred to in all the rest of Scripture. Their thoughts and influence are incredible. Peter uses these psalms, as does the author of Hebrews. Paul uses Psalm 110 in writing to the Corinthians. Jesus uses Psalm 110 for Himself in the synoptic Gospels. What is so vitally important about Psalm 2 is its identification of Jesus Christ as God's Anointed One. This psalm is the first of several psalms known as the Royal Psalms, depicting Christ as King of Kings. These psalms are different from the Enthronement Psalms because of their depiction of Christ in human terms, a king among men (Pss. 2, 20, 21, 45, 72, 110 and 144).

Their beauty lies in the exalted picture they paint of Jesus Christ and the awesome image set forth in their poetry. This heavenly prince rules all the kings of the earth, judges all the nations, crushes all God's enemies, defends and protects all God's people, marries His Bride, the church, and fulfills the promised hope of David's eternal throne. No wonder these seven Royal Psalms end with this exclamation: "Blessed are the people whose God is the LORD!" (Ps. 144:15).

The recent tragedies in the USA have caused a great wave of "spirituality" to arise out of the American soul. But absent – glaringly absent – is the preeminence of Christ in all of our prayers and professions. When in our National Cathedral, a clergyman invokes God with these words, "O God of Abraham, Jesus and Mohammed," the apostate soul of our nation is laid bare for all to see.

The church must recover its prophetic voice and proclaim without blinking that there is salvation in no one else than in Jesus Christ, that Son of the living God. And for the church to do so, our young people must recover the vision of a Christ-centered life and calling.

For that reason we pray this week for theological education that is devoted to capturing the minds of college students for Jesus Christ (2 Cor. 10:3-5) and committed to teaching a Christ-centered view of work, ministry, marriage, family and society. Such institutions challenge our future leaders to respond to the call of Christ upon their lives and futures. Hence, these Royal Psalms.

God has said, "As for Me, I have set My King on Zion, My holy hill" (Ps. 2:6). If we hope to hear our nation repeat these same words, then our young men and women in college must install Christ as Lord of all they are, all they do and all they hope to become. The nations are in an uproar over Christ, but let it not be so for our own nation. Let us pray for our university students, and for those who minister to them, that the Lord's Anointed might truly come to be the King of the nation.

## DAY 30 BOASTING IN THE LORD

# Read Psalm 20

*Some trust in chariots and some in horses, but we trust in the name of the LORD, our God.*

Psalm 20:7

Psalm 20 is a prayer: the prayer of the people of Israel for their beloved hero and king, David, the "Shepherd of Israel." He is the "anointed" (v. 6) of the Lord (*mashiyach* or "Messiah" in the Hebrew text). Therefore, he is a type of Christ (which means "anointed," *christos* in Greek). This prayer for King David by the church of the Old Testament, therefore, reflects the hope of the New Testament church in King Jesus, the "Good Shepherd" of the Israel of God (John 10:11; Gal. 6:16). This prayer expresses six hopes for the church, the Kingdom of God.

God's people pray for (1) answers to prayer, (2) security in office, (3) the aid of God's presence (*Shekinah* glory) (4) acceptance of our worship, (5) wisdom and success in counsel, and (6) fulfillment of all petitions (vv. 1-6). The reason for these bold prayers is simply that God loves His anointed and will undergird him. The hope of the church is not grounded in horses or chariots (i.e. vast human armies) but in "the name of the LORD, our God" (v. 7). In other words, the very character and nature of Jehovah is the basis of our confidence in Christ.

The church knows that Jesus is the Lord; He is God, in the flesh. Therefore "the name of the Lord" – Jesus – is the power of the church in her witness, work and warfare. In 1986 Phil McHugh, Gloria Gaither and Sandi Patti combined to write a popular chorus that went like this:

*There is strength in the name of the Lord, there is power in the name of the Lord, there is hope in the name of the Lord, blessed is He who comes in the name of the Lord.*

That is the hope expressed in Psalm 20.

Realizing the truth of this psalm, Jesus told His disciples, "'Truly, truly, I say to you, whoever believes in me will also do the works that I do; and greater works than these will he do, because I am going to the Father. Whatever you ask in my name, this will I do, that the Father may be glorified in the Son. If you ask me anything in my name, I will do it'" (John 14:12-14). The hope and power of the church is, as it has always been, in the name of the Lord Christ.

Our young people are living in an age of tremendous computerization, scientific advancements, worldwide networks of information and massive doses of higher education. The danger in all of this could be that our young people might come to trust, not so much in chariots and horses, but in techniques and technology rather than in the Spirit and the Word, in the name of Christ.

Our campus leaders and college professors must teach our youth by word and by example that Christ is more than sufficient for answers to modern man's problems – yes, even postmodern man's problems! A great system of doctrine, a biblical form of government, a well-educated clergy and a rich history of success may well qualify as "chariots and horses." The time to learn that the Lord gives success is early in one's life – in college.

Years ago, on *Face the Nation*, Billy Graham told the press that if he had to do it all over again he would travel less, preach less and pray more. May our young people learn this early in life and ministry: "Our hope is in the name of the LORD, our God."

## DAY 31 VICTORY IN JESUS

### Read Psalm 21

*He asked life of you; you gave it to him, length of days forever and ever.*
Psalm 21:4

Psalms 20 and 21 form a "diptych;" two psalms that belong together, like Psalms 9 and 10, or perhaps were once together, like Psalms 42 and 43. Michael Wilcock states that these two psalms face each other "like two hinged panels." In the church these two sacred hymns have been used in times of war and victory: Psalm 20 in times of tumult and danger, Psalm 21 in celebration of victory and the end of hostility. Derek Kidner adds, "A comparison of verse 2 with Psalm 20:4 suggests that Psalms 20 and 21 are paired as petition and answer." The church has also used Psalm 21 on Ascension Day as a coronation hymn to Christ the King.

Young people must indeed be taught that life is not a smooth passage from one rite to the other as a child grows into youth and youth into adulthood – an endless stream of graduations, acquisitions and accomplishments. No, for the Christian life is a great spiritual warfare with Jesus Christ at the front of the ranks. Kingdom perspective is necessary. Jesus is not what A. W. Tozer sarcastically called "the Utilitarian Christ," but rather the Captain of the well-fought fight.

Our hymnody reflects a change of view on what Christ and His church – the Kingdom of God – is all about in this world. Old hymns like "A Mighty Fortress," "For All the Saints," and "Onward Christian Soldiers" reflect a spiritual warrior mindset. (Note: The last of these three hymns has been removed of late from several main-line hymnals: too "militaristic.") Modern choruses prefer to sing of being "happy in Jesus," warm in His fellowship and "safe in His arms." Psalm 21 will not let us live in this dream world.

David reminds us of three realities affecting his life, Israel's life and our lives. He writes as a "type" of Christ. First, we do have enemies (spiritual and earthly) who will rise up against us and seek our ruin (Ps. 20). Second, God will give us victory over our enemies, who are really the enemies of Christ and only ours through association with Him (Ps. 21:1-6). Third, God will crush His and our enemies in order to protect us, build His kingdom and glorify Himself (Ps. 21:7-13). Unless our young people in college realize this reality, they will worship a false Christ, look for a false deliverance and cling to a false hope – a carefree and comfortable life in this world. This may be the promise of modern advertising, but not of the Gospel.

Many times the words of William W. How will prove true in our covenant children's lives: "Thou wast their rock, their fortress and their might; Thou, Lord, their captain in the well-fought fight; Thou in the darkness drear, their one true light." But just

59

as assuredly, Christ's spiritual triumph will also form the core of their joy in life. Bishop George Horne has accurately reminded us: "The joy of Christ Himself, after His victory, is in the strength and salvation of Jehovah, manifested thereby. Such ought to be the joy of His disciples, when God hath enabled them to vanquish their enemies, either temporal or spiritual; in which latter case, as they are called kings, and said to reign with Christ."

Spiritual preparation for our children's conflict and conquest in Christ must be a priority for campus ministers and college professors. We cannot keep the conflict from touching their lives, but we can prepare them to fight to win in the inevitable war of Christ. They must, early in life, be oriented to look not for "nice" life tomorrow, but for the glorious life yet to come! "But lo! There breaks a yet more glorious day; the saints triumphant rise in bright array. The King of glory passes on His way. Alleluia!" (How).

## DAY 32 THE PLEASING THEME

### Read Psalm 45

> My heart overflows with a pleasing theme; I address my verses to the king...
>
> Psalm 45:1

Young people always like music and their favorite music is the love-song. Rock 'n Roll makes its living on boy-meets-girl love ballads. Whether it's the Beatles crooning, "*I Wanna Hold Your Hand,*" or Dave Matthews pouring out the song, "*Crush,*" the formula is the same. Sometimes the love-song lasts for generations like "*We've Got a Groovy Kind of Love*" by Wayne Fontaine and the Mindbinders (when I was at the university) or Phil Collins and Genesis (when my children were in college). Love is the staple of life: love for God shared with mankind between a boy and a girl.

Psalm 45 is a love song. In fact, it is a "Royal Wedding Song," written for the nuptial festivities of Israel's King and His future queen-bride. It divides itself into two lovely – even "romantic" – sections: verses 1-9 about the King of Glory (sung by the bride), and verses 10-17 about the Bride of Beauty (sung by the King himself). This lovely psalm is a love-song about Christ and His bride, the church. This is the love of all loves.

In our Reformed witness to college students we must be very, very careful to avoid presenting our most holy religion as little more than a Scripturally mechanical method to "get the right answer" and nail down guaranteed justification. Our faith is a love affair with God in Christ, and as such is filled with all the passion, drama, and yes, "romanticism" of the best of love stories. In his book *The Godly Preachers of the Elizabethan Church*, Irvonwy Morgan described the Puritan clergy as the "Romantic Preachers." This "romanticism" in their preaching was displayed in the great theme of their sermons: spiritual warfare in which the rescue of sinners from eternal danger was accomplished by the heroic Christ, who was the champion of their souls and who loved them more than His own life. Never was there such a love story as this. It is, as J. R. Tolkien told C. S. Lewis, "The myth that is true!" And never were there love-songs that set forth, in poetry for music, this love affair between Christ and the church like Psalm 45.

The essence of our love life in Christ is clearly set forth in a series of three parallels in this psalm: Christ is blessed and that makes us (the church) beautiful; Christ is victorious and so we are established; Christ is anointed and so we are adorned. The glory of our husband, Jesus, becomes the glory of His bride, the church. This is heart-religion; that which provides the spark of passion to the wonder of truth.

Puritan pastor John Brown captured the ethos of this psalm when he wrote: "In singing this *song of the Lamb*, let me with open face behold his glory, and be changed into the same image from glory to glory, as by the Spirit of the Lord. Let my admiration of his excellency swell to the brim, and my love burn with a most vehement flame; and let my hopes of being for ever with him, be strong and lively. Let my heart be all wonder at his excellency, fullness, and grace – all subjection to his government and laws; and let my lips be filled with his praise and honour all the day." May this be the heart of all our young people in college – "love burning with a vehement flame" for Christ!

## DAY 33 A PRAYER FOR OUR NATION'S LEADER

### Read Psalm 72

*May prayer be made for him continually, and blessings invoked for him all the day.*

Psalm 72:15

On September 20, 2001 President George W. Bush addressed a grief-stricken and indignant nation in the tragic wake of terrorist attacks on New York City. His speech will be recorded in the annals of American history alongside those of other leaders in times of great crisis. Esther Margolis, Publisher of Newmarket Press, wrote: "President George W. Bush's address to the nation on September 20, 2001, has become one of those speeches that even while you're listening to it, you know will immediately impact the lives of hundreds of millions of people all over the world." In closing that speech, entitled "Our Mission and Our Moment," President Bush looked into the eyes of 270 million Americans and said: "I will not forget the wound to our country and those who inflicted it. I will not yield; I will not rest; I will not relent in waging this struggle for freedom and security for the American people. The course of this conflict is not known, yet its outcome is certain. Freedom and fear, justice and cruelty, have always been at war, and we know that God is not neutral between them. Fellow citizens, we'll meet violence with patient justice – assured of the rightness of our cause, and confident of the victories to come. In all that lies before us, may God grant us wisdom, and may he watch over the United States of America." Mr. Bush acknowledged that, without God's wisdom, grace and strength, no success or victory is possible. All good kings, prime ministers and presidents acknowledge this truth.

In Psalm 72, the people pray for the king – Solomon. The psalm is of his authorship and reflects the God-given wisdom of the Son of David, the King of Israel. He designs a prayer to be sung, a prayer containing five stanzas. Each stanza reflects a particular aspect of a just ruler and his righteous reign. Stanza one (vv. 1-4) prays for the nature of his administration: wisdom,

62

righteous rule, justice for all and the vindication of the oppressed. Stanza two (vv. 5-7) prays for his spiritual influence: promoting the fear of God, revival and reformation (an outpouring of the Spirit). Stanza three (vv. 8-11) prays for his international policies: dominance, victory, strength, influence and favorable trade balance. Stanza four (vv. 12-15) prays for his domestic policies: help for the poor and needy, the sanctity of life, and love for the people. And stanza five (vv. 16-17) prays for national prosperity: agricultural prosperity, urban renewal, support from the people and international fame. This psalm is a perfect "Prayer for Our Nation's Leader."

The psalm is obviously to be fulfilled in Christ, of whom Solomon is a type, the Messianic Son of David and King of the Jews and the church. These very blessings and beauties will mark His rule over, first, the church and then, the world. Our young people need to begin to see business, law, politics, medicine, education, science and the ministry as Christ sees them: part of the overarching cultural mandate to bring all things under the dominion of the true Solomon ("Man of Peace") – Jesus Christ (2 Cor. 10:3-5).

May our ministries to college students remind them that Christ has redeemed, gifted and called them to assist him in bringing His kingdom out of the shadows and into the light of His glory. That is our purpose and our prayer.

## DAY 34 AN ARMY FOR THE KING

### Read Psalm 110

*Your people will offer themselves freely on the day of your power, in holy garments; from the womb of the morning, the dew of your youth will be yours.*

Psalm 110:3

H. C. Leupold begins his exposition of Psalm 110 with these words: "It is not merely coincidence that this psalm is quoted more often in the New Testament than is any other. This fact is a testimony to its importance." This "New Testament" psalm written by David for himself but pointing to Jesus Christ for its fulfillment is a masterful poetic presentation of the kingship of Jesus Christ. "Christ the King" might rightly be the title, for indeed that is its subject and material.

The psalm divides itself into two paragraphs (i.e. strophes or stanzas). Verses 1-3 speak of the eternal reign of Jesus Christ, the Son of God. His divine sonship and rule are alluded to in the first two verses. God the Father, in eternity past, speaks to God the Son: "Sit at my right hand...." ... and "sends forth from Zion [his] mighty scepter" that his Son might rule. In verses two and three Christ is depicted as the warrior king: "Rule in the midst of your enemies." The second stanza (vv. 4-7) speaks of the present reign of Jesus Christ, the Son of God. He is pictured as a priestly-king, like Melchizedek of Abraham's time. Christ is a "priest forever," ever living to intercede for the saints (Heb. 7:25) and to apply His satisfactory blood atonement to their sinful souls (Heb. 9:22). Lastly, He is set forth as the king of judgment on the last day: "He will execute judgment among the nations" (v. 6).

What is so amazing (and pertinent to our young people in college) is that King Jesus gathers an army of volunteers (v. 3) around Him, in this life, who will serve His kingly purposes – in life and in death. "Your people will offer themselves freely on the day of your power [i.e. after Christ's resurrection], in holy garments; from the womb of the morning, the dew of your youth will be yours". Derek Kidner explains: "This gives the picture of a splendid army suddenly and silently mobilized." What a happy and holy thought: An army of young people equipped, energized and encouraged to join the ranks of the church and serve King Jesus!

Could it be that this "Generation-X," these "postmodern" sons and daughters of the self-centered Baby Boomers, will be the army of God to reform our churches, restore our cities and pray down the revival of religion, in their youth and our old age? Oh may it be so. May they "just appear" on the scene for Christ like dew shows up in the morning. May they cover the land with refreshing grace from God. May our Christian colleges prepare them well for "The Fight of Faith." And may the new song of our young people be the old song written by a college president, Timothy Dwight, for Yale University in the days preceding the Second Great Awakening: "I love Thy kingdom, Lord, the house of Thine abode; the Church our blessed Redeemer saved with His own precious blood.... For her my tears shall fall, for her my prayers attend; to her my cares and toils be given, till toils and cares shall end."

## DAY 35 BLESSED ARE THE PEOPLE

## Read Psalm 144

*Blessed are the people whose God is the LORD!*

Psalm 144:15

I was once told as a young Christian by a man discipling me, that whenever God's Word repeats itself it is a crucial point to grasp. For God only need say something once, but when He repeats it twice or more, He wants to be sure we grasp the truth. Twice in the Psalter this thought is expressed: "Blessed are the people whose God is the LORD!" (144:15), and "Blessed is the nation whose God is the LORD" (Ps. 33:12). What an important truth for our young people to grasp early in life.

One of the critical mistakes made by many church leaders is to assume that the world in which we live and the issues with which we struggle are those of the world of Calvin and the Puritans. This is not so. Our world is more like the world of Paul than the world of Luther. Christendom is disintegrating. (Malcolm Muggeridge wrote that it has died!) And the spiritual issues are more basic today than even thirty years ago when my denomination was born. The refinements of the Reformed faith, as lovely, life-giving and liberating as they may be are not the issues foremost in our young peoples' lives. They live in a neo-pagan world, "the twilight of a great civilization" (Carl F. H. Henry) and the beginning of a "new dark ages" (Chuck Colson). The world of Paul was a lot more brutal than the world of Luther. And the basic issue that separates those two worlds – like night and day – is this: "Who is God; Caesar or Christ?"

Our postmodern, post-Christian, secular, new-age Western

culture is polytheistic, superstitious and committed to "the religion of the state" – culture reigns supreme. Our campuses are faced with the vast and variegated sampling of life views and religions known only to Paul and the apostles before these days. What a mission field for Reformed ministries in the universities!

Psalm 144 sings of a "blessed people" who know, love and serve the Only and True God. They are blessed by a perspective of truth (vv. 1-4), by the protection of truth (vv. 5-11) and by the permanence of truth (vv. 12-15). The refrain of the psalm (vv. 7-8, 11) reminds us that our youth do not come to this truth unopposed: "Rescue me and deliver me from the many waters, from the hand of foreigners, whose mouths speak lies and whose right hand is a right hand of falsehood.." This psalm looks at life realistically.

But it also promises the future generations a blessedness that our fathers sacrificed on the altars of modernity and materialism. It promises spiritually strong sons, godly daughters, life free of want, success in their undertakings and the treasures of God's favor in their land: "May there be no cry of distress in our streets!" (v. 14b). Idyllic? Perhaps, but it is the prayer of the psalmist and the promise of God: "Blessed are the people to whom such blessings fall! Blessed are the people whose God is the LORD!" This is a prayer for returning to "old paths" (Jer. 6:16; 18:15; 31:21) and an outpouring of God's grace. Michael Wilcock summarizes this psalm, our prayer and the hope of our youth: "Then and now, whenever God's people are under assault they do well to remind themselves of all that their loving God has done for them in the past, insignificant though they are. They can quite properly ask him to act in ways that even in modern times might be described as the rending of the heavens, a bolt of lightning, rescue from a sea of troubles. They know that his, and their, chief weapon is the truth of the gospel, to destroy the lies which (like Samson's hair) are the secret of the enemy's great strength. They are sure that nothing but good can result, even from the most disastrous circumstances, when God's people are taking refuge in the Rock."

## DAY 36 THE GRACE OF GOD

## Read Psalm 6

*O LORD, rebuke me not in your anger, nor discipline me in your wrath.*

Psalm 6:1

The Penitential Psalms are a collection of hymns, in the Psalter, that have served the church for many years in both its meditation and its worship. Martin Luther lectured on these seven psalms of repentance in 1517. These lectures led to the publication of the messages on the Penitential Psalms – the first book Luther himself prepared for publication. He wrote it, he said, "Not for Nurembergers, that is, cultured and smart people, but for coarse Saxons, for whom Christian instruction cannot be chewed and prechewed enough even by my wordiness." He wrote the commentary for common folks.

Many of those who pray for both the reformation of our most holy religion and the revival of God's church, beseech God for a spirit of brokenness. The church of this twenty-first century has ignored cultural sins, shifted the blame for corporate sin and covered personal sin with psychological jargon. We are all victims, it seems; none of us are responsible. But Luther's theology of the cross challenges this cop out. Gerhard Forde, in his book entitled, *On Being a Theologian of the Cross,* points a finger at our irresponsible attitude toward our sins. "The language of sin, law, accusation, repentance, judgment, wrath, punishment, perishing, death, devil, damnation, and even the cross itself – virtually one-half of the vocabulary – simply disappears. It has lost its theological legitimacy and therefore its viability as communication. A theologian of the cross says what a thing is. In modern parlance: a theologian of the cross calls a spade a spade. One who 'looks on all things through suffering and the cross' is constrained to speak the truth." If this is so – and it is – where do we turn for sobriety, sanity and sound teaching about sin, repentance, confession and forgiveness?

The answer is obvious. We can turn to no one else than to our shepherds. Our preachers and pastors, must lead us into a clear apprehension of the Gospel and a confident appropriation of the grace that justifies and then sanctifies us in Christ. A sure indication that a church needs both reformation and revival is that it does not truly understand justification by grace through faith in Christ alone, nor does it fully grasp the truth of sanctification by grace through faith in the Spirit.

Our pastors must preach the Gospel, teach the Law and call all men to repentance and faith. They must both model and apply grace – the life of God in the soul of man. Without grace our religion dies, our churches decline and our culture decays in hopeless decadence. Men who truly understand and live in the Gospel must shepherd God's flock by means of the Gospel.

We must pray for Reformed seminaries and other institutions that supply men for the ministry to our churches. Unless our seminaries train our future pastors in how to call people to repentance, challenge people in faith, instruct people in the Gospel and comfort people with grace, all is lost. Richard Lovelace is correct: "During the last two centuries the understanding of sin has suffered a correlative decline in the church along with the apprehension of God.... One of the consequences of this remarkable shift is that in the twentieth century pastors have often been reduced to the status of legalistic moralists, while the deeper aspects of the cure of souls are generally relegated to psychotherapy, even among Evangelical Christians." Let us pray for seminaries to prepare men for the ministry who truly understand the exceeding sinfulness of sin and the awesome wonder of grace.

## DAY 37 CLASSIC CONFESSION

### Read Psalm 51

*Against you, you only, have I sinned and done what is evil in your sight.*
Psalm 51:4

Psalm 51 has been used throughout the ages of the church to confess sins to God. Known as the *Miserere*, the subtitle of this psalm tells us that Psalm 51 was written in the wake of David's sin with Bathsheba (2 Sam. 11–12). If we follow the paragraph divisions of the New American Standard Bible then David's classic confession is really a collection of five prayers: repentance from sin (vv. 1-4), recognition of sinfulness (vv. 5-9), renewal from sin (vv. 10-13), reformation from sin (vv. 14-17) and restoration from sin (vv. 18-19).

In this psalm there is a great theology of sin. It is summarized well by Bishop George Horne of Norwich (1730–1792) in these words: "The penitent's first ground for hope of pardon is his own misery, and the divine mercy which rejoiceth to relieve that misery. The riches, the power, and the glory of a kingdom can neither prevent nor remove the torment of sin, which puts the monarch and the beggar upon a level. Every transgression leaves behind it a guilt, and a stain; the account between God and the sinner is crossed by the blood of the great propitiatory sacrifice, which removes the former; and the soul is cleansed by the Holy Spirit, which takes out the latter." This psalm should be studied and applied by church pastors of our time.

Ours is an age where man's responsibility for sin and his duty of repentance are seldom heard. Years ago a popular Christian periodical ran an article entitled: "Repentance: The Forgotten Doctrine." What was forgotten in the eighties has been forsaken in the dawning of this twenty-first century. Evangelical Christianity seems to be headed the way of liberalism, with a Gospel that calls for no repentance. Within my own denomination there are parties preoccupied with the Law, but with little talk of grace. And, at the other end of the theological continuum are those preoccupied with grace to the point of being accused of antinomianism. Could it be that what both these dear brethren, and their schools of thought, desire is really a serious view of the Law, genuine repentance when we break that Law, and a Gospel that teaches grace without ignoring the terrible reality of sin?

Psalm 51 offers this Biblical balance. It clings to the reality of God's lovingkindness and His great compassion. At the same time, it acknowledges the reality of a sinful nature (v. 5) and the sinful actions that proceed from original sin: iniquity ... sin ... transgression (v. 3). David is not afraid to make full confession of sin because he realizes the full extent of God's grace. A true understanding of the Gospel does not make us lawless or "loose" with God's Law. Quite the opposite is true: Gospel living is a commitment to a holy life.

The late James Montgomery Boice recognized this dual emphasis in Psalm 51. He wrote: "Two things come together in these verses. The first is a fierce, almost desperate clinging to God's mercy. This is profound because, as many commentators have pointed out, mercy is the sole basis of any approach to God by sinners.... The only reason we dare come to God and dare hope for a solution to our sin problem is his mercy.... The second striking thing ... which comes together with the first, is David's profound awareness of his sin and its true nature."

Evangelicals often get bad press. We are called "mean-spirited." At other times we are labeled "worldly." Perhaps we've earned these labels because of our law focus or our loose grace! If we were humble about our sinfulness, honest about our sins and dependent upon God's grace we would be true to what we confess. We would please God more. And we would reclaim our good name among our neighbors.

## DAY 38 TIMELY CONFESSION OF SIN

## Read Psalm 32

*Therefore let everyone who is godly offer prayer to you at a time when you may be found.*

Psalm 32:6

Psalm 32 is commonly seen as the sequel to Psalm 51 and another chapter in the story of David's great sin with Bathsheba and its aftermath (2 Sam. 11). Alexander Maclaren correctly notes: "The old opinion that it records David's experience in the dark time when, for a whole year, he lived impenitent after his great sin of sense, and was then broken down by Nathan's message and restored to peace through pardon following swiftly on penitence, is still defensible, and gives a fit setting for this gem." It is a wonderful commentary on the pain and problems involved with unconfessed sin. The psalm divides itself into three parts that record the psalmist's gratitude for grace (vv. 1, 2), his groaning over unconfessed sin (vv. 3-7), and his guidance from God (vv. 8-11).

In parallel with Psalm 51, David provides us with a good anatomy of sin (Ps. 51:2, 3 compared with Ps. 32:5). He uses three words to describe sin. First sin is missing the mark, a falling short of God's glory and perfection (Rom. 3:23). Second, iniquity denotes an inward moral perversity or corruption; what we call original sin and total depravity – "the corruption of his whole nature" (Shorter Catechism, Q. 18). Third, transgression is wrongdoing, unrighteous actions, and law breaking, the trespassing or stepping over of the limits of God's Law.

In the *Book of Common Prayer* our Anglican and Episcopalian friends pray a prayer known as the General Confession which acknowledges all three aspects of sin: guilt, corruption, and law breaking. It serves as a beautiful pattern for confession of sin: "Almighty and most merciful Father; we have erred, and strayed from thy ways like lost sheep. We have followed too much the devices and desires of our own hearts. We have offended against thy holy laws. We have left undone those things which we ought to have done; and we have done those things which we ought not to have done; and there is no health in us." Would that we daily and specifically prayed such prayers.

In the Southern United States where I live and minister, saving face is more important than anything else. Therefore it is very rare to find people who will apologize, admit wrongdoing and ask for forgiveness. It is therefore not uncommon to find the absence of a Prayer of Confession in Southern worship services. In fairness to the South, I venture to guess that such confession-less Christianity is common throughout our land.

We tend to "let things go by." We want others to "just forget" about our sins against them. We tend to do penance rather than ask for forgiveness – we are extra nice to those we've wronged, in an effort to "set things right." It doesn't work. As a result of our unwillingness to confess our sins – to God and to others

71

we've wronged – we suffer the consequences. David put it this way: " For when I kept silent, my bones wasted away through my groaning all day long." (v. 3). Little wonder then that our churches are filled with people eaten up with bitterness, suffering with "depression" and subsisting on prescribed drugs from some therapist. Psychologists have been saying for years that the two chief causes of depression are unresolved guilt and bitterness in broken relationships. When will we pay heed to Psalm 32?

Holding grudges, living with unreconciled tension in relationships, saving face, explaining away our guilt and taking pills to replace penitence will only rob us of our birthright in Christ: "The joy of the Lord." Our pastors must learn to do more than talk about justification, grace and Gospel living. They have to teach and lead people through the biblical process of confession, reconciliation, restoration and restitution. Our people need to know that joy only comes to those who confess their sins to God and to those they've wounded. Only then can we say, "and you forgave the iniquity of my sin" (v. 5).

## DAY 39 SECOND THOUGHTS ABOUT FORGIVENESS

## Read Psalm 38

*O LORD, all my longing is before you; my sighing is not hidden from you.*
Psalm 38:9

Here is the third of the seven Penitential Psalms. It is an account of sin, sickness and social ostracism and David's plea for deliverance from God. David had sinned, falling into adultery and murder, and after a long period of impenitence he was confronted by the prophet Nathan. His account of his journey to repentance may well be recorded in these three psalms: 51, 32 and 38. H. C. Leupold believes this to be the case: "For it is the nature of the conscience and of the weak faith of man to raise the question of the finality of absolution, especially in the case of more grievous sins. So it is quite possible that the historical sequence may be this: Psalms 51, 32, 38, each reflecting a new phase of the writer's experience.... It cannot furthermore be denied that no deep sense of guilt is expressed. Penitence takes on various shades and forms, and the deeper sense of guilt has found expression in the other two psalms mentioned." Historically this psalm fits into that stage of David's life when Sheba rebelled (2 Sam. 20) and Absalom revolted (2 Sam. 15–19). Therefore David's sin is linked to sickness and interpersonal problems.

We must never forget that we live in a postmodern age where the ideas of absolute right or wrong, transgression against a perfect standard and genuine guilt are considered ridiculous, if not wrong. In fact, many therapists today tell us that guilt is bad; it is a feeling no "healthy" person should have. But they are wrong. A healthy conscience will always feel guilty when in fact the guilt of sin is warranted. When we do wrong we should feel guilty.

Our evangelical doctrine of justification by faith and the imputed righteousness of Christ should not rob us of the benefit of a guilty conscience. The elect are freed from the penalty of sin due to Christ's righteousness credited to them but that does not render them guiltless. And when they sin, until they confess that sin and deal with the consequences of their sin, guilt will be a genuine feeling with which to wrestle.

David's problems with feelings of guilt, physical sickness, family problems and political disruption may well be the judgment of God upon his grievous sins. And the same may be true of us. Anthony Evans has said that "every physical problem has a spiritual cause" somewhere down the line. We are uncomfortable with this, but remember: This is the age of "no fault," from no-fault divorces to no-fault car insurance. We are a nation of victims and victims never say, "I am the responsible one. I caused this. I am to blame."

Dr. John Reed Miller of the First Presbyterian Church in Jackson, Mississippi used to say to me quite often, "Until the church in America takes responsibility for our corporate sins, we will not see revival in America." This is a daunting task for America's pastors: To teach a nation of victims in an age of no-fault thinking that all our problems – personal and corporate – are ultimately our fault. That's the truth.

God sees our situation and hears our sad souls sigh with the burden of guilt, shame and complicated ramifications due to our sin (v. 9). He will not forsake us (v. 21) and He will make haste to help us (v. 22). When we His people take responsibility for our sins and the sins of our people, God will take responsibility for that which is His: restoration to grace. If America is not seeing this restoration, the problem lies with us and not God. "The Lord is not slow to fulfill his promise as some count slowness, but is patient toward you, not wishing that any should perish, but that all should reach repentance" (2 Pet. 3:9).

## DAY 40 A TIME FOR GRACE

### Read Psalm 102

> You will arise and have pity on Zion; it is the time to favor her;
> the appointed time has come.
>
> Psalm 102:13

Many commentators place Psalm 102 during the time of the Restoration, when Israel returned from exile in Babylon to rebuild the temple, Jerusalem and their way of life. The beauty of this psalm is that it recalls to our minds a wonderful truth about God and sin. When God disciplines us for sin, and when we repent, there inevitably comes a time for restoration. In truth, things may never be the same as they were prior to our sin and its serious ramifications: adultery may lead to divorce, alcoholism may lead to a DUI and imprisonment, and immorality may lead to disease and even death. But repentance always brings some sort of restoration.

The psalmist clearly states this in verse 13, "You will arise and have pity on Zion; it is the time to favor her; the appointed time has come." The seventy years of captivity were over. The time for restoring Israel to God's favor was at hand. And the psalmist saw the importance of this season of grace in the overall redemptive plan of God: "Let this be recorded for a generation to come, so that a people yet to be created may praise the LORD" (v. 18).

There is a great lesson here. When we have been severely disciplined due to our sin, it is possible to become genuinely embittered against the Lord. The discipline of God can often appear excessive. In due course, men may feel "hammered," chastised by the Lord more severely than seems right. But God is never wrong. He is slow to anger; in comparison to the length of time we remained in rebellion, His discipline is relatively short. For example: Judah's slide into more and more grotesque forms of idolatry went on for over 350 years! In comparison, God's discipline in the captivity was merely seventy years. Psalm 30:4, 5 points us to this wonderful truth: "Sing praises to the LORD, O you his saints, and give thanks to his holy name. For his anger is but for a moment, and his favor is for a lifetime. Weeping may tarry for the night, but joy comes with the morning."

We need a season of grace, a time for restoration in the West, and it is right for us to plead for that. Of course, we must realize that our sins may not have fully played themselves out, and our repentance as a people is surely lacking. But when we are disciplined by the Lord (and we shall be because of our godless ways from which we have not yet turned), and when God brings us to our senses and to remorse over our sins, then "times of refreshing … from the presence of the Lord" (Acts 3:19) will come as well.

Pastors in our nation must begin to say these things to their congregations. Let us not act like "Peace, Peace" when there is not peace but danger! (Jer. 8:11) And let us not be afraid to look foolish and warn the church of the indignation of a God who refuses to be toyed with. But let us also remind the saints that, after genuine repentance, God promises "a time to be gracious" to His church.

## DAY 41 GOD DOES NOT KEEP A COUNT

## Read Psalm 130

*If you, O LORD, should mark iniquities, O Lord, who could stand?*

Psalm 130:3

Psalm 130, the sixth of the seven Penitential Psalms, includes one of the most famous verses in the Psalter. Verse three, quoted above, makes reference to a truth all sinners must take note of, but over which Bible scholars disagree. What does this Song of Ascents, this pilgrim song, mean when it says: "If you, O LORD, should mark iniquities, O Lord, who could stand?" There are two standard opinions.

Joseph A. Alexander expresses the first view: "To mark is to note, take notice of, observe. To stand is to stand one's ground, maintain one's innocence, and perhaps in this case, to endure one's sentence. The question is equivalent to a strong negation, or an affirmation that none can stand." In other words, God does not keep a record and all men are hopelessly guilty before Him. H. C. Leupold reflects the second view: "To him sin is so serious a business that he realizes that, if all his sins were to be recorded against him and dealt with as they deserve, his case would be quite hopeless. In making that statement he momentarily envisions what would happen if God were on the alert, watching what sins a man may commit." In other words, God is not nit-picking us to death; if He did, not one man could survive His just wrath. In actuality these two positions are not mutually exclusive but rather complementary.

God does know all our sins, even more than we ourselves are cognizant of and therefore over which we are repentant. Yet He does not choose to discipline us for every single sin; He does not let the sins go by but deals with them in Christ rather than with us.

C. H. Spurgeon correctly pulls these two thoughts together and observes: "If men were to be judged upon no system but that of works, who among us could answer for himself at the Lord's bar, and hope to stand clear and accepted? Iniquities are matters which are not according to equity: what a multitude we have of these! Jehovah, who sees all, and is also our *Adonai*, or Lord, will assuredly bring us into judgment concerning those thoughts, and words, and works which are not in exact conformity to his law. Were it not for the Lord Jesus, could we hope to stand?" And, of course, this gives us great confidence before the throne of grace. We are able to confess our sins because God, unlike us, it not One to avoid the issue of sin but rather is One who deals with sin decisively. And He does so in the crucifixion of His Son. "For our sake he made him to be sin who knew no sin, so that in him we might become the righteousness of God " (2 Cor. 5:21). What a wonderful truth. And it is this truth that makes Psalm 130 so upbeat and so encouraging, even in the face of great sin.

But there is another truth to be found here. The older I get the more aware I am that the evangelical teaching about forgiveness is terribly warped and self-centered. We usually apply Psalm 130:3 to ourselves and forget how we treat others. Jesus will not let us do that. He repeatedly ties God's forgiveness of us to our forgiveness of others (Matt. 6:14, 15). If God does not "mark" our iniquities, should we keep a running tally of other peoples' offenses toward us?

We often say to others, or ourselves, "That's it! I've had enough! She did that once too often. I'm done. It's over! I just can't forgive her one more time." But if God's grace can mark your sins and cover them in Christ's blood, then God's grace in you can allow you to "let it go" one more time. After all, it really hasn't been "let go" by any means. For while Christ suffered on the cross, He paid for your sins against God and others' sins against you. That payment is what allows us to forgive.

It seems to me that there's a parable about this very thing in Matthew 18:15-35. Why not read Psalm 130, then Matthew 18:15-35, and then spend some time in prayer erasing that tally in your brain against those for whom God has already suffered in Christ? Do it! You'll be a much freer person when you let go of that which God took hold of in Christ.

## DAY 42 FOR THE SAKE OF THY NAME

### Read Psalm 143

*For your name's sake, O Lord, preserve my life!*

Psalm 143:11

The last of the seven Penitential Psalms is Psalm 143. It is a lovely psalm of a man with a broken and contrite heart. It is "an act of contrition." Years ago, as a young Catholic boy, I used to pray "The

Act of Contrition," a prayer that went like this: "O, My God, I am heartily sorry for having offended Thee. And I detest all my sins because of Thy just punishments, but most of all because they offend Thee, my God, who art all good and deserving of all my love. I firmly resolve, with the help of Thy grace, to sin no more and to avoid the near occasions of sin, through Christ our Lord. Amen." In a very real sense, these words express the sentiments of Psalm 143.

David remembers God's goodness (vv. 5-6) and he pleads with contrite heart that God would teach him to sin no more (vv. 7-9). In the end, he asks for forgiveness for God's sake: "For your name's sake, O Lord, preserve my life! In your righteousness bring my soul out of trouble!" (v. 11). The ultimate aim is God's sake – God's pleasure, God's purposes and God's praise. Before all other things that sin is, it is first and foremost of all a great offense, a personal injury and a direct insult to God. Evangelical and Reformed people, whose theology has at its core a "personal relationship with God" should realize this more than anyone else.

In the end, it is the honor of God that is at stake when we sin, for the sins of the saints who profess to have a personal relationship with God, dishonor the Lord more than the iniquities of the reprobate. David Dickson states, "It concerneth God in His honour, to revive the spirits of the contrite ones, when they have their recourse to Him."

Saints must realize that sin is ultimately the disfavor, disrespect and dislike of God bubbling up from our foul souls. When we are profane it is because we are angry with God. When we are covetous it is because we are critical of God's provision for us. When we break the Sabbath we are telling God that He means little to us. When we strike a man we do so to abuse the image of God in others. In the end, sin is always aimed at God by a heart that, even for a moment, hates God.

That is why David prays, "For your name's sake, O Lord, preserve my life!" (v. 11). He is asking for a renewal of love in his own heart for God the Good One.

Our Catholic friends are correct: God is all good and all

deserving of all our love. When we withhold that love, in any way, the Bible calls it sin. Many scholars believe Psalm 143 was written by David in the wake of Absalom's rebellion. In the Septuagint the subscription tells us that it was written when he fled from his son, Absalom. J. J. Stewart Perowne comments, "It is probably that the deep tone of sorrow and anguish which pervades the psalm, and the deep sense of sin, led to the belief that it must be referred to the occasion." The psalm then is the anguish of a father who deserves his son's love but instead received his hatred. And it is the psalm about a man who realizes that his Father-God deserved all of his love but received his sin instead.

May our future pastors teach us, by word and by example that our greatest duty is to love God. And our greatest act of love is an obedient and holy life. "For this is the love of God, that we keep His commandments; and His commandments are not burdensome" (1 John 5:3).

## DAY 43 THE RESTORATION OF GOD

## Read Psalm 60

*O God, you have rejected us, broken our defenses; you have been angry; oh, restore us.*

Psalm 60:1

In the Psalter the Holy Sprit's reviving work is often referred to as "restoration." Time and again the psalmists pray, "Restore us, O God, . . ." and in so doing ask God for revival. The Psalter includes seven Psalms of Revival – psalms that pray for regeneration, revival, reformation and restoration. In the next seven devotions we will pray through these Psalms of Revival (Pss. 60, 71, 80, 85, 137, 126, 138).

Psalm 60 is the first of these prayers for restoration, and it was written at a time in David's life when he felt duress during time of war. David was trying to subdue his northern enemies, Philistia and Syria, while his southern enemies, Edom and Moab, attacked his flank. He cried out to the Lord not to discipline him with defeat but to "restore" him in victory. He saw the invisible hand of

God behind the political and social events of his life and times.

How far we have fallen from that worldview! We deny that tragedies, attacks of enemies, a poor economy, natural disasters and social unrest are the remedial judgments of God. We say to ourselves, "These things just happen!" But how can people who believe in a sovereign God, who teach predestination and who profess the doctrine of providence really believe anything "just happens"?

We say, "Prosperity does not mean God is blessing us, nor do tough times mean God is judging us." But are we unwilling to look at the "pain indices" by which sociologists measure societal decay and deny that these reflect a culture in decline: rising crime, greater disparity between rich and poor, more and more divorces, fewer births, proliferation of immorality, declining trust in government and the delegation of religion to the periphery of life? Can we say that "these things just happen" and that they are not the judgments of God? We may want to explain these things away, but the writers of the psalm see such social problems as the heavy hand of God upon a sinful people. We should heed again the words of Moses: "'Have not these evils come upon us because our God is not among us?" (Deut. 31:17).

Old Testament Israel experienced times of revival. We see revival in the book of Acts. And we have historical records of reformations, great awakenings and local revivals many times in this Church Age. Habakkuk, Jeremiah, Isaiah, Daniel, Ezra, Nehemiah, and the psalmists wrote inspired prayers for revival. We are foolish and negligent, in addition to being proud, not to teach, preach and pray these prayers.

In his book *Can We Pray for Revival?* Brian Edwards calls us to do exactly that with these words: "If, in the past, God has given His people this experience in their times of need, and if His character leads us to believe that it may be ours as often as we need it, plead for it, and He chooses to give it, then we are challenged to pray for it." For what? For the regeneration of dead souls, for the renewal of tired saints, for the revitalization of stalled congregations, for the revival of the church, for the reformation of religion and for the restoration of our nation. Yes! God has been grieved. God is displeased. God has judged. But God can and will revive, reform and restore ... when we pray!

## DAY 44 UP FROM THE DEPTHS OF THE EARTH

## Read Psalm 71

*You who have made me see many troubles and calamities will revive me again; from the depths of the earth you will bring me up again.*

Psalm 71:20

One modern scholar recently wrote concerning the evangelical hope for revival that such longing for another Great Awakening was "a myth" that should not be believed. He said, "Here was a mythic understanding of revival that could never be fulfilled across a vast and variegated modern nation like the mid-century United States." In other words, twenty-first century America is too pluralistic and multi-cultural to allow for revival – a spiritual phenomenon that can only occur in the homogenous cultures of Christendom. But I don't believe that for a moment!

In Psalm 71 the psalmist prays to "a God for all seasons." This God is the "trust from [his] youth" (v. 5), "his strong refuge ... in the time of old age" (vv. 7-9), and the power for future generations, "all those to come" (v. 18). In fact, the heart of his prayer comes when he asks God for reviving power and grace for his offspring yet to be born in the future: "O God, from my youth you have taught me, and I still proclaim your wondrous deeds. So even to old age and gray hairs, O God, do not forsake me, until I proclaim your might to another generation, your power to all those to come. Your righteousness, O God, reaches the high heavens. You who have done great things, O God, who is like you? You who have made me see many troubles and calamities will revive me again; from the depths of the earth you will bring me up again. You will increase my greatness and comfort me again" (vv. 17-21).

The History of the Bible is the history of revivals and reformations, both in Old Testament and New Testament times. Ernest Baker, in his little book *The Revivals of the Bible* (1906), studies eighteen revivals in Scripture. Wilbur M. Smith, in his book *The Glorious Revival Under King Hezekiah* (1959), mentions sixteen "Biblical revivals." Likewise Walter C. Kaiser, Jr., in his book *Revive Us Again* (1999) examines sixteen revivals in the annals of both testaments. Modern scholars, made cautious by sociology, psychology and political science, may have come to doubt the possibility of revival, but the men of old did not. James Burns's classic book *Revivals: The Laws and Leaders* (not a book on "revivalism" but on genuine Spirit-sent, sovereignly-given awakenings) opens with these confident words: "In the history of religion no phenomenon is more apparent that the recurrence of revivals." And so it is.

Our theology of God and man demands that this be so. The wages of sin – death! – is exacted in every facet of fallen and depraved mankind's existence. Sin causes marriages to fail, families to fall apart, communities to rot out, nations to slip into decadence, churches to dry up, and souls to die in eternal perdition. God is the God of new beginnings, of second chances, of new births. We call His life-giving work regeneration, renewal, reformation, revival and restoration – depending upon who receives His life giving, restarting graces. All things human will eventually die unless God supernaturally infuses into these human endeavors grace. Grace is best defined as the life of God in the soul of man. How can grace-based, Gospel-driven, sovereignly reborn people, like Calvinists in my denomination, the PCA, doubt these truths?

The writer of Psalm 71 prays for his children's children, in their vast and variegated modern nations to hear of the revivals of old and experience a revival of new! This prayer has been answered again and again: in Jerusalem, Judea, Samaria, Antioch, Macedonia, Greece, Rome, Wittenberg, Zurich, Geneva, Edinburgh, London, Northampton, Rochester, New York City, Wales, Shantung, Zaire and elsewhere. Tell me, why can it not happen again in this vast and variegated twenty-first century America?

## DAY 45 THE SMILE OF GOD

# Read Psalm 80

*Restore us, O Lord God of hosts! let your face shine, that we may be saved!*

(Psalm 80:3, 7, 19)

When God the Spirit has been grieved by sin and quenched in His work, He withdraws and in so doing, He causes His people to lose their joy and strength (Neh. 8:10). Although God is always with His people, they do not always experience a sense of His favor (Read Deut. 31:17). Therefore, the Old Testament writers often speak of God's "shining face." They often pray for God to "cause His face to shine upon us." Always concrete thinkers, the Hebrews liken a smiling countenance to a "shining face." These saints are praying for God to smile upon them once again. That very request is the three-fold refrain of Psalm 80 (vv. 3, 7, 19).

People who need revival soon come to the conclusion that God's favor is absent from them for one chief reason: very few people are being converted and the vast majority of the land are spiritually lost and dead. Jeremiah tearfully recognized this in his day: "The harvest is past, the summer is ended, and [still] we are not saved" (Jer. 8:20). During the days of the Assyrian dispersion, Asaph wrote Psalm 80. Derek Kidner pinpoints correctly: "Not the fall of Jerusalem, it seems, but the last days of its northern counterpart, Samaria, about a century-and-a-half earlier, gave rise to this strong cry for help ... between 734 and 722 BC" The nation was lost, not only militarily and socially, but even more so spiritually.

Asaph cried out for God to revive the people of God: Israel in dispersion and Judah under duress. He pleaded: "But let your hand be on the man of your right hand, the son of man whom you have made strong for yourself! Then we shall not turn back from you; give us life, and we will call upon your name!" (vv. 17-18). Asaph prayed for God to send "the anointed one" – Messiah or Christ – to revive His people again. For in Christ, and Christ alone, is there new life and in Him only is the favor of God found, the smiling face beheld in glory: "we have seen his glory, glory as of the only Son from the Father, full of grace and truth" (John 1:14). The apostle reminded us that "in him was life, and the life was the light of men" (John 1:4).

C. H. Spurgeon understood what this prayer for revival was all about: "Under the leadership of one whom God had chosen the nation would be kept faithful, grace would work gratitude, and so cement them to their allegiance. It is in Christ that we abide faithful: because he lives we live also. There is no hope of our perseverance apart from him. If the Lord gives life out of death, his praise is sure to follow. The Lord Jesus is such a leader, that in him is life, and the life is the light of men. He is our life. When he visits our souls anew we shall be revivified, and our praise shall ascend unto the name of the Triune God."

America's churches are not growing. Thousands of congregations shut their doors every month. Conversion rate is near zero for all evangelical churches. Larger "mega-churches" grow mostly due to transfer growth from smaller congregations. We have lost most of the vestiges of our Christian culture. Society has transformed us, for surely we have not transformed it. The harvest of previous revivals has passed. The summer of evangelical growth has ended. And still, America is not saved. Oh, let us begin to pray for revival in our nations. Let us begin to draw near to God. Let us seek "the man of God's right hand" – Jesus Christ. God sees us. His eye is ever upon us. Oh that He would smile upon us and lay His hand of favor on our dry and dusty souls!

## DAY 46 REVIVE US AGAIN!

## Read Psalm 85

*Will you not revive us again, that your people may rejoice in you?*
Psalm 85:6

Many conservative Christians are afraid of the subject of revival. The very word conjures up visions of either emotional manipulation (revivalism) or ecstatic excesses (Pentecostalism). Walter Kaiser, Jr. summarizes the problem many evangelicals have with the concept of revival: "What then is revival? Probably this is one of the church's most abused terms. Some see it as a synonym for mass evangelism or a special week of meetings in the local church aimed at winning the lost to Christ. Others regard the term with suspicion and automatically associate it with bizarre happenings in church meetings held under heavy orgies of emotion…. But neither of these understandings can claim biblical support for what is distinctive or normative about revivals."

Many in my denomination are also reluctant to talk about, pray for, or seek outpourings of God's grace. There is a sort of scholasticism that has infected us; many of us are intellectually and theologically too sophisticated for revival. Dr. Martyn Lloyd-Jones blames this on our Reformed Puritan heritage: "I have known a number of men belonging to the Reformed constituency who really seem to be controlled by some such thoughts as this. 'After all,' they say, 'a man like John Wesley had a prominent part in the revival of the eighteenth century.' From that they seem to deduce that there is something undesirable and wrong about revival. 'Can any good come from such a quarter? If men like Wesley and Finney and other Arminians can be involved in revival and used in it, well we ought to be suspicious of revival.' … But perhaps the most important and most serious matter is this. The Puritans themselves do not seem to teach us anything about revival. Oh, that I could have quoted copiously and extensively out of the Puritans! But I cannot do so. As far as I can find, they did not write on the subject. Did they even recognize it?"

What then do we do with Psalm 85? This psalm was written as a "twin psalm" to Psalm 80 (yesterday). Psalm 80 was written by Asaph during the Assyrian dispersion, while Psalm 85 was written by the sons of Korah after the Babylonian captivity (circa 539 or later). Can we pray this prayer today? Or is this psalm "contextually fixed" – to be used only by one generation and none other? I believe the psalm is for all times. This psalm yields a three-fold perspective to our prayers for revival, and for that reason serves the purposes of our generation.

First it speaks of a *past* perspective of the grace of God

(vv. 1-3). Then it speaks of a *present* plea for the grace of God (vv. 4-7). Finally it speaks of a preparation for the *future* grace of God (vv. 8-13). In other words it ponders restoration (vv. 1-3), it pleas for revival (vv. 4-7) and it purposes reformation (vv. 8-13). The sons of Korah are saying, in so many words, "Lord, you began a good work of restoration in us; do not leave off, do not forsake Thy work. Revive us and reform us. Finish what you began!"

Can we not plead this before God? Alexander Maclaren rightly points us to this truth: "God leaves no work unfinished. He never leaves off till He has done. His beginnings guarantee congruous endings. He does not half withdraw His anger; and, if He seems to do so, it is only because men have but half turned from their sins."

We cannot finish the task God set before us without massive infusions – outpourings – of reviving grace. The church in the Old World needs reviving as much as the church in the New World needs reformation. May God give us this restoring, reviving, reforming grace so that His people may rejoice in Him!

## DAY 47 SONG OF THE EXILES

### Read Psalm 137

> By the waters of Babylon, there we sat down and wept, when we remembered Zion.
>
> Psalm 137:1

When I was a young lieutenant in the U. S. Army, a singer named Linda Ronstadt came out with an album of songs, and one of them began with this soulful lament: "By the rivers of Babylon when we sat down, there we wept when we remembered Zion. Those who carry us away to captivity require from us a song, but how can we sing King Alpha's songs in a strange land?" I didn't know it then, but that old negro spiritual was a rendition of Psalm 137:1, 3. It touched me then as a young, unconverted man. It does so even more, thirty years later.

Psalm 137 is the first half of twin psalms (Pss. 137 and 126). Both have to do with the Babylonian Captivity – three waves of refugees carried off from Jerusalem to Babylon in 605, 597 and 586 BC. One can almost see the agony of heart and the anguish of soul as these parched and weary exiles stagger toward the Tigris, Euphrates, or their tributaries for a drink of life sustaining water, only to hear the Babylonian soldiers taunt them: "Come now! You Jews love to sing! Sing us one of those psalms about Jehovah your King!"

A few years ago, while on vacation, I ran to a supermarket late one evening to get Tylenol for a sick child. While in the store I was confronted by an irate (and drunk) African-American lady. She heaped insult after insult upon me. Meanwhile seven Black men stood by, smiling, chuckling, giving her an "Amen" to one racial slur after another. The Black clerk turned her head and pretended not to see. When I left the store I shook with anger, fear and humiliation. I wanted to cry and I wanted to strike back. What had I done to incur such wrath, such hatred, such blatant racial mistreatment?

But then it dawned on me: This is what these men and women have swallowed for three centuries or more, at the hands of my ancestors and friends. Perhaps what I felt was what they felt – daily. And perhaps this was what Israel felt "by the rivers of Babylon." They were under God's discipline. They were experiencing remedial judgment for "the sins of their fathers." They were helpless, hurt but unable to strike back.

When you and I feel outraged by forty million abortions, frustrated by an anti-Christian media, let down by a politically-correct government, slandered by the homosexual alliance and misrepresented by liberal neighbors, we may well be paying for the wages of our fathers' sins; sins we benefited from and the fruit of which we enjoyed. What shall we do? What can we do?

The thing to do is to remember: to remember Zion (the golden age of the church, v. 1), to remember Jerusalem (the City of God, v. 6), and to ask God to remember us in our affliction (v. 7). This remembering, this weeping, this agony of soul over the fruit of our fathers' sins is the first step to revival. For just as remedial judgment comes before reviving joy, so sorrow over sins' fruit always comes before repentance from sins' folly.

We will once again sing the songs of Zion, King Alpha's songs. But only after we've been purged of our love for the world so that our love for God is once again renewed.

## DAY 48 LIKE MEN IN A DREAM

### Read Psalm 126

*When the Lord restored the fortunes of Zion, we were like those who dream.*

Psalm 126:1

Psalm 126 is the second half of the twin psalms, Psalm 137 (yesterday) being part one. It is "A Song of Ascents," a song of "degrees" or "goings up;" that is, a Pilgrim Song for Israel's annual journeys to Jerusalem for the high holy days. J. J. Stewart Perowne sets Psalm 126 in its historical context of Ezra 1:1–2:70: "The first colony of exiles had returned to Palestine. The permission to return had been so unexpected, the circumstances which had led to it so wonderful and so unforeseen, that when it came it could hardly be believed. To those who found themselves actually restored to the land of their fathers it seemed like a dream. It was a joy beyond all words to utter. God, their fathers' God, had indeed wrought for them, and even the heathen had recognized His hand."

This psalm's laughter answers Psalm 137's tears. This dream of the restoration reverses the nightmare of exile. The Pilgrim songs sung with joy make up for the songs of Zion unable to be sung for sorrow. In the euphoria of this happy day in 539 BC, the psalmist prays, "Restore our fortunes, O Lord, like streams in the Negev! (v. 4). This is a prayer for revival (which was answered in the days of Ezra and Nehemiah!).

Their beginning is certainly inauspicious. They are "the remnant" – a small portion of a nation remaining and returning to Israel's land. Only 49,897 people returned to rebuild the temple, Jerusalem and the Hebrew way of life. And yet, because God had begun to pour forth reviving graces – even if at first just a trickle – they had assurance of greater grace yet to come. They pray, with confidence: "Those who sow in tears shall reap with shouts of joy! He who goes out weeping, bearing the seed for sowing, shall come home with shouts of joy, bringing his sheaves with him." (vv. 5-6). The sorrow of repentance had sowed the seed of revival's harvest. The hard work of reformation would yield the joyful fruit of restoration. John Stott explains: "The exiles have returned to a city and temple in ruins, and to fierce Samaritan opposition. Their restoration has been only a tiny beginning, like the sowing of seed…. Indeed, they are confident that their present hard work will be crowned with success, just as the farmer who sows in tears will reap in joy. Thus, the joy experienced when the Lord first restored their fortunes will be renewed."

The inauspicious beginning of a reform movement in my denomination, almost thirty years ago, can be expected to yield a great harvest of souls and to bring a restoration of favor to the land under God's "rain of revival" (Hosea 6:1-3). And the wonder of it all was this: Just as all the nations saw the destruction of Jerusalem and the deportation of Jews, so the whole world acknowledged the reviving work of God. "They said among the nations, 'The Lord has done great things for them.' The Lord has done great things for us; we are glad " (vv. 2-3). And the wonder of it all will be when the nations see the great outpouring of grace upon our land and all the seeds of our reforming work sprout up in a great harvest of godliness and godly souls. Then the nations will smile and say, "The Lord has done great things for America. We are glad!" And we will be glad too.

## DAY 49 THE LORD WILL ACCOMPLISH HIS WORK

## Read Psalm 138

*Though I walk in the midst of trouble, you preserve my life…. The Lord will fulfill his purpose for me …*

Psalm 138:7, 8

Ours are troubled times. We seek to describe them with such labels as "post-Christian," or "postmodern," or "neo-pagan." Carl F. H. Henry writes about *The Twilight of a Great Civilization.*

Malcom Muggeridge proclaimed *The Death of Christendom*. Chuck Colson warned us of a new Dark Ages in *Against the Night*. All in all, most people don't see much hope for the church in America or Christianity in the West. One senses little hope for "times of refreshment ... from the presence of the Lord" (Acts 3:19).

Psalm 138 thinks otherwise. David writes of God's reviving grace: "Though I walk in the midst of trouble, you preserve my life." (v. 7). He seems certain of such, no wishful thinking here. And he gives us the ground of his confident assertion: "The Lord will fulfill his purpose for me" (v. 8). And why is he so certain of this (as Paul is in Phil. 1:6)? The answer is "the steadfast love of God" referenced in verses 2 and 8. The word in Hebrew is *chesed* – one word in Hebrew that can be translated accurately only by a whole phrase in English: the covenant love and loyalty of God. Because God has sworn a covenant with those who trust in Christ, He will not fail to build His church worldwide and fulfill all His promises.

Joseph A. Alexander informs us, "The work begun and yet to be completed was the whole series of God's gracious dispensations towards David and his seed, beginning with the first choice of the former and ending in the Messiah." David thus prays, "Do not forsake the works of Thy hands" (v. 8). And the understood reply from God is, "Don't worry. I wont'!"

David refers to "the words of your mouth" and to "the ways of the Lord" – God's pronouncements and God's patterns. These are further reinforcing truths that God will revive His church worldwide. Despite her troubles, God will pour forth His Spirit on the works of His hands – the church – and will raise her up in glory and gladness.

Tell me, is it so outlandish to conceive and too difficult for God to revive the Church of Rome? Can He not raise up the Coptic Church, the Byzantine Church and the Armenian Church in Spirit and Truth? Is the Eastern Orthodox Church impenetrable when it comes to the Holy Spirit? Could the Neo-orthodox mainline churches ever be impregnated again with born-again life? Would it be impossible for God to remove the worldliness, the arrogance and the shallowness from evangelical churches? Do you think God could or would ever take away the Reformed Church's intellectual pride and replace it with spiritual passion? Why not? Were not all these churches once "the works of God's hands" and are they not still the love of His life?

Troubled though they all are, they all were once His church. The Lord once had a great plan for them all. And that plan is not finished. "The Lord will fulfill his purpose for me." And what concerns the church everywhere is a great revival of religion!

## DAY 50 THE BEAUTY OF UNITY

### Read Psalm 133

*Behold, how good and pleasant it is when brothers dwell in unity! It is like the precious oil on the head, running down on the beard, on the beard of Aaron, running down on the collar of his robes!*
*It is like the dew of Hermon, which falls on the mountains of Zion! For there the Lord has commanded the blessing, life forevermore.*

Psalm 133

Each year, in my denomination, our General Assembly ends by singing a metric version of Psalm 133 from *The Trinity Psalter*. Each year our teaching and ruling elders return to their fields of ministry with this prayer for unity. One of the Pilgrim Songs of the Church, Psalm 133 celebrates both the beauty and the blessings of brothers who "dwell together in unity" (v. 1).

Would you pray for the beauty of balance, the blessings of unity, the fruit of reformation and the gift of revival for your denomination? Perhaps you could keep these seven weeks of devotions in the Psalms and use them again and again; or share them with another or a small group, praying together for your denomination. If there are two things the church of Jesus Christ needs, they are the profitableness of reformation and the unity of revival — truth and love. This song celebrates these two jewels of true religion.

Scotsman David Dickson summarizes this psalm and all our prayer efforts over these past seven weeks. He states: "The fruits of peace in the reformation of religion and civil judicatories, so redound to the comfort of all families and private persons, that the good of concord may be demonstrated sensibly. Such a concord is genuine, and worthy of the name, which uniteth the members of the visible church, as brethren, or children of one father, in the true religion, for the mutual discharge of all the duties of love. Some things are pleasant and not profitable, and some are profitable and not pleasant, but the concord of God's people, or holy peace within the visible church in any place, is both pleasant and profitable. This blessing is not to be expected by any, but through Christ, on whom the oil of gladness, and all the graces of the Spirit are first poured out, and then from him are carried to the meanest member of his body."

Pray for the "Blessing" for your denomination. And may the brethren pray with you!

# Part Two

## God Our Redeemer
## Celebrating God the Son - Jesus Christ
## His Redemptive Work and
## Headship Over the Church

*"And they remembered that God was their God
and the Most High God their redeemer...
so He shepherded them according to the integrity of
His heart, and guided them with His skillful hands."*

*Psalm 78:35, 72*

## DAY 51 A GUEST IN GOD'S WORLD

### Read Psalm 39

*Hear my prayer, O LORD, and give ear to my cry; hold not your peace at my tears! For I am a sojourner with you, a guest, like all my fathers.*

Psalm 39:12

We begin our second fifty days of prayer together in this section by looking at three psalms that are part of a mini-collection. Klaus Seybold calls Psalms 38-41 "Prayers for the sick." We examined Psalm 38, one of the Penitential Psalms, in our previous section (p. 72). We now look at Psalms 39–41. James Luther Mays observes of our psalm for today: "The prayer seems to be a penitential supplication of one who is grievously ill. But the suffering is portrayed less as a case of personal and social affliction (contrast to Psalm 38) and more as a matter of the general human predicament of transience and futility. The whole prayer is pervaded with a melancholy about the human condition."

The psalmist "muses" over the evil and sorrows of life in a fallen world (vv. 1-3) and then he "speaks" – he prays. Three times he addresses the "LORD" (vv. 4, 7, 12) and these three vocatives become his three prayers. He asks God to help him understand the brevity and transience of his own life, "a mere breath" (vapor) and a "shadow" (literally: a reflection or image; namely the "image of God"). Time, it seems, is running out. Second, he asks God to "deliver me from all my transgressions" because he senses that God's hand is against him, in fact, afflicting him due to his sins (vv. 10-11). God has taken away what is "dear to him" in order to reprove him – health, prosperity, security and shalom, his wholeness and welfare. Third, he asks God to turn His angry gaze away from him so that "I may smile again" (v. 13).

He has learned his lesson and this is it: "For I am a stranger with You, a guest, like all my fathers" (v. 12) The English Standard Version renders it this way: "I am a guest, like all my fathers" (i.e. ancestors). We exist in God's world as God's guests and only as such. He invites us here by birth; He determines how long we visit in life; He sends us back from whence we came through death.

Brother James is right: "Yet you do not know what tomorrow will bring. What is your life? For you are a mist that appears for a little time and then vanishes" (Jas. 4:14).

As we pray for our beloved homeland, let us remember three things. First, life is short. Terrorists, nuclear bombs, war, space shuttle disasters, crashing economies, and the daily stuff of cancer, heart attacks and accidents, remind us that life here is transient – brief, moving on, over soon. Second, we share a fallen humanity with all men in our broken world. All our suffering is ultimately due to the Holy Hand pressing against the sinful image. God is preparing His world of men for the return visit of Jesus. Third, we Christians must see life as Christ did. We, like He, are mere sojourners in this world. Much as we love it, this land is not our home. We are passing by in time, passing through in history, passing on in glory. We belong to another place. We say, with Christ, "My kingdom is not of this world" (John 18:36). Like Paul, "our citizenship is in heaven" (Phil. 3:20). As we pray for our homeland we ask for three things – and three things only: for time that God might do His work in us, for forgiveness that God might shed His grace on us, and for safe passage as Christ travels with us, leading us home, to where we really belong: The City of God.

## DAY 52 WHEN THE HEART FAILS

### Read Psalm 40

*For evils have encompassed me beyond number; my iniquities have overtaken me, and I cannot see; they are more than the hairs of my head; my heart fails me. Be pleased, O LORD, to deliver me!*
Psalm 40:12-13

It is easy to be "spiritual" when everything is going well. But when "evils ... beyond number" surround us, well that's a different story. In Psalm 40 we have the third of the "Prayers for the Sick" in the Psalter. This beautiful song is part hymn of praise (vv. 1-10) and part lament (vv. 11-17). David runs the gamut of emotion, from confident trust to serious discouragement.

He begins by praising God for past deliverances (vv. 1-10).

God has heard his prayers, delivered him and blessed him. And his response is pure praise. He even remarks that God's gracious works toward him are too numerous to recount. His love and admiration overflow: "None can compare with you!" (v. 5). He has openly shared his testimony with many others (vv. 9-10). But things have changed.

Suddenly his tune changes from praise to lament, just as suddenly as his circumstances have changed. Now he says, "my heart fails me" (v. 12). He is on the way to the Temple, but this time not to offer a sacrifice of thanksgiving (v. 6), but rather to plead his case before God. His prayer is as straightforward as his praise: Evils due to his own sin again threaten to destroy him and he needs God to be his Champion and Deliverer once again (vv. 13-17). He feels almost panicky: "Do not delay, O my God" (v. 17).

But David sees not just his sinful self in dire distress. The Holy Spirit opens his eyes to see Christ. In verses 11-12 he mentions the steadfast love (Hebrew *chesed*: the covenant love and loyalty of God the Redeemer). He loses sight of himself – "My iniquities have overtaken me, and I cannot see" (v. 12) – but not of the Messiah. Henry Law explains what David "saw" with the eyes of his soul: "To the eye of faith the blessed Jesus here conspicuously appears. 'All we like sheep have gone astray; we have turned every one to his own way, but the Lord hath laid on Him the iniquities of us all.' 'He was made sin for us, who knew no sin, that we might be made the righteousness of God in Him.' Thus He stands before God, by imputation as the greatest sinner ever seen on earth. He denies not His sin-laden position. He accepts all the iniquities of all His people, as verily His own. He acknowledges their grievous weight. They so depress Him that He cannot raise His eyes. In numbers they exceed all power to count. In devout consciousness of the immensity of relief, with what fervour will the believer bless His burden-bearer – His sin-sustainer – the Lamb of God, that taketh away his sin!"

But how did he come to see Christ? Look back in verses 6 and 7. When he came into the Temple to pray, he heard the

Levites reading the Law of God, more than likely the Book of Deuteronomy, the Book of the Covenant, the Gospel in the Old Testament. God's Word lifted him, once again "from the pit of destruction, out of the miry bog" (v. 2) of his own foiling and filth. And the good news put a "new song" in his mouth (v. 3). H. C. Leupold says, "This happens to be one of the clearest testimonies to the importance of the Word or law of the Lord for the people of the Old Covenant."

When we stupidly return to "wallowing in the mire" (2 Pet. 2:22) of our once atoned for and previously forgiven sins, we have two choices. We can stare at the moral and spiritual cesspool that seems ever to leak out of our souls, and in the process lose heart. Or we can go to God's Word, open to any page, and soon see Christ and the cross. Quickly the stories of grace in Christ will remind us of previous works of grace in our own lives. And we will bow before God, confess our sin, and sing with a heart of praise: "Blessed is the man who makes the LORD his trust" (v. 4).

So take your eyes off your mess and gaze across that pool of pollutant sin. Look long. Look hard. Squint if you have to. You will see Him, there on the other side – the Lord Jesus Christ, beckoning you to draw near and saying to you, "Come to me, all who labor and are heavy laden, and I will give you rest" (Matt. 11:28).

## DAY 53 THE HEALING OF A HEAVY SOUL

### Read Psalm 41

As for me, I said, "O LORD, be gracious to me; heal me, for I have sinned against you!"

Psalm 41:4

Psalm 41 is the last selection in Book One of the Psalter. It is a fitting end to Volume One of "The Prayers of David." And it is linguistically and positionally linked to Psalms 39 and 40, the "Prayers for the Sick." Michael Wilcock comments, "The threads are drawn together one more time in the final psalm of the first David Collection. Again there is sin that needs forgiving, ... and sickness that needs healing.... Again there is the malice of enemies; again a cry for help gives way to new confidence; and the opening words of this psalm echo those of the very first one, 'Blessed is the man who...'"

Once again David sees life more holistically than we do. He refuses to compartmentalize things the way postmodern men do. To him all of life is a seamless garment of God's grace and man's sin and the complex tapestry these two needles weave together. His sickness, his sin and the reality and recklessness of his enemies all fit together. We refuse to see life that way: to us things "just happen." Children just rebel against godly parents, evil befalls us and we are always innocent (i.e. victims), financial ruin comes upon us due to providence ("bad luck" in the world's lingo) but never because we failed somehow. Gone, it seems, are responsibility, guilt and consequences. We have become a nation of whiners, and certainly, a nation of victims.

In David's world sin was a weighty thing, as was God. In fact, God was described as possessing "glory" (Hebrew *kabod*) — a word that really meant heaviness. Sin was a heavy-duty thing: it caused sickness, brought sorrow, cried out for salvation and guaranteed serious consequences. Sin brought guilt, not just shame. Shame is a feeling whereas guilt is a state, a reality, a condition that necessitates remedy. When sin loses it weightiness, faith falls apart. David F. Wells, in his wonderful book entitled *Losing Our Virtue: Why the Church Must Recover Its Moral Vision*, has this to say: "The problem with all of this is that where sin has lost its moral weight, the cross will lose its centrality, Christ will lose His uniqueness, and His Father will no longer be the God of the Bible." Yet God has constructed mankind in such a way that sin will really, in the end, prove to be the wake-up call to people in an age of "the lightness of being."

Wells explains: "If, then, we in this generation have lost our ability to name our sin — and we have — we have nevertheless not lost our sin. We may call it by other names, we may not even recognize it at all, and we always misinterpret it. Our moral radar is defunct. And yet, moral reality keeps intruding into our experience; the threads of a moral existence are ever present. It is thus that creation is the great ally of the Gospel, while culture and the fallen self are its great enemies. This is the awful contradiction that cuts through all of life, and it offers the most telling entrée for the Gospel into the postmodern soul." And that is what Psalm 41 is: David's poetic entrée for the Gospel into the postmodern soul.

In fact, loved ones, things *do not* "just happen." God has made a world of cause and effect. The cause of all evil is always our sin. And the cause of all good is forever God's grace. And life is caught between the same two bookends that Psalm 41 is: The Blessed Man who flees to God for help ... the Blessed God who remains the Friend of sinners. This is not a truth to be argued with, explained away or ignored. This is the Truth of Life: Men sin; God delivers. And the man who is able to make any sense of life knows the weightiness of this warp and woof of existence. Sin is a heavy thing, an overwhelming thing. And the only force heavier than sin is the grace of Christ the Redeemer.

## DAY 54 THE MORNING PSALM

## Read Psalm 3

*I lay down and slept; I woke again, for the LORD sustained me. I will not be afraid of many thousands of people who have set themselves against me all around.*

Psalm 3:5-6

Psalms 3 through 10 make up a sub-collection of psalms that may be referred to as "The Golden Chain of Trust." These eight psalms are songs of trust and prayers for deliverance in the face of wickedness and evil men. Psalms 3 and 4 make up the first pair of psalms in the Psalter – hymns that belong together, side by side (e.g. Pss. 9–10; Pss. 42–43; Pss. 127–128). Psalm 3 is known as the Morning Psalm, Psalm 4 as the Evening Psalm. Both belong to the time of David's life when he fled from his rebellious son, Absalom (2 Sam. 15–17). These psalms fit into that group of psalms known as "The Songs of the Fugitive." Alexander Maclaren sheds light on this group of psalms: "The psalms which probably belong to the period of Absalom's rebellion correspond well with the impression of his spirit gathered from the historical books.... We may well allocate with a fair amount of likelihood the following psalms to this period – 3, 4, 25, 28, 58, 61, 62, 63, 109, 143. The first two of these form a pair; they are the morning and evening hymn."

Psalm 3 is the psalm that will not let us dismiss the concept of evil or wickedness. Psalm 2 puts the struggle between good (God) and evil (world) in its cosmic context of Revelation 12 and 13. But Psalm 3 brings wickedness down to the personal level. While you and I sleep the wicked do their evil work. Things that go bump in the night are dangerous. For the second time in the first three psalms a key word appears: "wicked" (Hebrew *rasha*). Jean-Pierre Prevost makes an insightful observation: "The whole drama of the psalms is played out in the opposition between the just person and the wicked." And we are uncomfortable with this. We have a difficult time using those two words often seen in the Psalter: evil and wicked. These are not just two adjectives. They point to certain kinds of people. All around us are evil men who live in wickedness and do wicked things.

We can't help but notice how politicians have rediscovered these words with these truths since September 11, 2001. Terrorists are "evil" men and their networks are "wicked." And "just" nations who display "righteous" indignation are justified in their assessments and reactions. David – a government man himself – agrees: he tells us that there are "many thousands of people ... against me all around" every night he sleeps (v. 6).

But David knows something postmodern men don't. He knows the heavenly math. And he knows therefore that the One Good God infinitely outnumbers myriads of terrorists, infinitely overpowers millions of nuclear warheads and infinitely controls all the networks of evil in this vast and wicked world.

God sees and answers from "His holy hill" (v. 4). *Selah*, the composer writes: pause. Contemplate that deeply. Abide in that truth. While we slept in the valley of evil, God was awake – all night – on His holy mountain! Now it's time to shower, grab a bite, brush our teeth and comb our hair and get on to work. God is on the job.

## Day 55 The Evening Prayer

## Read Psalm 4

*Be angry, and do not sin; ponder in your own hearts on your beds, and be silent. Selah Offer right sacrifices, and put your trust in the LORD.*

Psalm 4:4-5

As we mentioned previously, Psalms 3 and 4 are related: one is the Morning Psalm, the other the Evening Psalm, respectively. J. J. Stewart Perowne connects the two in this manner: "David had said in the previous Psalm, 'I laid me down and slept:' he says in this, 'I will lay me down in peace, and sleep.' These words evidently connect the Psalms together. That was a morning, this is an evening hymn…. The interval between the two Psalms or the occasions to which they refer may only have been the interval between the morning and evening of the same day. The thoughts and turns of expression in the one are not unlike those in the other." David's day, full of evil men and wickedness has come and gone, now as he retires to bed he does what many of us do – he lays awake and rehearses the day in his mind. And he prays.

It was a rough day, and David does not want a sleepless night, tossing in anger, wakeful in fear. He prays like we often pray – first he speaks in his heart to God (v. 1); then in his mind to his enemies (vv. 2-3); then in his soul to himself (vv. 4-5); and once again to God (vv. 6-8). The war of the inner world rages until the *shalom* (peace) of the Lord closes his eyes in rest.

John Calvin sees verse 4 as that which the Psalmist says to the wicked, continuing the line of conversation from verses 2 and 3: "Tremble, and do not sin; meditate in your heart upon your bed, and be still." Calvin sees the psalmist saying to the ungodly: "You turn what is honorable into something reproachful, you love what is worthless, and you aim at lies and fantasy. Repent of these things. Learn to abhor them. Become indignant against them." Luther follows the same line of thought and artfully defines this trembling anger: "And this is what it means to be angry and indignant, to be inflamed and to burn with a holy wrath against vanity and lies." But David may not be speaking to his myriad of enemies but to himself.

"Be angry and do not sin," is how Paul quotes this verse in Ephesians 4:26, using the Septuagint (Greek O. T.) version. And Scripture interprets Scripture. Evil men and their wickedness will upset, unsettle and anger the soul, causing what Perowne aptly calls "any sort of disquietude, or strong emotion, the agitation of anger as well as fear." We've all felt this: The other car runs the red light, misses you by inches, and causes your heart to leap out of your chest into your throat and your infant in the car seat next to you to cry. Later that night the flood of emotion arises – tears of relief, the fear of a near miss, and anger (indignation) at the lawless driver who nearly took from you your precious child and your life.

But the voice within calms your trembling soul, "Shhhh! Be still! God has rescued you again." Once more Jesus' prayer for you has been answered: "Deliver them from evil." You were saved because "the LORD has set apart the godly for himself" (v. 3). Go to sleep! You dwell in safety because the God of peace is with you (v. 8).

And David hears the Spirit's comfort. He tells the Lord, as he drifts off to sleep, "You have put more joy in my heart than they have when their grain and wine abound. In peace I will both lie down and sleep; for you alone, O LORD, make me dwell in safety" (Ps. 4:7-8). Life is still rough. Absalom is still after him, he is still a fugitive and there is no assurance that tomorrow will be any brighter or better. But he glows with the glad thought that even death cannot ruin him: God belongs to him, and even more wonderfully, he belongs to God. He retires and rests in that preeminent source of assurance: "My sheep hear my voice, and I know them, and they follow me. I give them eternal life, and they will never perish, and no one will snatch them out of my hand. My Father, who has given them to me, is greater than all, and no one is able to snatch them out of the Father's hand" (John 10:27-29).

## DAY 56 ORDERING YOUR PRAYERS ARIGHT

# Read Psalm 5

*O LORD, in the morning you hear my voice; in the morning I prepare a sacrifice for you and watch.*

Psalm 5:3

Psalm 5 picks up where Psalm 4 left off and continues "The Golden Chain of Trust" that runs through this sequence of readings in Psalms 3 through 10. Michael Wilcock reminds us of the *sitz en leben* (the situation in life) of Psalm 5: "With Psalm 3 the king woke to this first day of exile, with Psalm 4 that day ended, and with Psalm 5 he wakes again to see the same situation, but now with maturer thoughts about it. He sees the broader scene. His opponents represent all God's opponents – the wicked (v. 4), and his supporters represent the righteous (v. 12). The Psalter opened with the making of that basic distinction in Psalm 1." Again and again David speaks to God about these two humanities, as he alternates between "You and them" and "You and me" perspectives. Wickedness and evil are again in focus (v. 4).

The enemies of God and His saints are described in seven terms. They are boastful (v. 5), false, violent (v. 6), unreliable, destructive, flattering (v. 9), and rebellious (v. 10). Their lives are bent toward one purpose: to manipulate men and situations to their ends, to the harm of the godly and in opposition to God. But this plentitude of wickedness does not unsettle the shepherd of Israel. Why not? He has prayed. There is the key to his security and stability.

"O LORD, in the morning you hear my voice; in the morning I prepare a sacrifice for you and watch." (v. 3). The Hebrew of this verse is difficult. It has been translated as "I will make preparations," or as "I will draw up my case," or unfortunately "I prepare a sacrifice." Perhaps the best translation is this: "As soon as morning comes, I shall set (my prayer) in order for Thee and then keep watch (for an answer)" (Leupold).

The gist of David's words is that he has thought through his circumstances and his resulting prayer. He knows he is under

103

God's judgment yet he also knows that evil men are responsible for their wickedness. He knows that he loves the Lord and trusts in Him. And he knows that God is able to sort all of life out and do what is both righteous and gracious, as the situation demands. As his difficulty comes into clearer focus, as the lines are more clearly drawn between good and evil, God and men, the realization crystallizes: Only God can sort this out and do what is best.

David's prayer is masterful because it reflects God's perfect promises, his own sinful condition and the reality of a world full of wickedness. David prays, as we should: God will fulfill His Word, God will forgive our sins, and God will foil the wicked. Our duty is three-fold and simple. We must order our prayers aright. We must trust in the goodness of God. We must wait and watch for the Lord to act. Let the words of Puritan William Gurnall encourage us to pray like this: "O Christian, stand to your prayer in a holy expectation of what you have begged upon the credit of the promise." Let it be so, Lord, with us. Let it be so!

## DAY 57 GOD IS A RIGHTEOUS JUDGE

### Read Psalm 7

*God is a righteous judge, and a God who feels indignation every day.*
Psalm 7:11

This psalm bears the inscription: "A Shiggaion of David, which he sang to the Lord concerning the words of Cush, a Benjaminite." Now there was no love lost between David and the tribe of Benjamin. The Benjamites were the tribe of Saul and were naturally loyal to the king from their clan who sought the life of young David (See 1 Sam. 18–27 and 2 Sam. 20). J. J. Stewart Perowne says of this inscription: "It is more probable that this Benjamite named Cush, belonging to Saul's tribe, was conspicuous among the calumniators of whom David complains to the king." Others speculate that this unknown Benjamite was of the period and ilk of Shimei who cursed David as he fled from Absalom (2 Sam. 16:5-8). This Benjamite named Cush (whoever he was)

was certainly of the sentiments of Sheba the Benjamite who sided with Absalom and against David and said, "We have no portion in David, and we have no inheritance in the son of Jesse; every man to his tents, O Israel! [i.e. "to arms!"]" (2 Sam. 20:1).

One of the most painful things in life is that people misinterpret our actions and motives, draw unfair and inaccurate conclusions about us, spread these hostile feelings to others and pass on prejudices from generation to generation. How often in the ministry I have had to step between factions in the church (cf. 1 Cor. 1:11-13), some bearing the grudges of fathers and "clans" set against each other, and in the end find myself labeled, by one or both, as an enemy as well. When this happens it hurts. But it also forces us to the God who is a righteous judge.

David pleads before this judge his innocence. He is blameless. He does not claim that he is sinless, but rather that he is neither guilty of the false accusations nor disloyal to anyone. In truth, David never sought the office of king from Saul nor did he ever speak against him. Nor did he ever raise a violent hand against his own son, Absalom, even when the boy sought the father's life. Instead, David pleaded with his generals to "Deal gently for my sake with the young man Absalom." (2 Sam. 18:5), once his forces had regained his throne. And he buried the bones of Saul and Jonathan with honor and cared for Saul's descendants all his life – despite what the Benjamites had done to him (2 Sam. 19:24-30 and 21:10-14).

Rather than strike back in bigoted rage – justified in the eyes of men – David pleads his case before God. He reminds both himself and Jehovah that "God is a righteous judge, and a God who feels indignation every day." This is the God who has watched His own Son be murdered simply because men hated Christ's Father! So David says, in effect, "Lord, you be the judge. If I am as bad as my accusers say (vv. 3-5) then 'lay my glory in the dust' (i.e. kill me and remove from me the glory of the image of God). If my enemies are evil, then get them (vv. 6-16). 'If a man does not repent' (v. 12) – either they or I – then You judge and destroy."

In a culture where Black cannot forgive what White did to

ancestors decades ago, where South still resents North, where denominational divisions still carry on in a loss of true fellowship, and where it doesn't take but one slip-up to ensure that our children will pay for our sins at the hands of another man's offspring, it becomes increasingly important to examine one's own life and actions (vv. 3-5), to repent of wrongdoing (v. 12) and to leave the rest to God the righteous judge.

## DAY 58 WHAT IS MAN AFTER ALL?

### Read Psalm 8

*When I look at your heavens, the work of your fingers, the moon and the stars, which you have set in place, what is man that you are mindful of him, and the son of man that you care for him?*

Psalm 8:3-4

Psalm 8 continues "The Golden Chain of Trust" poetically expressed in Psalms 3-10. It is another Evening Psalm, this time probably when David was but a shepherd boy. For this reason Psalm 8 may be one of the earliest – the first? – of the psalms of David. David muses over God's greatness, the vastness of the creation and the irony of both man's littleness and man's wonderfulness, as he tends the flocks by night and gazes upon the nighttime sky (vv. 3-4).

Psalm 8 is a majestic hymn. "This psalm is an unsurpassed example of what a hymn should be, celebrating as it does the glory and grace of God, rehearsing who He is and what He has done, and relating us and our world to Him; all with a masterly economy of words, and in a spirit of mingled joy and awe" (D. Kidner). We sing this same psalm in the modern, upbeat version made so popular by singer Sandi Patti – "How Majestic Is Your Name."

The complexities of life that burden David the king (or a modern premier, prime-minister or president) are somehow put into perspective by this song written by a teenage shepherd boy lost in the wonder of his God, his sheep and his own little but important life. Three stanzas celebrate the three great mysteries of life. First, God's greatness is seen in the massive and limitless expanse of the cosmos with the glory of heaven above even that, but also in the little, weak and helpless baby who suckles at the breast or toddles along in his first awkward steps. Who can create and control a universe out of nothing? And who can make and mold a man out of a baby? Only God, and God alone (v. 2).

Second, God's goodness is seen in His manufacturing for Himself a vast array of galaxies – heavens, moons and stars, other suns and other worlds – apparently in a wasteful display of glorious creativity; but also creating and caring for a finite number of men – each one a personal project of God. God knows and names each moon, sun and planet. God knows and names every single creature who bears the label "human being" (vv. 3-4).

Third, God's grace is seen in His setting out the nature and work of man, this creature who lives between two worlds. He is *imago dei*, a little less than the angels (v. 5) but the lord of all those creatures known as the animals (vv. 6-8). He is not able to be a god and should never consider himself "a naked ape." He bears his own place in what the Medievals called "The Great Chain of Being" – and a noble place it is. He and his helpmate are the vice-regents of God's creation, the prime-minister of God's plan and the pro-creators of God's race of mankind (Gen. 1, 2).

That is what surrounds us all, from boys who shepherd sheep to men who guide and guard nations: God's greatness, God's goodness, God's grace. And for reasons inexplicable, people – like you and like I – play a key role in creation, culture and the church, and this by God's design. The refrain of this hymn that both opens and closes the psalm is this: "O LORD, our Lord, how majestic is your name in all the earth!" (vv. 1, 9). And since God's name is majestic our nature is marvelous. Since God is great, good and gracious, we who have been created in His image ought to reflect that which is noble, upright and grateful. May it ever be so with us!

## DAY 59 WHAT YOU DON'T KNOW WILL HURT YOU!

### Read Psalm 9

*And those who know your name put their trust in you, for you, O LORD, have not forsaken those who seek you. ... Put them in fear, O LORD! Let the nations know that they are but men!*

Psalm 9:10, 20

Psalms 9 and 10 may well have once been one psalm. They are linked together in the Greek *Septuagint* as they are in the Latin *Vulgate*. In Book One of the Psalter (Pss. 1–41) only Psalm 10 and Psalm 33 lack an inscription or title, perhaps indicating that Psalms 9 and 10 were also one in the Hebrew text. Psalm 9 is the first of nine acrostic or alphabetical psalms (9, 10, 25, 34, 37, 111, 112, 119 and 145). F. B. Meyer makes the observation, "In the *Septuagint* this psalm refers to the death of the Divine Son, and recites His victory over death and the grave, and all our foes."

David writes as the King of the Jews, the shepherd of Israel, and therefore as a type of Christ. His enemies are then a type of the enemies of Christ and His church. The theme of the psalm is therefore the victory of God in Christ. A. F. Kirkpatrick writes: "Psalm 9 is a triumphant thanksgiving, rarely passing into prayer (vv. 13, 19): its theme is the manifestation of God's sovereign righteousness in the defeat and destruction of foreign enemies of the nations." In his musings over the great cosmic warfare in heaven, reflected here on earth, David reminds us that what we know makes all the difference in eternity.

The first half of the psalm ends with verse 10: "And those who know your name put their trust in you, for you, O LORD, have not forsaken those who seek you." In other words, when the elect come to see God for who He truly is they will put their faith in Him and be saved. In commenting on this very verse Charles Simeon, the English evangelical leader and pastor of Trinity Church in Cambridge in the nineteenth century, observed that when we encounter God for who He really is we are struck by His name which imparts not only His identity but also His "essential perfections" (attributes) and his "diversified dispensations" (actions). And thus we come to know what we should do with this God: "renounce all false confidences" (repentance) and "rely solely on God" (faith). As a result we will "study the Holy Scriptures" and we will "follow the example of the Scripture saints." In other words, knowing God (to borrow J. I. Packer's book title) will transform our whole existence.

The second half of the psalm ends with verse 20 which refers to the men of the world: "Put them in fear, O LORD! Let the nations know that they are but men!" There is a striking emphasis here. Men must come to know their own frailty and weakness, their humanity (Hebrew *enosh*) in comparison with the omnipotence of God Himself. Boy! What greater and better lesson for our postmodern society to learn: "that they are but men." Men of finite aptitudes, finite resources and finite opportunity cannot solve an infinite and eternal problem: the fallenness of our race!

David realized what, hopefully, our national leaders, our pastors and our parents will begin to learn: Only God can "fix" what man has broken. Only trust in Jesus Christ will guarantee success in things that are immortally and inevitably significant. Ours is an age that needs to know two key truths: The name of God and the nature of man. Once we know these things we will "renounce the devil and all his works and pomps" and reject the arm of flesh for deliverance. And we will trust in the Lord and tell others the truth: "What you don't know (and may not want to hear) will indeed hurt you … forever!

## DAY 60 THE MACHINATIONS OF A REPROBATE MIND

## Read Psalm 10

*Why does the wicked renounce God and say in his heart, "You will not call to account"?*

Psalm 10:13

Psalm 10 is a difficult psalm to place. Most scholars believe it was originally the last half of a Psalm 9 and 10 combination. (See introduction to Psalm 9, yesterday.) But then again, Psalm 10 seems to stand on its own, both linguistically and thematically. A. F. Kirkpatrick rightly observes, "Psalm 9 however appears to be complete in itself, and it seems preferable to regard Psalm 10 as a companion piece rather than as part of a continuous whole." I agree.

Psalm 10 pulls back the sheets and reveals for us what lies beneath the warfare of good versus evil, rehearsed in Psalms 1 to 9. The underlying problem of evil and wickedness in our world is a reprobate mind, a hardened heart, a dead soul. Four times in Psalm 10 the Holy Spirit reveals to the psalmist the musings and machinations of the unconverted mind. In each of these four revelations of reprobate thought, the writer is careful to point out that men never really say these things; no, rather they think them. The refrain is heard four times: "All his thoughts are (v. 4) ... He says to himself (v. 6) ... He says in his heart (v. 11) ... [He] say[s] in his heart (v. 13)." He reasons away the truths of Psalm 9 – God's Holy Name and his own human weakness.

Here is what his heart and mind say to each other. First, he believes, "There is no God" (v. 4). He does not deny the existence of God, but rather acts as if God does not exist. Like men who spurn an enemy at a social gathering, so the wicked treat God. They act as if God were a "non-person"; someone not worthy of recognition. "He goes about his scheming as though there were no God. He knows there really is, but he acts as though there were not ... the persons involved do not deny the existence of God; they merely despise Him" (Leupold). We find these men all around us. They go to church, they pray and they say things like "God bless America!" and "God Save the Queen." But when we interject God into business dealings and race relations (vv. 2-5); honesty in relationships (v. 7), social responsibilities (vv. 8-9) and moral conduct (v. 14), we get the cold shoulder and God gets ignored. Why?

The last three thoughts expose the motives of the fallen heart and deadened conscience: "I shall not be moved; throughout all generations I shall not meet adversity. (v. 6) ... God has forgotten, he has hidden his face, he will never see it. (v. 11) ... You will not call to account!" (v. 13) In other words: "I am fixed for life, God is too old and too busy to see what I do, and if He did He wouldn't do anything about it anyway. Men get away with these sorts of things all the time! God is the least of my concerns!"

The psalmist thinks more clearly: "But you do see, for you note mischief and vexation, that you may take it into your hands" (v. 14). First he sees the nail-pierced hands of Christ who atoned for evil. The *rashim* (the wicked) must realize what the righteous know. God is. God sees. God grabs hold of and acts. God requires an "accounting."

When I was a little fellow, I was always amazed at how well my mother knew my heart and could read my mind. As she zipped up my coat and tied my scarf she would often say, "Now be careful, Michael, and remember: When no one else is around, God is watching you!" She ruined many an occasion of "mischief and vexation" (v. 14) with those words! But she was right. And it's a good thing for us "grown ups" to remember as we button up our wool dress coats and grab hold of our leather briefcases each morning: When no one else is around, God is. And He sees who we are and what we do. And, someday soon, He's going to want to talk to us about it!

## DAY 61 THE FOLLY OF SIN

### Read Psalm 52

*See the man who would not make God his refuge, but trusted in the abundance of his riches and sought refuge in his own destruction!*

Psalm 52:7

Psalm 52 begins a sub-grouping of psalms that were written by David during the years of danger when Saul and his associates pursued David in order to kill him. They concern danger and call upon God for both justice and deliverance. Five of them are called a *miktam* and fit into the fugitive years of David, prior to Saul's death when David lived in the wilderness. These five psalms (Pss. 56–60) along with Psalm 16 (also one of the six *miktams* in the Psalter) are called "The Fugitive Psalms." These nine psalms[1]

---

[1] See Part One: God Our Refuge for devotionals in Psalm 58 (Day 16) and Psalm 60 (Day 43).

remind us that evil men are a very real threat to godly men in this life.

Paul recognized this fact of life when he wrote to Timothy saying, "Indeed, all who desire to live a godly life in Christ Jesus will be persecuted" (2 Tim. 3:12). If we side with God in this world then we pit ourselves against evil – against the world (1 John 2:15-17). Our worldly evangelical church does not want to acknowledge this truth. They do not want to admit that all human culture is fallen and must be confronted and converted (brought under Christ's control – 2 Cor. 10:3-5). We hear from sociologists the myth, "There is no such thing as bad people, only those whose environment has created anti-social norms." Nonsense! The Psalter divides the world into two humanities: the wicked (bad men) and the righteous (bad men who have been redeemed). In fact, the Psalter begins with this fundamental division of mankind in Psalm 1 (See Ps. 52 in comparison with Ps. 1 for identical imagery). The reality of evil men engaged in wickedness is something we must grasp for purposes of both godly living and Gospel mission.

Psalm 52 divides itself into three stanzas (paragraphs). Psalm 52:1-4 speaks of the *Fact of Evil* described in three poignant terms: destruction, deceit, devouring. The next paragraph (vv. 5-7) speaks of the *Folly of Evil*. Wicked men are, perhaps surprisingly, described as people who trust in prosperity rather than God. What a similarity to the worldview of most middle-class evangelicals! Finally Psalm 52:8-9 speak of the *Faith of the Godly*. The Christian trusts in God, not only in this life, but also with a view toward "forever and ever" (v. 8). The gist of the whole psalm is this: The proud thoughts, the wicked ways and the false values of the worldly man come to a disappointing end. "See the man who would not make God his refuge, but trusted in the abundance of his riches" (v. 7). How sad is his life, how catastrophic his death.

In the second book of his four-volume set of books about Christ and modernity, *God in the Wasteland: The Reality of Truth in a World of Fading Dreams*, David F. Wells describes postmodernity as "worldliness": placing God at the periphery of life and making sin seem normal and godliness look odd. The worldly man — oftentimes a churched man — puts personal peace and affluence at the center of his life. The godly man does the opposite. His life is theocentric. And for this reason the unworldly, godly man is an effective witness in the world. Far from hating his fallen culture and hiding from his broken community, he ventures out into "the world" and shows to others the real peace and eternal prosperity of a life with God at the center. His mission is to show forth the folly of worldliness (sin) and the blessedness of godliness — life with God at center of all we are and do.

## DAY 62 A LESSON TWICE LEARNED

## Read Psalm 53

*The fool says in his heart, "There is no God."*

Psalm 53:1

One of my seminary professors used to say, "When you find something repeated verbatim in the Holy Scriptures, stop, study and meditate upon those words." Psalm 53 is almost a verbatim repeat of Psalm 14 (See Day 91 reading, p. 162). Both psalms are ascribed to David. Under the inspiration of the Holy Spirit, the psalmist of Israel was led to pen two hymns — almost identical. The difference between the two is verse 5. H. C. Leupold correctly states that a man (the psalmist) "having the familiar text of Psalm 14 before him, desired under certain circumstances so to change the psalm as to make it applicable to a situation that was prevailing at his time."

Most scholars believe Psalm 14 is the earlier of the two psalms, mainly for two reasons, both literary in nature: The use of Elohim (God) in Psalm 53 instead of Yahweh (Lord) in Psalm 14; and the inclusion of Psalm 53 in Book Two of the Psalter, considered a later collection than Book One. But if Psalm 53 is rightly included in "The Fugitive Psalms" timeframe, it may well be the mother of Psalm 14.

The focus must surely be on the first verse: "The fool says in his heart, 'There is no God.'" What does David mean? Notice that the fool (unconverted man) speaks the words "There is no God" in his heart, either his mind or will. Hengstenberg believes this is a matter of the desire, not the thought, of fallen man: "The discourse here is not of the atheism of the understanding but the atheism of the heart." In other words, the sinful man knows that indeed there is a God but he surely wishes there were not! Matthew Henry explains: "The fool cannot satisfy himself that there is no God, but he wishes there were none, and pleases himself with the fancy that it is possible there may be none; he cannot be sure there is none, and therefore he is willing to think there is none."

This explains why the fool is so hostile to the Christian and why they "eat up my people as they eat bread" (v. 4). If the world could just eliminate (or silence) the people who believe in God and live as though God were real, then the fantasy of a godless world and life could cruise on unhindered. As long as there are people who want to live as if God were real the battle between good and evil will continue. Saul certainly knew there was a God (Jehovah), but he wished there was not so that he could dispose of David without guilt.

This is why Christian witness is so important. God has set aside His own people so that they might live in the world as if God were both real and relevant. In doing so, they remind the world of fools – and all of us are fools until enlightened and transformed by the Holy Spirit – that God exists and is a force to be reckoned with and a Being to whom all are answerable. Also, in our desire for God's presence and power in our lives we are indeed the happier and healthier lot of people. Is this not David's prayer? "Oh, that salvation for Israel would come out of Zion!" Oh that God would work graciously in the world through His church so that foolish mankind could accept two undeniable facts: God exists and God is good. To know Him is to know life and to desire Him is to find happiness. Foolish men can believe these truths when God's people live as though God is real and God is relevant – He is to be gloried and He is to be enjoyed, now and forever.

## DAY 63 CORAM DEO

# Read Psalm 54

*They do not set God before themselves.*

Psalm 54:3

Psalm 54 is set against the background of 1 Samuel 23:13-29, "The Ziphites went up to Saul at Gibeah, saying, "Is not David hiding among us?'" It fits into "The Fugitive Psalms" of David's life. Saul, obviously aware that God had chosen David, over him, to be the King of Israel sought to kill David and thwart God's design. In my study Bible I have written over the title of Psalm 54 "The Reason Evil Exists in God's World." For that is the great question of Theodicy: Why does a good God allow evil to exist in His world? Psalm 54:3 answers that question.

David states, "For strangers have risen against me; ruthless men seek my life; they do not set God before themselves" (v. 3). This statement makes Psalm 53 and 54 twin psalms, both lamenting a practical atheism (See Ps. 53:1). The key to understanding this godless way of life is the phrase "They have not set God before them." Joseph A. Alexander comments, "To not set God before them is to act as if they did not remember or believe in His existence and His presence. The *selah* indicates a pause of indignation and abhorrence."

In the historical context Psalm 54:3 reminds us that men often (usually?) live as though God can not see what they are doing. Saul and the Ziphites were guilty of this stupid miscalculation: "They have no regard for God's will, and no fear of His judgments ... as it was they were simply fighting against God in making themselves the tools of Saul's blind rage, for it must have been well known that God intended David to be Saul's successor" (A. F. Kirkpatrick).

This is a common way of life. The same verse appears again in Psalm 86:14, a composite of other psalms. This tendency to act as if God does not see who we are and what we do has a name. Puritan John Brown called it impiety. We moderns seem to have lost this word in our vocabulary. Perhaps it too was jettisoned along with "worldliness." "Piety" is that word Paul uses repeatedly in the pastoral epistles, alongside the word "doctrine" (*didaskalia* = teaching). It is the Greek word *eusebeia*, translated "godliness" or "religion," better "piety."

Piety is devotion to God and to the things and ways of God. To be "pious" is not a bad thing; it is to be sincerely "religious" and concerned about the kingdom of God. Piety is what develops in us when we live each day *Coram Deo*, before the face of God, in His presence. It results in personal "devotions," Sabbath keeping, witnessing, tithing, fasting and prayer and a sobriety of life that truly believes that God is watching us and Christ is with us. Piety thrives in the claiming of this promise from Jesus, "And behold, I am with you always, to the end of the age" (Matt. 28:20). Hence, the Great Commission is fueled by a biblical piety. One writer labeled it "practicing the presence of God."

When men think that God is too far away to care, that Christ is too removed to be involved, that the Holy Spirit is just "a force" rather than the personal presence of God in us, then men try to get by with what they know they could never do if they were before the face of God. *Coram Deo* – that is the truth that separates the wicked from the righteous. And that is the reason the saints "do good" in a world that loves evil.

## DAY 64 THE DISTRESS OF A GODLY MAN

### Read Psalm 55

> *Cast your burden on the LORD, and he will sustain you; he will never permit the righteous to be moved.*
>
> Psalm 55:22

Psalm 55 could rightly fit into one of two periods of David's life: when Saul persecuted and pursued him or when Absalom, his son, rebelled against him. An ancient Syriac version places Psalm 55 in the time of Absalom's rebellion: "Of David when he lamented over the death of his son Absalom." John Calvin and others assign it to the Sauline persecution. Placed by the Levites in Book Two, among "The Fugitive Psalms" (Pss. 53–60), we must agree with Calvin.

David laments that evil men surround him and have turned his life into a veritable hell. He is most saddened by the fact that those closest to him – once his dear and intimate friends – have now turned on him. He means, of course, his father-in-law, Saul, and his wife, Michal, and others in Israel once his friends. He expresses the thoughts of many of us when life becomes painful: "Oh, that I had wings like a dove! I would fly away and be at rest; yes, I would wander far away; I would lodge in the wilderness" (vv. 6, 7). Translated: "I'd retire, build that log cabin in Ohio, move away from civilization and only see people when I went to the store, needed the doctor, or went to a football game." Believe me, I've been there. So have you. The pipe dream may be different – perhaps a tin-roofed fishing shack on the Gulf or a ski lodge in the Rockies – but the sentiment is the same. If we could just eliminate the pain of people in our lives, we would be happy and at rest. Not so!

Psalm 55 expresses the emotions of David at a raw and restless time of his young life. We share the advantage of seeing how God used what was behind Psalm 55 to prepare David for the pressure-filled life of royalty. Just like Jesus, of whom he was a type, David "learned obedience through what he suffered" (Heb. 5:8). He learned to cast his "burden upon the LORD" (v. 22) and to find endurance in the grace of the Messiah – also a man given to suffering (1 Pet. 2:21-25). What these evil and traitorous people intended for evil God used for good in David's life (Gen. 50:20; Rom. 8:28).

A life of peace is not a life that builds Christlike character. That is the truth behind Psalm 55, Peter's first epistle, and the warp and woof of the Christian life. William S. Plummer reminds us, "There are several reasons why the truly pious man should be sore pained (v. 4). God loves them and so afflicts them. The world and the devil hate them and so trouble them. They are very jealous of themselves, and so they continually prove and humble themselves. Religion refines their sensibilities, and so they are more distressed at a vain thought than ungodly men are at a naughty deed." Hence Psalm 55 picks up where Psalms 53 and 54 end: Piety develops a sensibility of soul that causes the saints to grow in grace through difficulty and distress.

When Paul said he wanted to know Jesus much more intimately, he prayed to know "the power of his resurrection", and share "his sufferings" (Phil. 3:10). So it must be with us. To be persecuted, forsaken, betrayed by friends, hounded by in-laws, even deserted by a spouse, hurt beyond words. But these things also build piety, perseverance and participation in the sufferings of Christ on behalf of His church (Col. 1:24). No sense whining about it or dreaming of "flying away." The only reasonable response is to "cast your burden upon the LORD" and know that He will "sustain you" and "will never permit the righteous to be moved" (v. 22).

## DAY 65 GOD'S BOTTLE, GOD'S BOOK

### Read Psalm 56

*You have kept count of my tossings; put my tears in your bottle. Are they not in your book?*

Psalm 56:8

In Psalm 55:6, 7 David sang, "Oh, that I had wings like a dove! I would fly away and be at rest; yes, I would wander far away; I would lodge in the wilderness." Psalm 56 is to be sung to that same tune, known in Hebrew as "*Jonath elem rehokim*" (the silent dove in far off lands). In the collection of "The Fugitive Psalms," the first four (Pss. 52–55) concern themselves with being betrayed and let down by close friends. The last five (Pss. 56–60) concern the reality of Saul's pursuit of David. Psalm 56 opens up this second subset of "Psalms of Distress."

Psalm 56 builds itself around a refrain repeated, in substance, twice (vv. 3-4 and vv.. 10-11): "When I am afraid, I put my trust in you. In God, whose word I praise, in God I trust; I shall not be afraid. What can flesh do to me?" (vv. 3-4) The honesty of David, quite frankly, makes modern men quite uncomfortable. We are an arrogant age which has convinced its generation that grown-up people are not afraid ... of anything! Hence the macho man of Bowflex country and the postmodern vixen of *Sex in the City*. Fearless Folks!

Truth is – let's "get real" – we are all afraid. We fear losing our jobs, losing our lovers, losing our pastorates, losing our kids and losing our virginity. We fear the city streets at night, the stress-filled office at dawn, and the lonely apartment in the evening. We fear how we look, how others see us, how much others will find out about the real us.

This fear lies behind postmodernity's penchant for re-imaging, the preference of style over substance. We have come to really believe that if we change the way we think of ourselves and what others think of us we can alter reality. Why else would our times be known as "the age of the therapeutic"? How sad. Fear still lives and lurks in the one place we cannot re-image – the soul.

The wise man knows that there are three great forces in the world to be genuinely feared: The devil against us, the sin inside us, and the world around us. He is not immobilized by these fears. But they do make him take seriously the Christian answer to these fearful forces. God is greater than the devil and sovereign over him. Christ shares his human nature and has conquered his sin. The Holy Spirit is in this world, in him, and has given him His Word. He faces fear with faith and says, "in God I trust; I shall not be afraid. What can flesh do to me?"

The reality of evil in our world and fear in ourselves causes David to talk of God's bottle and God's book. When he fled from Saul in Israel to the Philistines of Gath (1 Sam. 21), he knew fear – fear at home and fear abroad. So he says, "put my tears in your bottle. Are they not in your book?" (v. 8). Meaning: God is attentive to the dangers men often want to pretend don't bother them at all. Bishop George Horne, a man who lived in a day when brave men acknowledged fear, sums up this psalm: "Known unto God are all the afflictions of his servants; while banished, like David, from their abiding city and country, they 'wander' here below. The 'tears' of penitence are had in remembrance, and, as so many precious gems, will one day adorn their crown. How dear, then, in the sight of God, were the 'wanderings' and 'tears' of the holy Jesus, submitting to perform penance for their sins which He never committed!"

Christ feared the cross – just look at Him in Gethsemane! – but

119

He trusted in God and went forward into fear. God bottled His tears and recorded His fears, then delivered Him from death. And so shall God do so for us who walk in faith in the midst of fear.

## DAY 66 BE EXALTED, O GOD

### Read Psalm 57

*Be exalted, O God, above the heavens! Let your glory be over all the earth!*

Psalm 57:5, 11

In 1977 Brent Chambers wrote a chorus or "praise song," that is now included in many hymnals as a standard selection, entitled "Be Exalted, O God." This song was taken from Psalm 57 and its twice-repeated refrain in verses 5 and 11: "Be exalted, O God, above the heavens! Let your glory be over all the earth!" Derek Kidner observes, "The stirring refrain of verses 5 and 11 punctuates and binds the psalm together."

Psalm 57 is one of "The Fugitive Psalms" of David (Pss. 16, 56–60). It was written in the same time as a number of psalms written during his "outlaw years" when he was sought by Saul and remained on the run. David wrote this psalm while in one of his hideouts in the desert. He likens his refuge in God to that of hiding in the cave. Alexander Maclaren picks up on this and comments: "What truer or richer description of trust could be given than that which likens it to the act of a fugitive betaking himself to the shelter of some mountain fastness, impregnable and inaccessible? What lovelier thought of the safe, warm hiding-place which God affords was ever spoken than that of 'the shadow of Thy wings'?"

And so it should be with us. We should know that "a soul which trusts has a right to God's gracious dealings" (Kidner) and we should not be reluctant to plead our case before God in hope and trust. David did so and even united this belief to the refrain that God is exalted when He deals graciously with His saints.

More than we realize, God's reputation in the world of men depends upon His treatment of the children of the Church. Time and again Moses, David and the prophets bemoan the fact that when God disciplines His saints the world thinks lowly of Him. God is just and must punish sin but God prefers to be gracious and show mercy to His saints. When God acts in covenant love and loyalty to us (the Hebrew word *chesed* usually translated "steadfast love") men are drawn to our God.

When David left Gath and hid in the caves of Adullam (1 Sam. 22:1), from where he wrote this psalm, it seemed as if he'd hit rock bottom – alone, a fugitive, like an animal cowering in a cave. But such was not the case. Michael Wilcock explains: "Soon others came, happy to make common cause with him, but at the outset he would have been alone. Isolation and solitude are not the same. He had felt the first in Gath; now he had to cope with the second as well.... Strangely, he felt better. We sense a growing confidence. He may have been a fugitive hiding in a cave, but he was also a believer taking refuge in the shadow of God's wings.... And David's escape from both Saul and Achish itself shows that God's covenant love and faithfulness are looking after him."

There is something about "hiding in God," about "resting in Christ," about "fleeing into the security of the Spirit" that honors God and brings men to Him. God is not impressed with self-sufficient men, with wealth and power and position. No! Trust is what touches God and, in some inexplicable way, draws other men to Him in repentance and faith.

## DAY 67 THE DOGS OF THE DEVIL

### Read Psalm 59

*Each evening they come back, howling like dogs and prowling about the city.*

Psalm 59:6

Psalm 59 is set in the backdrop of 1 Samuel 19 when Saul sent men to stake out David and Michal's house and ambush David. Psalm 59, one of "The Fugitive Psalms," is a lament psalm, an individual lament, the complaint of a soul who has been wronged. Yet it includes a very strange verse; one that has made the scholars question the historical setting of the psalm. The verse in question is verse 5: "You, LORD God of hosts, are God of Israel. Rouse yourself to punish all the nations; spare none of those who treacherously plot evil." How is it that in an individual lament the psalmist mentions "the nations"?

H. C. Leupold, the late evangelical Lutheran professor of Trinity Lutheran Seminary in Columbus, Ohio explains: "It does not seem far fetched to us to assume that at the very time outside enemies of the nations, especially the Philistines, were harassing the nation in one way or another. As a result, when David reflects on his own distress he felt that, when God took his case in hand, He would at the same time work deliverance from the distress into which the nation had been brought by attacks from the heathen.... From that point of view the psalm is a good example of how private concerns did not make a man like David indifferent to matters of national import." Here is a lesson for the modern church.

In writing these devotionals I fear that I will present God Our Redeemer in purely personal and psychological terms: The Savior who tends to our hurts and worries, the "Utilitarian Christ," as A. W. Tozer called Him, who is there to make life successful and easy for us. In her study of modern Protestant preaching *All Is Forgiven*, sociologist Marsha Whitten points to how both liberal and evangelical preachers have turned God into a "daddy" who spoils His children and a "fellow sufferer" who works through therapeutic ways to help the kids feel great! God forbid that I should present such a Redeemer to you.

The refrain of Psalm 59 will prohibit that distortion. This refrain is one we wouldn't want to sing today: "Each evening they come back, howling like dogs and prowling about the city" (vv. 6 and 14). That is how David saw Saul's henchmen and the Philistine militia – a pack of wild dogs prowling the city at night!

Last year I spent three weeks in Africa. While in Uganda I slept in a cinder-block cell room adjacent to a hospital. My biological clock was not in sync; I was awake most nights from 2:00 a.m. until morning. As I tossed and turned in bed, I could hear howling and growling animals in the night. These were sounds I never heard in Ohio, Illinois, Texas, Tennessee, South Carolina, Mississippi and the other places I've slept in America. This was a different world, a much more dangerous world. This was the world of wild beasts, both the four-legged type and Idi Amin — both of them man-eaters! This was a world in which men went to bed at night but did not awake in the morning – the dogs would come!

I couldn't help but think of my life and theirs: how safe mine was, how small (almost petty) my concerns. But how different and more dangerous was the existence of my brothers and sisters in this land of wild dogs! I could not help but pray for them and weep for all they had been through. And as I left my room each sunny morning to preach to them and teach them, I thanked God for one more day, and for protection from that which howled in the night and prowled in the city ... the dogs of the devil.

## DAY 68 RESTORING THE FOUNDATIONS

### Read Psalm 11

*If the foundations are destroyed, what can the righteous do?*

Psalm 11:3

Today we begin a sequence in which we read through seven "Psalms of Trust" (Pss. 11, 16, 23, 27, 63, 73 and 91). These are hymns and prayers in which the psalmist's confidence in God is the central theme of the composition.

Psalm 11 is difficult to pinpoint in the life of David. Some see it set in the persecutions of Saul. Others believe that it fits into Asbalom's rebellion. Cheyne calls it simply, "a persecution psalm" that has much in common with similar psalms written by David in difficult times. We classify it as a "Psalm of Trust."

In an extremely difficult time people are saying to David, "All is lost! Flee! Run for your life! The very foundations of society and the fabric of culture are gone. Ruined! We have labored for nothing. What can we do? Nothing! All is lost!" But David does not panic. He hears the voice of fear and realizes fear is the opposite of faith.

Alexander Maclaren sees through this fear for what it is as well: "The implication is, Why wage a hopeless conflict any longer

at the peril of life? All is lost; the wise thing to do is to run."
This kind of fear can be seen in the evangelical church throughout
America. We see the foundations of education destroyed and
so we withdraw from public schools. We see the foundations of
our cities destroyed and so we hide in the suburbs. We see the
foundations of theology destroyed and so we fill ourselves with
"feel good" books with titles like *Warmly in His Hand* and *He Still
Works Miracles*. We seem to have forgotten that God is not one to
lose in the long run and we are not ones who should seek for
safety but rather live in service.

David denies the fears of verse 3 and counters with the truth of
verses 4-7. The Lord is at home, on the throne and in charge. The
foundations of life rest on Him and not in schools, neighborhoods
or even our systems of belief. God holds everything together, all
by Himself! And, incidentally, since we do not possess heaven's
perspective, things are never as bad as they appear.

Maclaren summarizes our duty when the foundations are
destroyed, or at least seem to be crumbling: "The foundations are
not being destroyed, however many and strong the arms that are
trying to dig them up. The righteous have done much, and can do
more, though his work seem wasted. Self-preservation is not a
man's first duty; flight is his last. Better and wiser and infinitely
nobler to stand a mark … and to stop at our post, though we fall
there, better infinitely to toil on, even when toil seems vain, than
cowardly to keep a whole skin at the cost of a wounded conscience
or despairingly to fling up work, because the ground is hard and
the growth of the seed imperceptible…. The only reasonable
attitude is obstinate hopefulness and brave adherence to duty."

When things are tough and the going is rough, it remains for
the church to double her efforts and invest all she has in God's
cause. The church is not a stock market. When things are bad we
don't pull out, sell high and buy low. "When the foundations are
destroyed, what can the righteous do?" Answer: They can renew
their faith in God, renew their efforts in ministry and renew their
support for the church of Christ, the "kingdom which cannot be
shaken" (Heb. 12:28).

# DAY 69 THE LINES HAVE FALLEN IN PLEASANT PLACES

## Read Psalm 16

*The lines have fallen for me in pleasant places; indeed, I have a beautiful inheritance.*

Psalm 16:6

Of all the seven Psalms of Trust none is more worthy of the title than Psalm 16. This beautiful song of faith is full of poetic expressions of faith and prophetic statements of hope. It may well be the most beautiful of all David's psalms. The subtitle calls it "A *Miktam* of David." No one really knows what a *miktam* is, but only six psalms bear that word. Five of the six are in Book Two of the Psalter (Pss. 56–60) and these have to do with David's "outlaw years." More than likely Psalm 16 belongs to that grouping and historical period.

David was dispossessed and often dismayed in those years between his anointing and his coronation; years in which he was betrayed by a wife, hunted by the king and rebuffed by many. Yet he kept his focus squarely on target: "The LORD is my chosen portion and my cup; you hold my lot. The lines have fallen for me in pleasant places; indeed, I have a beautiful inheritance" (vv. 5-6). David lost his home, wife, land and place in society. No matter; his riches were in God and his future was tied to God's will, not Saul's ways. In due time God would exalt him and humble all his enemies. Of this David was sure. He trusted in God.

Little wonder then that Peter and Paul chose this psalm to point to Jesus Christ and the hope of the resurrection (Acts 2:25 and 13: 35). Jesus, like David who was His "type," seemed to have lost everything – family, friends, success, a future and even life itself. His service for God seemed to cost him all He was and all He had. But such was not the case.

Because Christ trusted in God, the Father rewarded Him with a resurrection to glory that placed Christ at the preeminent place in all the universe (Phil. 2:5-11). The fact that God did not allow Christ to decay in death shows forth "the path of life" to those who would follow David and Christ to glory in the Way of Faith.

Bishop George Horne helps us see the connection between David's faith, Christ's trust and our hope in the Lord: "The return of Christ from the grave is beautifully described by Jehovah 'showing,' or discovering to him a 'path of life,' leading through the valley of the shadow of death, and from that valley to the summit of the hill of Zion, or to the mount of God in heaven, on which he now sits enthroned. There, exalted at the right hand of the Father, that human body, which expired on the cross, and slept in the sepulcher, lives and reigns, filled with delight, and encircled by glory incomprehensible and endless. Through this thy beloved Son and our dear Saviour, 'thou shalt show' us likewise, O Lord, 'the path of life;' thou shalt justify our souls by thy grace now, and raise our bodies by thy power at the last day; when earthly sorrow shall terminate in heavenly joy, and momentary pain shall be rewarded with everlasting felicity."

No one said it would be easy to live by faith; tithing by faith, praying in faith, persevering in faith and working in faith. But although not easy, the life of faith is the only "sure bet" in this life. It is the "path of life." It is the narrow way that leads to life. Few are they who find it. But rewarded they are, nevertheless.

## DAY 70 GOD, OUR SHEPHERD

## Read Psalm 23

*The LORD is my shepherd, I shall not want.*

Psalm 23:1

What can one possibly write new and refreshing about Psalm 23? It is, without any argument, the most popular of all psalms over all times. The accolades attributed to the psalm are incredible. C. H. Spurgeon writes, "This is the pearl of Psalms whose soft and pure radiance delights every eye." J. J. Stewart Perowne says: "This Psalm breathes throughout a spirit of the calmest and most assured trust in God: it speaks of a peace so deep, a serenity so profound, that even the thought of the shadow of death cannot trouble it." Alexander Maclaren observes, "The lovely series of vivid pictures, each but a clause long, but clear-cut in that small compass, like the fine work incised on a gem, combines with the depth and simplicity of the religious emotion expressed, to lay this sweet psalm on all hearts." John R. W. Stott calls it the "best known and best loved of all the psalms." J. M. Boices's comments on its use in the church: "Millions of people have memorized this psalm, even those who have learned few other Scripture portions. Ministers have used it to comfort people who are going through severe personal trials, suffering illness, or dying. For some, the words of this psalm have been the last they have uttered in life." Perhaps H. C. Leupold summarizes it best: "Expositions vie with one another in describing the rare beauty and charm of this psalm."

But there is a danger in all of this admiration for Psalm 23. Over time this psalm of David has become, like the hymn "Amazing Grace," the public property of the American culture. Like the hymn that has been recorded by everyone from bagpipers and marching bands to Judy Collins, Psalm 23 has been read at funerals of nonbelievers, inaugurations of godless presidents and commencement exercises at secular universities. A rude awakening is in store for most Americans: Psalm 23 only belongs to those who are true Christians, those who have made, by faith, Jesus Christ their Good Shepherd (John 10).

This psalm is not a guarantee of a trouble-free life but of the fact that Christ will be with us and, in fact, will be before us in all our difficulty – even in the valley of the shadow of death. Derek Kidner catches this truth: "Depth and strength underlie the simplicity of this psalm. Its peace is not escape; it contentment is not complacency: there is readiness to face deep darkness and imminent attack, and the climax reveals a love which homes towards no material goal but to the Lord Himself."

Our modern church is caught up with the idea that the Lord owes us all "personal peace and affluence." If that were the case we would not need faith and Christ's life would not be the pattern for all believers. Our struggles with sacrifice, service, suffering and stewardship ultimately result from a defective view of life. We are not here to "settle down" and get comfortable, but to travel with

Christ through this dangerous life to the "house of the LORD." We will not fear, nor lag behind. The Lord is with us. And our future is secure: We will "dwell in the house of the LORD forever" (v. 6). But let these truths not ensnare us in what William L. Holladay calls "the sentimentalizing" of Christianity: "The danger, then, as I have already said, is the sentimentalizing of the psalm, shaped by Sunday-school pictures, and, to the extent that the psalm defines our faith, a sentimentalizing of our faith." Let the reader of Psalm 23 beware!

## DAY 71 A HOLY PLACE FOR HOLY HOURS

## Read Psalm 27

> One thing have I asked of the LORD, that will I seek after: that I may dwell in the house of the LORD all the days of my life, to gaze upon the beauty of the LORD and to inquire in his temple.
>
> Psalm 27:4

Psalm 27 is a lovely psalm that befuddles some critics. The psalm divides itself into two equal parts (vv. 1-6; vv. 7-12) with a conclusion (vv. 13-14). But the two halves are diametrically opposite in tone. The first half is a "Psalm of Trust," the second half, a "Psalm of Lament." Hans-Joachim Kraus comments, "The principle question in the form analysis of Psalm 27 comes up in view of the remarkable break that is to be noted between verses 6 and 7. Whereas verses 1-6 are replete with trust and confidence, verses 7-14 have the sound of lament and prayer." This has caused many commentators to postulate that the two parts are really two separate psalms, written at different times but later forced together by a compiler. But a focus on verse 4 yields the key to understanding the whole of the psalm.

David is surrounded by enemies: the men of Saul, the forces of Absalom, the Philistines or others. We know not what enemies; just that there were "a host" encamped against him (v. 3). David seeks solitude not in the Tent of Meeting – The Tabernacle – but rather the tent he erected in Jerusalem to house the Ark of the Covenant for a time. (The Tabernacle was in Gibeon until Solomon took it to Zion in 2 Chron. 1:3-4.) He goes there not to seek sanctuary but to meditate or inquire – to pray and think.

In that quiet and holy place, a place of prayer and security in God, David revels in God's love and is refreshed by God's grace. But as he steps out of the tent, in battle garb, the reality hits him: All seem to have forsaken him (even his family, v. 10), and all are against him. He senses the danger and feels the tension. Then he recalls: Had he not faith in God he would perish. But as it is, he will "see the goodness of the LORD in the land of the living" (v. 13). So he waits on God and takes courage in grace.

Let me transfer this to our modern world. Perhaps what we moderns lack are "holy places" – sanctuaries, chapels, prayer rooms – that we regularly visit and in which we meditate and pray. Medieval men made space for God in both their schedule and their neighborhoods. They went to Morning Prayer at church on the way to work as the sun rose and Evening Prayer on the way home as the sun set. They learned to withdraw from the world in order to get closer to God. Was that such a bad idea? Such a "Catholic" mispractice?

Whenever I am in London, I make it a part of my itinerary to go to Evening Prayer (Evensong) at St. Paul's Cathedral. I "decompress." I can hear London, faintly, outside – big, busy, godless, "a host encamped" against God. The solitude of the vaulted sanctuary, the reverence of those in prayer and the far away sounds of "the land of the living" help me focus on what lasts forever, what fades away and where my first love must be (1 John 2:15-17). It is good for my soul to "behold the beauty of the LORD and to meditate in His temple," that holy place (v. 4).

Am I just a sentimental old man, with still a bit too much of his Catholicism in him, to hope that once again someday evangelical Christians would discover the joy of holy places, holy hours of prayer and the renewing joy of daily withdrawal to be with God for a season? Could we ever see again in our cities, towns and suburbs morning and evening prayer? Would we be better men in the world if we went more regularly to "the cover of His tent" (v. 5). May it be so once again: "The goodness of the LORD in the land of the living."

## DAY 72 THIRSTING FOR GOD

# Read Psalm 63

*O God, you are my God; earnestly I seek you; my soul thirsts for you; my flesh faints for you, as in a dry and weary land where there is no water.*

Psalm 63:1

Psalms 61 to 64 make up yet another sub-collection in the Psalter. These psalms appear to have come from the time in David's life when he fled from Absalom and hid in the wilderness, waiting for his restoration to the throne (2 Sam. 15–19). In his delightful little book, *The Life of David as Reflected in His Psalms*, Alexander Maclaren writes: "The sixty-third psalm is by the superscription referred to the time when David was, 'in the wilderness of Judah,' which has led many readers to think of his long stay there during Saul's persecution. But the psalm certainly belongs to the period of his reign, as is obvious from the words, 'The king shall rejoice in God.' It must therefore belong to his brief sojourn in the same wilderness in his flight to Mahanaim when, as we read in 2 Samuel 17:29, 'The people were weary and hungry and thirsty in the wilderness.'"

David is in the "dry and weary land" of the trans-Jordan wilderness. His soul feels like his body – hot, dry, tired and dusty. He longs for that place of refreshment (the same place he spoke of in Psalm 27), the sanctuary of the Tabernacle or Tent of Meeting. He left that behind, as he fled from Absalom's forces. The king sent Zadok the high priest and the Levites back to Jerusalem as they tried to flee with David and take the Ark of the Covenant with them. "Then the king said to Zadok, 'Carry the ark of God back into the city. If I find favor in the eyes of the LORD, he will bring me back and let me see both it and his dwelling place. But if he says, "I have no pleasure in you," behold, here I am, let him do to me what seems good to him'" (2 Sam. 15:25-26). David was thinking correctly.

He said, in effect, "No! The Ark of the Covenant belongs in God's tabernacle, among God's people, in Zion, God's city. I am the fugitive, not God. I am under God's righteous discipline and His tender mercy. God will do what is right; but for now I must be driven away. God remains as He always is; may He bring me back to Him." Psalm 63 reflects the prayer of David composed in this trying hour. Psalm 63 is the prayer of a broken and repentant man with confidence in God's covenant of grace and restoring mercy.

Derek Kidner comments, "Once more the worst has brought out David's best, in words as well as deeds.... There may be other psalms that equal this outpouring of devotion; few if any that surpass it." When we are disciplined and suffer the due consequences of our sins how do we respond? How often we say, "Why is this happening to me?" Or we whine, "Has God forsaken me and left me on my own?" Then some ask, "Where is God when you need Him?" And many often stay away from church and, quite frankly, pout. These are not the responses of true piety.

The parallel is easy to draw: The life of a Christian becomes weary, dusty, and dry when he departs from the Lord and withdraws from the public ordinances of the church. But God remains at church – in His regular place, if I my say it that way. And in His lovingkindness, His covenant loyalty, He draws us back to Himself, and back to His covenant people, the church. Our sins may cause a time of wilderness wandering for our souls. All the same, God is ever where He should be, in His preached Word, in prayer, in the Lord's Supper and in the fellowship of His saints (Acts 2:42). David Dickson reminds us, "Because the power and glory of God are nowhere so clearly seen as in public ordinances, therefore should the ordinances be loved and earnestly sought after, that we may find communion with God in them."

Feeling dry of spirit and dusty of soul? When was the last time you went to church?

## Day 73 Whom have I in Heaven but Thee?

### Read Psalm 73

*Whom have I in heaven but you? And there is nothing on earth that I desire besides you.*

Psalm 73:25

Contentment is something all of us struggle with at one time or another and often repeatedly. Few of us have grown spiritually to the place where Paul abided, who said that he had learned the "secret" of contentment (Phil. 4:10-12). In fact, our lives are often filled with the struggle that Asaph records in Psalm 73 — envious over the wicked and embittered because of the ungodly. C. H. Spurgeon is correct: "Here begins the narrative of a great soul-battle, a spiritual Marathon, a hard and well-fought field, in which the half-defeated became in the end wholly victorious." This is a common problem we all face: "Why do the ungodly prosper while the righteous do not?" In a very real sense this question is related to the whole issue of Theodicy: why a good God allows evil in His creation. It is a question about the moral government of God.

J. J. Stewart Perowne puts the question in perspective: "There are some questions which never lose their interest, some problems of which it may be said, that they are ever old and yet ever new. Not the least anxious of such questions are those which deal with God's moral government of the world. They lie close to man's heart, and are ever asking and pressing for solution. They may differ in different times, they may assume various forms; but perhaps no man ever looked thoughtfully on the world as it is without seeing much that was hard to reconcile with a belief in the love and wisdom of God." These are the questions behind Psalm 37, the book of Job, Solomon's Ecclesiastes and Psalm 73.

Psalm 73 takes its life again and again, in a thousand different ways, in our hearts. Why do perverted men get elected, escape impeachment and maintain such high ratings? Why don't conservative, reformed, serious churches grow faster and larger? Why is it the unconverted are always so rich? How is it that the more godless the scholar, the more his books are published and the more he is in demand as a conference speaker?

Asaph struggles with these very issues until ... he says, "But when I thought how to understand this, it seemed to me a wearisome task, until I went into the sanctuary of God" (vv. 16, 17). He gives us no theological solution, no psychological perspective, and no "insights" that cause it all to make sense. He simply says, "When I went to Church it dawned on me: The smug and happy reprobate is doomed. He is on a slippery slope (v. 18) and he is sliding luxuriously to a Christ-less eternity!" In the light of the unconverted man's imminent and eternal ruin, this saint feels blessed beyond measure.

Part of living by faith is to trust that God has indeed "granted to us all things that pertain to life and godliness" (2 Pet. 1:3). God has not "short-changed" us at all. If there is something we desire but do not have – more money, a bigger church, that PhD, a certain woman as wife – then the only explicable reason is that desire would rob us of our chief desire: the nearness of God (Ps. 73:25-28).

Therefore, the wise man of faith will often find himself praying this strange but profound prayer of trust: "O God, thank you for not giving me all my desires, for not answering all my prayers, for withholding from me that which would withhold from me the one great treasure and joy of life forever – You!"

## DAY 74 IN THE SHADOW OF THE ALMIGHTY

### Read Psalm 91

*He who dwells in the shelter of the Most High will abide in the shadow of the Almighty.*

Psalm 91:1

When I was a fairly new Christian, twenty-five years ago, Psalm 91 made quite an impression upon me. It was from this psalm that a book about missionary martyr, Jim Elliott, received its title: *The Shadow of the Almighty*. Everyone at my newfound church home seemed to be reading that book. Also, my new bride brought with her a record (remember those things? – precursors to the CD!) that was a recording of a professional reader who was reciting psalms with instrumental background music. By far the most beautiful "cut" on the record was Psalm 91. I listened to it over and over again. The serenity and strength of this psalm deeply impressed this restless young convert.

Of all seven Psalms of Trust, Psalm 91 may rightfully claim the preeminence. Few songs rise to the grandeur of this precious ode to God by a man of faith. Rowland Prothero, in his delightful little book, *The Psalms in Human Life* begins his historical survey of the psalms in the life of the church with these words: "Above the couch of David, according to Rabbinical tradition, there hung a harp. The midnight breeze, as it rippled over the strings, made such music that the poet-king was constrained to rise from his bed, and, till the dawn flushed the eastern skies, he wedded words to the strains. The poetry of that tradition is condensed in the saying that the Book of Psalms contains the whole music of the heart of man, swept by the hand of his Maker." One cannot help but wonder what awoke David the night he composed this magnificent hymn of Trust: "The Shadow of the Almighty."

Modern men are not supposed to get scared, to be frightened or intimidated by anyone or anything. It is part of the arrogance of the modern that bravado has replaced common sense. But, in fact, we ought to be afraid, for we live in a dangerous world; a world in which Luther wrote: "And though this world with devils filled should threaten to undo us ..." It is not such a foolish thing for men to be wary of evil, nor is it cowardly to "hide oneself in God."

Psalm 91 reminds us that God is BIG, important, strong, capable, confident, sure, dependable and our true champion. He has at His command legions of angels (v. 11). He is able to spread his "pinions" – those big wings of massive expanse owned by all birds of prey – over his saints to both hide and shield them. He casts a "big shadow" over the cosmos, and, like children on a playground who feel secure as long as Dad looms over them, His saints dwell securely in His presence.

The blessings of abiding under God's care are innumerable: lack of fear, safety, victory, answered prayer, and eternal security. The best of both worlds is afforded to those whose lives are centered under the Shadow of the Almighty: "With long life I will satisfy him and show him my salvation" (v. 16).

Take it from a man who's lived outside the shadow of God for one-half of his life and under the shadow of the Almighty for the other half. There is no comparison: the life of faith is the better life. It is such a great joy to arise each morning and be able to say, "My refuge and my fortress, my God, in whom I trust" (v. 2).

## DAY 75 THE COMFORTS OF HISTORY

# Read Psalm 77

*I will remember the deeds of the LORD; yes, I will remember your wonders of old. I will ponder all your work, and meditate on your mighty deeds..*
                                                    Psalm 77:11-12

Most people do not enjoy history. There's a reason for that. It seems that most of us had a high school history teacher who was also the football coach. His view of history was last week's game and a list of names and dates to be memorized. I have been fortunate. I have been blessed by God with history teachers, in elementary and high school, who loved the subject and made the past come alive. God likes history. Three-fourths of His Bible is historical in nature and content.

Psalm 77 begins our new sequence of readings, a collection of psalms I have entitled "Psalms for a Nation in Decline." Psalm 77 is a lament but it also focuses on history. Asaph's answer to his grief over God's estrangement from His people Israel (vv. 7-10) is found in remembering the past. "I will remember the deeds of the LORD; yes, I will remember your wonders of old" (v. 11). The cure to a melancholy spirit over the spiritual demise and decline of our people is a rehearsal of God's dealings with us in the past.

God is immutable; He does not change. He is indeed "the same yesterday and today and forever" (Heb. 13:8). If He showed favor to our land in days of old, He will do so again. Here is where history becomes an ally. People will say, "But I hate history!" and I say, "Not so!" A wife will press flowers and put them in a book for remembrance – a historical memento of a time of romance. A man will frame a picture of his son and himself when his boy shot his first buck – a historical reminder of a special day. Photo albums, plaques on the wall, yearbooks, souvenirs and the old National Championship cap we wear all indicate our desire to remember great moments of the past.

So Asaph reminds us: When we muse on the historical record of God we will be encouraged. "I will ponder all your work, and meditate on your mighty deeds. Your way, O God, is holy. What

135

god is great like our God?" (vv. 12-13). God redeemed us in the past (v. 15); surely He will reform, revive and restore us in the future.

Years ago I went through a very difficult and trying time in my life and ministry. I was flat on my back for six weeks. During that time I was introduced to a book by Peter Marshall, Jr. and David Manuel, entitled *The Glory and the Dream*. It was a narrative history of America from the voyages of Columbus to the Revolutionary War. But the focus was spiritual: What God had done in and for America – the ebb and flow of Christianity in the New World. Marshall and Manuel followed this book with two more volumes, *From Sea to Shining Sea* and then *Sounding Forth the Trumpet* – from the Revolutionary War to pre-Civil War days. I await anxiously the next volume on the Civil War.

The books have fueled my hope for revival and my faith that God has not forsaken this Puritan Hope, this Pilgrim Pride called America. God has rescued and restored this land and its people before. He can do it again, and oh that He would! He is still the God of history – my nation's history. Of Him we continue to say, "You are the God who works wonders; you have made known your might among the peoples" (v. 14).

## DAY 76 TEACH YOUR CHILDREN WELL

### Read Psalm 78

*We will not hide them from their children, but tell to the coming generation the glorious deeds of the LORD, and his might, and the wonders that he has done.*

Psalm 78:4

When I was in graduate school a rock 'n roll group known as "The Super Group" – Dave Crosby, Stephen Stills, Graham Nash and Neil Young – recorded a song entitled *Teach Your Children Well*. That is what Psalm 78 could be subtitled. For Asaph states, "We will not hide them [the Lord's precepts] from their children, but tell to the coming generation the glorious deeds of the Lord, and his might, and the wonders that he has done. He established a testimony in Jacob and appointed a law in Israel, which he commanded our fathers to teach to their children, that the next generation might know them, the children yet unborn, and arise and tell them to their children..." (vv. 4-6). In this psalm, one of the longest in the Psalter, Asaph reviews Israel's history from Moses to David, from Exodus to monarchy.

Psalm 78 is a set of divine cliff-notes for the survey of Exodus to 2 Samuel. And the lessons taught in these historical books are to be passed on to five generations: the fathers, their children, the generation to come, their children and then their children (v. 6). William S. Plummer rightly observes, "Those great religious truths which suit one generation, are no less applicable to all who come after them.... The Bible is for all times."

Any people who lose the sense of their own history soon fall into ruin. Three things make up every culture: a common language, shared religious values, and a chronicle of definitive historical events. When, for instance, the people of America forget Columbus Day, ignore the Civil War, no longer celebrate Memorial Day and revise history in high school so that it is politically correct, then the seeds of the collapse of culture have been sown. If Americans are more tuned into the ABC Evening News and current events than the History Channel and memorial events then the loss of the American soul is guaranteed.

The same is true for the people of God, the church. The more and more our Christian bookstores become full of "how to" books, the endless volumes on family, feelings and finances, and the dime-novel books that can be churned out every three months by our publish-for-hire authors, the more we lose the sense of who we are. Read Psalm 78 – slowly. There is no "feel good" word-smithing in its seventy-two verses. This isn't a manual for success and security. This is a survey of a people's life with God – warts and all – for almost half a millennium.

There is something lasting, worthy of exploration, transferable to other generations about the lessons of history. Read Hebrews 11 if you don't believe me. Paul tells the Corinthians,

"Now these things happened to them as an example, but they were written down for our instruction, on whom the end of the ages has come" (1 Cor. 10:11). We fail our children greatly when all we give them are Veggie Tales and cartoon characters of the Bible. We need to rediscover the art of storytelling and passing down to the next generation the epic stories of our most holy religion. What our ancestors in Christ experienced is very much determinative of who we are. And what they did is a guideline for how we live. Teach your children well, for what they learn of days gone by will prepare them for days yet to come, and time even beyond that.

## DAY 77 THE SADDEST PSALM OF ALL

### Read Psalm 88

*O LORD, God of my salvation; I cry out day and night before you.*

Psalm 88:1

Psalm 88 is the gloomiest, saddest, darkest psalm in the Psalter. To this fact all scholars agree. It is an individual lament: the cry of a person in deep distress and sorrow. In all the other laments of the Psalter, both individual (personal) and corporate (national), the cries of complaint are met with hope in God somewhere in the psalm, but not in Psalm 88. H. C. Leupold calls this psalm "the gloomiest psalm found in the Scriptures." J. J. Perowne says it is "the saddest, darkest psalm in all the Psalter. It is one wail of sorrow from beginning to end." And Joseph A. Alexander refers to it as "the most despondent psalm in the collection, in which the complaints and lamentations are relieved by no joyful anticipation or expressions of strong confidence." It is characteristic, A. F. Kirkpatrick observes, that the last word is "darkness."

Why is this psalm in the Psalter? Why did the sons of Korah and Heman the Ezrahite (son of Zerah; 1 Chron. 2:6) collaborate to produce such a melancholy, depressing psalm? The answer may not please most of us, but here it is: There are situations, circumstances and events in life that crash into our world with such devastating and horrible force that we are sent reeling and grasping for answers that never come. Notice the structure of Psalm 88. The New American Standard Bible divides it into three paragraphs: the psalmist complains of feeling forsaken by God (vv. 1-9), feeling bewildered by God (vv. 10-12) and feeling rejected by God (vv. 13-18). He cries out, as Michael Wilcock puts it, "praying in total darkness."

The first year I was a Christian, back in 1977, my father died of cancer at the age of only fifty-five. That September afternoon, as we walked away from the grave in Columbus, Ohio, the minister gave my mother a memento – a cross. Looking down at the emblem of death in her hands, she turned to me with tears in her eyes, and lamented, "Thirty years together and all for this? Just this?" and then began to sob. Margie entered into the darkness of the valley of death that day; her life had drawn "near to Sheol" (88:3). She wanted answers: Why such a painful and untimely death for a relatively young man?

But answers did not come then. They have not yet, a quarter of a century later. There will be no answer to that question in this life. That is the realism of this living Psalter – not every question is answered, every sorrow removed, every wrong made right – in this life. In spite of this, my mother has found her solace in that cross that now hangs on her wall and has done so since 1977.

The cross my mother held in her hand is the answer. And, yes, all of life is about that cross. For there was a dark day, the day Jesus died, a day answers refused to come. Yet, in the end, the cross is the answer to sickness, sorrow, sin and its wages. It seems fitting that the Anglican Church has reserved Psalm 88 for Good Friday – the day the Good Man died for bad men. We may hold the cross in our hand, in our darkest moments when there appear to be no answers, and ask ourselves, "Is this all there is? Just this?" And the answer is, "Yes; and this Cross is all we need ... forever!"

## DAY 78 I WILL GO TO THE ALTAR OF GOD

## Read Psalms 42 and 43

*Then I will go to the altar of God, to God my exceeding joy, and I will praise you with the lyre, O God, my God.*

Psalm 43:4

Psalms 42 and 43 once apparently made up one psalm. The refrain (42:5,11; 43:5) divides the combined psalm into three reasons why the sons of Korah felt despair of soul and disturbance of heart. First, the psalmist is somehow unable to go to the sanctuary; perhaps exiled from Judah. His soul is dry. He is experiencing spiritual declension (42:1-5). Second, he feels overwhelmed by the difficulties he now faces. He feels drowned in a sea of sorrows or a river of trouble (42:6-11). Third, he is surrounded by a godless nation. It depresses him (43:1-5). Derek Kidner speculates, "It is the lament of a temple singer exiled in the north, near the rising of the Jordan, who longs to be back at God's house."

Would we "spiritualize" this psalm too much if we drew a parallel to the sorrows of backsliding? A person falls away from the church: "how I used to go with the throng and lead them in procession to the house of God" (42:4). But as he drifts from church he drifts from God – work, golf, fishing, the newspaper and television replace Sunday worship. Soon he's in over his head and difficulties overwhelm his life: "All your breakers and your waves have gone over me" (42:7). Eventually this backslidden and discouraged soul realizes he has forsaken the communion of the saints for the company of a godless society: "Vindicate me, O God, and defend my cause against an ungodly people, from the deceitful and unjust man deliver me!" (43:1). What the sons of Korah have set forth in poetry, Puritan Phillip Doddridge (1702–1751) called *The Rise and Fall of Religion in the Soul*. This is a common problem that calls for renewal of faith in the individual, the reformation of religion in the church, and the revival of the church in the land.

The answer to this problem is to turn and go back, as Jeremiah puts it, on "the ancient paths" (Jer. 6:16; 18:15 and 31:21). The solution is to return to what you left. "Then I will go to the altar of God, to God my exceeding joy" (43:4). For renewal the Korahite knew he needed to get back to the Temple for worship; the saint knows that his renewal begins by going back to worship, at church, on the Lord's Day. As a young Catholic altar boy, we used to begin the Mass with the words of Psalm 43:4: "I will go to the altar of God, the God who gives joy to my youth" (*Vulgate*). I now understand this verse differently: in Christ.

What causes spiritual declension is not our forsaking the church but rather distancing ourselves from Christ and His cross. In the church, through the means of grace, Christ feeds, refreshes, enfolds and encourages His saints. Under the shadow of the cross we blossom and grow as Christians, "little Christs." Once we leave the Gospel fellowship, forsake the Gospel meal, forget the Gospel message and forfeit Gospel prayer we wither and dry up. When we return to Christ and His community of the cross we are renewed.

Richard Lovelace, in his marvelous book *Dynamics of Spiritual Life: An Evangelical Theology of Renewal*, reminds us that returning to the cross is the source of joy for a believer, the fountain of renewal for a congregation, and the catalyst for revival of Christianity. The more we conform ourselves to what Luther called "theologians of the cross" the more we experience the joy of Jesus. The farther we stray from the shadow of the cross the more we will be asking ourselves, "Why are you in despair, O my soul? And why are you disturbed within me?" Whenever we sense that spiritual declension is setting in, it is time to turn around, go to the altar of God – Calvary – and refresh our souls in the Shadow of the Cross.

## DAY 79 A WAKE-UP CALL FOR GOD

### Read Psalm 44

> *Awake! Why are you sleeping, O LORD? Rouse yourself! Do not reject us forever!*
>
> Psalm 44:23

Psalm 44, a psalm of the sons of Korah, is much discussed and debated concerning its date. Calvin and not a few scholars assign

Psalm 44 to the intertestamental age of the Maccabean conflict, perhaps even to the persecution of Antiochus Epiphanies IV. But modern commentators have revisited the issue and are more and more prone to ascribe Psalm 44 to the age of David's monarchy.

Here is the problem: Israel has been faithful to God, yet God has allowed some crushing defeat to slam into His people (vv. 17-19). The people are therefore bewildered. The king (the "I" in the psalm) prays on behalf of the people (the "we" in the psalm). He focuses on God's glory: the old days of glory (vv. 1-3), the hope of future glory (vv. 4-8), the loss of present glory (vv. 9-16), the hunger for renewed glory (vv. 17-19), and the prayer for restored glory (vv. 20-26). Although he never actually mentions the word "glory," in fact that is what he hungers for – the glory of God in the land once again. This national lament reflects the puzzling question: "Why has God allowed us to be attacked when we were trying to be faithful to Him?"

Perhaps this is how Americans felt in the wake of the terrorist attacks in 2001. Americans were minding their own business and then, *Wham*! Some pastors said, "This is a wake-up call from God; a discipline from heaven; a remedial judgment." Others put their e-mails and newsletters out saying, "This is no judgment, these things just happen. Let's use it as an opportunity to preach the Gospel and model justice and mercy." But perhaps there is a third option.

The sons of Korah write the strangest thing in verse 23, speaking to God Himself: "Awake! Why are you sleeping, O Lord? Rouse yourself! Do not reject us forever!." The sons of Korah see this psalm as – are you ready for this – a wake-up call for God! We may be offended by such choice of words, even scandalized by the directness of the prayer. But H. C. Leupold is right: "Since a tone of absolute reverence pervades the psalm, these unusual expressions dare not be charged too heavily against their writer."

The psalmist's words are not only not irreverent, but also actually biblical. He remembers the words used by Moses in the wilderness. When the ark was hoisted up and carried forward on the march, the prophet would exclaim, "Arise, O Lord, and let your enemies be scattered." But when the ark once again came to rest, the lawgiver said, "Return, O Lord, to the ten thousand thousands of Israel" (Num. 10:35, 36).

In my devotional Bible I have written my own title for each psalm. To Psalm 44 I have affixed the words, "A Prayer for Revival," for that is what it truly is. The psalm asks God to awaken that His people might have an awakening. It asks God to beat back the enemy that peace may reign again. And in the wake of all the American nation has gone through in these last few years, God's people there need to pray that God return, in glory, to His church (revival) and awaken the dead souls of their unconverted neighbors, and yes, their enemies. It is time for God to wake up for our nations, rise up for the church and put down our enemies – His enemies, too. And it is time for the church to pray that once again glory fill our lands, and the lands of those who hate us.

## Day 80 The God who is There

### Read Psalm 50

*These things you have done, and I have been silent; you thought that I was one like yourself. But now I rebuke you and lay the charge before you.*

Psalm 50:21

Patrick Morely, the author of *The Man in the Mirror* and other books for men, has said repeatedly that there are two gods we all must deal with: The god whom we like and the God who is. Francis Schaeffer referred to this real God as "The God Who is There." Psalm 50 develops this very thought. The author of this psalm is Asaph: Levite, musician and singer, appointed by David to compose and perform psalms (See 1 Chron. 15:16-22; 25:1ff and Ezra 2:40-41). Asaph wrote twelve psalms: Psalms. 50 and 73–83.

In this psalm God rebukes His Old Testament church, not for their religious practices but for their mental image of Him. He says clearly, "Not for your sacrifices do I rebuke you; your burnt offerings are continually before me....These things you have done, and I have been silent; you thought that I was one like yourself. But now I rebuke you and lay the charge before you" (vv. 8, 21). The two sins Asaph rebukes are formalism and hypocrisy.

Perhaps it was from this psalm that John Bunyan drew his imagery for a scene in *The Pilgrim's Progress*. Pilgrim Christian comes upon two fellow travelers, Formalism (vv. 7-15) and Hypocrisy (vv. 16-21), who entered into the Celestial City (heaven), not by the narrow gate of faith in Jesus alone, but by climbing over the wall. When warned by young Christian that their false entrance will be exposed at the judgment seat, they reply, "'Custom, it being of so long a standing, as above a thousand years, would doubtless be admitted as a thing legal, by an Impartial Judge. And besides ... if we get into the way, what's matter which way we get it? If we are in we are in; thou art but in the way, who, as we perceive, came in at the gate; and we are also in the way that came by tumbling over the wall. Wherein now is thy condition better than ours?'" But Christian knew better. So did Asaph. And so do we.

Formalism (going through the truly-reformed motions of worship, doctrine and "custom") needs to be reminded that God is spiritual. Hypocrisy (saying the right things but doing the wrong) needs to be reminded that God is true. Jesus put it this way: "But the hour is coming, and is now here, when the true worshipers will worship the Father in spirit and truth, for the Father is seeking such people to worship him. God is spirit, and those who worship him must worship in spirit and truth" (John 4:23-24). Beyond Reformed practice there is an inner response to grace; beyond conservative ethics there is a true response to law. Jesus made this the heart of true religion and called it "spirit and truth."

Men are satisfied with formalism and hypocrisy. Wives will take flowers for payment of sin; parents will take outward obedience in lieu of true holiness; pastors will settle for attendance and money instead of commitment, but God is different. "You thought I was just like you" (see v. 21), "but you were wrong – dead wrong," says God. For at the time Asaph wrote this psalm God was changing kings in Israel, and He told the people why. When He selected David to replace Saul, He told Samuel, "Do not look on his appearance or on the height of his stature, because I have rejected him [i.e. Eliab, David's brother]. For the LORD sees not as man sees: man looks on the outward appearance, but the LORD looks on the heart" (1 Sam. 16:7). And God found a man of spirit and truth in a teenage shepherd boy; a man with a heart after God to do all His holy will (1 Sam. 13:14; Acts 13:22). God is still seeking such people.

## DAY 81 CONSIDER THE COVENANT

## Read Psalm 74

*Have regard for the covenant, for the dark places of the land are full of the habitations of violence.*

Psalm 74:20

This psalm was probably written a decade or two after the destruction of the Temple and the plundering of Jerusalem by Babylon in 587 BC The reference to "the perpetual ruins" (v. 3), a pillaged and ruined sanctuary (v. 4), the sacking of the city by pagans (vv. 3-8) and the absence of the prophets (v. 9), all point to the Babylonian captivity. Asaph is the author, but probably not the Asaph of David's time. More than likely this Asaph was a descendent of his, bearing the same name or one of the "sons of Asaph" employed in temple liturgy and psalmody. This national lament calls upon God to remember His people, consider His covenant and redress the wrongs done to Israel by the Babylonians. This psalm is cousin to Psalms 79 and 137 and the Lamentations of Jeremiah, all produced at the same time.

Things looked hopeless – no Temple for worship, the very heart of Israel, was gone. The *Shekinah* glory had left, the very presence of Jehovah was gone. The prophets were all dead or carried away in bondage; the very voice of God was gone. All was lost, or so it seemed.

Yet there remained one anchor for the pillaged and plundered soul of our Old Testament brethren: the Covenant of Grace with God. And to that one remaining hope Asaph clings: "Have regard for the covenant, for the dark places of the land are full of the habitations of violence." The world seems full of evil. The "dark places of the land" – for Israel the caves and hills of Palestine; for us the alley-ways and vice-filled corners of our cities – seem full of violent, cruel and godlessly wicked men. And so they are.

They have always been. But when God is in the land His presence (the Holy Spirit), His voice (the Word preached) and His holy habitation (the godly church) keep evil at bay. Like spiders and reptiles and rodents, evil men crawl back into their stink holes when glory fills the land. When, however, God becomes grieved, and withdraws His favor, the society feels His absence, the community lacks His voice (when preaching is in decline) and the church itself becomes carnal, even wicked. Historians refer to these times as the "dark ages" (See Deut. 31:17).

The ray of hope remains: God has made a covenant with His people. Asaph remembers God's Word, uttered almost a millennium earlier, "But truly, as I live, and as all the earth shall be filled with the glory of the LORD" (Num. 14:21). The Covenant of God promises this truth.

In the Peter Jackson film, *The Lord of the Rings: The Two Towers*, the movie climaxes with a "resurrected" Gandalf returning, "in the east, at dawn, with an army" to the dark and cruel world that is overwhelming Rohan and a beleaguered band holed up at Helm's Deep. As his horse rears up in the glory of dawn, the picture reminds us of a powerful biblical truth: In this world full of dark recesses of evil, God reigns supreme. In the end good always conquers evil because the Son of God goes forth to war to fulfill the covenant His Father made with His people: "I am Your God and you are My people; I will never leave you or forsake you." Yes, beloved, we often forget God and even forsake Him, but God always remembers the covenant and redeems us from evil.

## DAY 82 COVERING ALL THE BASES

## Read Psalm 25

*The troubles of my heart are enlarged; bring me out of my distresses. Consider my affliction and my trouble, and forgive all my sins. Consider how many are my foes, and with what violent hatred they hate me.*

Psalm 25:17-19

It is symptomatic of a postmodern age that we are against any absolute except this one: I am always right. Ever notice how people today believe in nothing except their own innocence, integrity and rightness of cause? That's why John F. MacArthur refers to America as "a nation of victims" – we are always in the right while others are always doing us wrong! Not so with King David. When he penned Psalm 25, at a time when political troubles from without, personal troubles from within and his own sin combined to make life difficult, he prayed with amazing objectivity. Such objectivity could only be inspired by the Holy Spirit as a pattern of prayer for all of us in tough times.

We have an expression in America, one of our idioms: "Covering all the bases." We get that colloquial statement from the American pastime, baseball. To "cover all the bases" is to make sure every angle of thought and every possible outcome is considered; like baseball players guard first, second and third bases, as well as home plate.

In Psalm 25 David "covers all the bases" in his prayer. He prays about his troubles and he does so comprehensively. Four repeated themes arise in the twenty-two verses of this psalm. First David prays for deliverance from his enemies, a theme never far from any of David's psalms and prayers (vv. 1-3, 15, 19-20). Second, he confesses his own sin and realizes it, too, has caused him great trouble (vv. 6-7, 11, 16-18). Third, he asks God for guidance and wisdom (vv. 4-5, 21-22). Finally, he confesses his faith in God in a series of creedal statements about God, His character and His ways (vv. 8-10, 12-14). Why does David pray this way? Is he just rambling through a prayer? Is there no common theme to his prayer?

The answer is simple: humility. Psalm 25 is the prayer of a humble man. He prays, "The troubles of my heart are enlarged; bring me out of my distresses. Consider my affliction and my trouble, and forgive all my sins. Consider how many are my foes, and with what violent hatred they hate me" (vv. 17-19). When troubled he prays, in effect, "Lord, I am not sure if all this is happening to me because my enemies are evil, I am sinful or there are things You want me to learn from all this. But I do know that You are trustworthy to deliver, faithful to forgive and gracious to impart wisdom." Could there be a more balanced, objective and humble prayer?

I often find myself in difficult situations as a pastor. I find myself asking God, "Is my trouble due to sinful people striking out at me because I faithfully preach the Word? Or is this due to my own sins and their consequences? Or am I just thick-headed and You, Lord, are teaching me a lesson I should have already learned?" Truth is, probably all three of these things are true – all at the same time. The good news is that I don't have to figure out what is happening and why, but simply how to learn and grow from it. The better news is that God knows and is working in me for my growth in grace. "The friendship of the LORD is for those who fear him, and he makes known to them his covenant" (v. 14). My job is to "cover all the bases." God's task is to make the right call. I am confident He'll do His job. The question is, will I do mine?

## DAY 83 THE PRAYER OF A MAN OF INTEGRITY

### Read Psalm 26

*Vindicate me, O LORD, for I have walked in my integrity, and I have trusted in the LORD without wavering. ... But as for me, I shall walk in my integrity; redeem me, and be gracious to me.*

Psalm 26:1, 11

Years ago, when I was first converted, an older man began to disciple me. One of the first spiritual disciplines to which he introduced me was Scripture memory. One of the earliest verses I memorized was from Proverbs 20:6, "Many a man proclaims his own steadfast love, but a faithful man who can find?" Translated:

We all think we have peerless integrity but a man of such character is rare indeed.

Why then does David seem to mention his own integrity so much? (See Pss. 15, 24, 26, 73, etc.) Does David fall under the rebuke of Proverbs 20:6? Probably so, for David was sinful (i.e. prideful) like all of us. Some commentators find great difficulty in what David writes. Buttenweiser comments, "Nor does it even ring true." Koenig calls David "self-righteous." But more than likely David is praying with honesty and humility.

Psalm 26 is the second Psalm of Petition we are reading this week (Pss. 25, 26, 61, 64, 70, 86, and 94). These seven Psalms of Petition may well be entitled "Defeat for Us Our Enemies," for that is their common theme. Here in Psalm 26 David prays that God would deliver him because he is a man of integrity.

David appears to be praying to God in a situation where he has been falsely accused. He asks God to take his case in hand and prove him innocent of the charges. Like any man on a witness stand he delivers "character witness" – only he is his own witness to God the Judge. His defense is two-fold.

First, he reminds God that he is not accustomed to the fellowship of "men of falsehood … hypocrites … evildoers … the wicked" (vv. 4-5). He is like the blessed man of Psalm 1 who "who walks not in the counsel of the wicked, nor stands in the way of sinners, nor sits in the seat of scoffers" (Ps. 1:1). The accusation does not fit the pattern of the company he keeps.

Second, he reminds the Lord that his chief concerns and first love have always been the House of the Lord: "O LORD, I love the habitation of your house and the place where your glory dwells" (v. 8). For proof of this read 2 Samuel 7. A man concerned with God's glory and God's rituals is not the kind of man who also delights in evil.

One of the marks of a spiritual man is truthfulness. When he is truthful about God he displays faith. When he is truthful about others he is honest. When he is truthful about sin and wickedness he is righteous. When he is honest about himself he displays integrity. Jesus would not admit to false charges about Himself, tolerate misinformation about His Father, or allow men to be too hard on others. Christ was the paradigm of integrity – neither false nor proud, just truthful. And Christ remains committed to upholding the man of integrity.

All of us will face false charges, after all "all men are liars" (Ps. 116:11). All we can do is to follow David's plan: "But as for me, I shall walk in my integrity ... in the great assembly I will bless the LORD" (vv. 11, 12). We know that the Judge can tell the difference between a self-righteous man and a man of integrity as soon as he opens his mouths in prayer. So, beware!

## DAY 84 GOD IN THE WILDERNESS

### Read Psalm 61

*From the end of the earth I call to you when my heart is faint.*
*Lead me to the rock that is higher than I.*

Psalm 61:2

A few years ago David F. Wells wrote four books well worth reading. The first was his Prolegomena (introduction to theology) entitled *No Place for Truth; or Whatever Happened to Evangelical Theology?* (1993) The second was his theology proper (doctrine of God) entitled *God in the Wasteland: The Reality of Truth in a World of Fading Dreams* (1996). The third book was his anthropology (doctrine of man) entitled *Losing Our Virtue: Why the Church Must Recover Its Moral Vision* (1998). Recently (in 2005) he completed the fourth and final book *Above All Earthly Pow'rs - Christ in a Postmodern World* - his Christology. These are four of the best books I have ever read, and I must say that the titles are worth the price of the books. It was, in particular, the second title that intrigued me most: *God in the Wasteland*. The book jacket pictured the crumbled ruins of a church. How thought provoking – title and artwork!

Psalm 61 begins a short grouping of Psalms (Pss. 61–64) that could well be entitled "The Wilderness Psalms," for they reflect the weary soul of David as he hid in the wilderness of Mahanaim, a fugitive from Absalom's rebellion. These four psalms share a common theme: "At a distance from the sanctuary and in peril of his life, the psalmist throws himself upon God. What he longs for above all things is the sense of God's presence, as he realised it in the worship of the sanctuary" (A. F. Kirkpatrick). The postmodern man, and the contemporary Christian share a common need with this ancient composer, David.

We live in a wilderness, what Wells calls metaphorically, "the Wasteland." We live in a world full of the ruin and rubble of "fading dreams," consumerism and cheap substitutes for a culture too busy for depth and development. Values replace virtue. Celebrities replace heroes. Style replaces substance. Therapy replaces theology. Shame replaces guilt. Mysticism replaces spirituality. And the self replaces God as the center of life.

The problem, it seems, is that we haven't lost enough yet to find God. We haven't been forced to let go of all the stuff in order to grab hold of Christ. We are a people still trying to "fit God into" an already overloaded schedule and lifestyle. The result is "the Wasteland" – that strange world where there are lots of "things" but nothing seems to hold together.

David had lived there too, you know. Oh yeah! He'd been very successful, very sexy and very satisfied. And in building that self-centered world he took a man's wife and then a man's life, and everything fell apart. A few years later David lost it all. But in so doing he found all that matters, "Lead me to the rock that is higher than I" (v. 2). In other words, "Let me rebuild my life on something greater, more noble and more lasting than self – God!" David came to see the only One upon whom life could be built to last ... forever. Somehow, he saw again, the footsteps of God in the sand of the wilderness. David Wells puts it this way, "There are footprints in our world whose size and shape speak of Another. He is out of proportion to what is merely natural and is the only explanation for what is natural. This is the external coordinate." And the footprints through the Wasteland lead to the "rock that is higher than I" – Jesus Christ. Deep down men need something greater than self, larger than life, lasting forever. They need God in the Wasteland. Blessed are we that Christ knows the ways of the wilderness well, and travels the back roads of ruined lives, lifting them up on The Rock!

## DAY 85 THE PSALM FOR WEDNESDAY

# Read Psalm 94

*When the cares of my heart are many, your consolations cheer my soul.*
Psalm 94:19

In the time of the Second Temple, in days of the Restoration from Babylonian captivity, the Levites set forth seven psalms as "The Daily Psalms." Psalm 94 was the "Psalm for Wednesday." The *Septuagint* bears the inscription for Psalm 94 as "*A Psalm of David for the Fourth Day of the Week*." Speaking of the training of Hebrew children in Christ's day, Alfred Edersheim states, "The earliest hymns taught would be the Psalms for the days of the week." Therefore every Wednesday at morning prayer, our little Lord Jesus would recite from memory, with His family, Psalm 94.

This Psalm for Wednesday appears to be almost out of place in the Psalter. It separates Psalm 93 from Psalms 95–99, "The Enthronement Psalms" which celebrate the kingship of God. Yet, in theme, it fits into this subset of psalms because the idea of king, and judge of vengeance go hand in hand. The first half of the psalm expresses the psalmist's concern about the wicked (vv. 1-11) and the second half his confidence in God (vv. 12-23). The psalmist correctly thinks of God's vengeance, a thought moderns are often uncomfortable expressing. W. Graham Scroggie reminds us, "As we may not attribute to God human passion, vengeance here cannot mean heated personal feelings, but the necessary punishment of wrongdoing .... Yahweh-El has both the right and the power to judge evil, and He is here bidden to demonstrate both." It is in remembering this that a lot of peace of mind and soul can be found.

Years ago I was filling in as a guest lecturer at a seminary. The class was on ecclesiology, the doctrine of the church, and one student took exception to my ideas. He informed me that, prior to the emergence of marriage and family therapy, the church had "failed miserably" in helping those in emotional stress. I asked him if he was saying that prior to the rise of psychology in the last century the saints of old were without emotional and psychological aid from God. He said, "That's right." Psalm 94 would prove otherwise: "When the cares of my heart are many, your consolations cheer my soul" (v. 19). Meditating on God's righteous judgment is comfort for a troubled soul.

Much of modern therapy deals with the victimization of people and therefore by nature, centers on another, evil, guilty party. People in this sort of therapy often find it difficult to forgive and they cannot let go of old hurts until "justice is served." These poor souls are in for a life of bitterness, mistrust, broken relationships and isolation. God may well take longer to right the wrong than their therapy demands. But right the wrong He will.

Marvin E. Tate summarizes this psalm well: "Psalm 94 summons those with weak faith and lax commitment to a renewed perception of the work of Yahweh which would permit them to join in the acclamation of His kingship .... The Great King is coming to judge on earth with equity and faithfulness. He did not overlook the sinfulness of early generations of Israel and He will not ignore wickedness." The author of Hebrews reminds us of this truth: "For we know him who said, 'Vengeance is mine; I will repay.' And again, 'The Lord will judge his people'" (Heb. 10:30).

This truth served as satisfactory therapy for hundreds of generations of God's people. Isn't it interesting that with the demise of the psalms in life we see a rise in psychology? As men become less spiritual and more secular they become more psychological and less secure. Perhaps we would do better and feel better if we all read Psalm 94 more often, say ... every Wednesday!

## DAY 86 NO SHADES OF GRAY (OR IS IT GREY?)

### Read Psalm 70

*But I am poor and needy; hasten to me, O God! You are my help and my deliverer; O LORD, do not delay!*

Psalm 70:5

With minor changes, the short Psalm 70 is identical to Psalm 40:13-17 (See Part 2, Day 2). More than likely Psalm 40 is the original version. Psalm 70 was separated from its longer, original text and used, more than likely, in public worship. Psalm 70 is an intensification of Psalm 40:13-17. There is more of an urgency about it. It is sharper, more intense and more pointed in application.

Psalm 70 is a chiasmus of sorts: an a-b-b-a pattern. The compiler (and editor) of David's psalm places a request for himself in the first and last verse. In between he prays against the wicked and for the godly. There is a primitive, and therefore beautiful, simplicity about this psalm. It draws upon the truth of life's number one lesson: God punishes the wicked but rewards the righteous. This is, you know, how the Psalter begins: "For the LORD knows the way of the righteous, but the way of the wicked will perish" (Ps. 1:6).

Psalm 70 reminds us of two things postmodern men really don't believe. Darwinism and the evolutionary myth have robbed us of the fact that there is a moral order to God's universe. Accountability, judgment, reward and punishment are everyday parameters of life and ultimate realities for every angel and human being (See Rev. 20).

Second, in the moral order of this universe, there really are no shades of gray. Issues in life do indeed get hazy and fuzzy for us creatures, but to the Creator God all is black and white. Even evangelicals have a hard time with this. Pastors appear less and less willing to make public pronouncements about sin. In fact, we are advised that to do so will confuse and alienate the postmodern man who sees sin differently than God does. Perhaps there is some wisdom here.

Yet our duty as Gospel people should be to help clarify life's graying issues. Michael Wilcock reminds us that God will soon do that: "In the last analysis there will be no greys. We have here in another form the psalmist's frequent longing for God's judgment, which will show up everyone for what he or she really is. The distinctions will be made anyway at the end of time." Let me add, that God needs no help from you, me or His pastors in distinguishing between the black and the white. But we do.

Psalm 70 reminds us that rather than pontificate, point fingers, yes, and even preach about the wicked and the godly, the best thing we can do is pray about them. And we can pray with a blunt and urgent honesty. We can name the wicked and identify the godly, in prayer. If we are wrong – as we may well be at times – then only God hears, and after all, only God really knows.

Here is where we really find out whether we believe in the infallibility of God's Word. Can we pray this "primitive" psalm in these postmodern times, or do we need to practice a form of spiritual censorship? Perhaps if we argued less and worried less about the various shades of gray (for Americans) and grey (for the English), and prayed Psalm 70 more frequently and fervently, things would begin to clear up a bit for us all. Regardless of whether or not you agree, you have to admit this: Since the Holy Spirit repeated this psalm, almost word for word, in the Psalter, He would like us to pray it at least twice as often as the other psalms. Think about that. No ... better yet ... pray about that, using Psalm 70!

## DAY 87 THE MOSAIC OF THE GODLY MAN

### Read Psalm 86

*Preserve my life, for I am godly; save your servant, who trusts in you – you are my God.*

Psalm 86:2

Another of these "Psalms of Petition" that call upon God to defeat for us our enemies, is Psalm 86. This psalm is the only psalm of David in Book Three of the Psalter (Pss. 73-89). All the other psalms in this book are from Asaph (Pss. 73–83), the sons of Korah (Pss. 84, 85, 87, 88) and Ethan the Ezrahite (Ps. 89). Also unique about this psalm is its almost exclusively including expressions found in other psalms; so much so that it is often referred to as "The Mosaic Psalm." Psalm 86 is also one of the only five psalms entitled a *Tephillah* (prayer). This prayer is a mosaic of a godly man.

This prayer of David divides itself into three parts, according to the NASB: verses 1-10, 11-13 and 14-17. These three parts (paragraphs) speak of the heart of the godly man (vv. 1-10), the nature of the ungodly man (vv. 14-17) and a prayer that separates the two (vv. 11-13). This psalm carries on the theme of the entire Psalter, set forth in Psalms 1 and 2, the Psalter's introduction: There are two humanities in the world, the righteous and the wicked (Ps. 1). And they will be, throughout history, caught up in the great warfare between God and the devil, the church versus the world (Ps. 2). This great warfare between God and Satan in heaven, has found its parallel here on earth (Read Rev. 12).

A. Chouraqui describes the conflict of the godly against the ungodly: "The two actors in this duel between life and death, facing each other from start to finish, are the Innocent and the Rebel. They each refuse to give in. One rejects the way of light; the other, the way of darkness. One says no to the iniquity of the world; the other refuses the eternity of God. These refusals are at the heart of the tragedy. This conflict between two opposing wills ... is the source of the horror which erupts into the world and wounds the joy of creation."

But how do we spot a "godly" man and distinguish him from the "ungodly." David tells us in his prayer. The godly man is a man whose life can be described as one who trusts in God (v. 2). As a result his life is full of prayer, joy in the Lord, confession and forgiveness, worship, wonderment over God's work and a concern for the nations to know and love this God (vv. 1-10).

The ungodly, on the other hand, can be described as those who "do not set [God] before them" (v. 14). Hence they are self-focused and self-willed (arrogant), and prone to enforce their will contrary to God's (violent). They hate the godly (v. 17) because they, deep down, despise God.

To put all this in another way: The godly are God-oriented people; the ungodly are self-oriented people. As John Piper would put it, the godly have a God-ward life. The ungodly do not. The difference between the two is the prayer of verses 11-13. Godly people pray for God's insight and wisdom, for hearts attuned to God's will, for a worshipful attitude toward God, and they give thanks to God for His grace.

To be godly does not mean to be super-holy, sinlessly perfect or even deeply mature in spirit. To be godly is to live each day *coram deo ... contra mundum* (before the face of God ... against the world). John would describe this orientation in 1 John 2:15-17. It's all a matter of who or what is the love of our lives.

## DAY 88 CONSPIRACY THEORY

### Read Psalm 64

*Hide me from the secret plots of the wicked, from the throng of evildoers.*

Psalm 64:2

A few years ago my kids came home one Friday night from college with a video of a movie called *Conspiracy Theory* with Mel Gibson and Julia Roberts. They pulled me away from a ball game on TV and popped in this film. The riveting story involves an ex-CIA agent whose brain has been fried, whose life is a paranoid wreck and whose eyes see a grand conspiracy behind every news headline. In the end, we found out that he wasn't so weird after all. There was a conspiracy under foot and his life was in danger. In Psalm 64 David puts forth a conspiracy theory as well.

In Psalm 64, one of the psalms of David's wilderness years when he hid from Absalom, the deposed king writes: "Hide me from the secret plots of the wicked, from the throng of evildoers, ... They search out injustice, saying, 'We have accomplished a diligent search'" (vv. 2, 6). We moderns would say, "Oh, Dave! Get a life. Look, you screwed up. Absalom is reacting. Get off the conspiracy theory thing and face facts: You've got a seriously dysfunctional family. Get help." So David doesn't tell us about his conspiracy theory; he tells God. He prays and asks God to uncover the plot and destroy the conspirators.

Theologically, David is on target. He realizes that behind his son's rebellion and the revolution in Israel is a powerful force: the sinful human heart. "For the inward mind and heart of a man are deep!" (v. 6). Michael Wilcock expounds: "Behind them, the conspirators, is the all-pervading wickedness of the human heart."

As Jeremiah put it, four centuries later, "The heart is deceitful above all things, and desperately sick; who can understand it?" (Jer. 17:9).

Truth is there is a grand conspiracy out there and all men are part of it – even your girlfriend, your family, your old CIA buddies, and, yes, you yourself! And this conspiracy against God (code word: The World) controls everything – even at times the church! Behind it lies a mastermind and he works his demonic schemes through a beautiful agent known in God's files as the Whore of Babylon.

But God has cracked the code, has a list of the principles and contacts, and has fatally undermined the network of evil. He has sent His own man into the world in order to discover and destroy the conspiracy. The deliverer of those caught in the plot of evil is not Julia Roberts but Jesus Christ. David calls Christ's mission "the work of God" (v. 9) and assures himself (and us who eavesdrop on his prayer) that Christ will expose the plot and expunge the evil from the world. "Then all mankind fears, they tell what God has brought about and ponder what he has done" (v. 9).

In the movie, *Conspiracy Theory*, my kids were amazed that the theme song, by Frankie Vallie, was one I used to listen to in college: "*Can't Take My Eyes Off of You.*" Perhaps that would be a good song to remind us of the truth of this psalm. In this psalm, as all the psalms, "Jesus is Himself the singer" (Augustine). And we could well sing of Christ, God's conspiracy breaker: "You're just too good to be true, can't take my eyes off of You; You'd be like heaven to touch." Thanks be to God that heaven has touched our world in Christ and delivered us from the grand conspiracy. We must not take our eyes off Jesus. Look to Christ and be saved from the world.

## DAY 89 A PSALM FOR POSTMODERN MEN

# Read Psalm 12

*Save, O LORD, for the godly one is gone; for the faithful have vanished from among the children of man.*

Psalm 12:1

Jesus taught us to pray, "Deliver us from evil." That is the theme of the current sequence of psalms: God's deliverance of us from evil and the evil one. Psalm 12 begins this sequence of focusing on seven "Psalms of Lament."

Jesus warned us, "And because lawlessness will be increased, the love of many will grow cold" (Matt. 24:12). I find it interesting that while Jesus spoke these words in AD 30, referring to our "last days," David had already expressed the same sentiments a thousand years before Christ. "Save, O LORD, for the godly one is gone; for the faithful have vanished from among the children of man" (v. 1). He decries the fact that disloyalty, lying, manipulation and injustice characterized his day and his culture.

He lived in an age when men boasted, "With our tongue we will prevail, our lips are with us; who is master over us?" (v. 4) How incredibly postmodern that sounds! Ours is the age of the deconstruction of language, the power of the crafted word, the omnipresence of the media, and the willingness of people to accept style for substance, word for deed, and promise in lieu of production. No one has to do the right thing any more; they just have to say the right thing. Ours has become an "information culture" where three men rule the day. Prophets, priests and kings have been replaced by consultants, lawyers and politicians – men of words. The modern ages have reflected this drift from truth in action to words in manipulation: the Age of Theology (1500s–1600s); the Age of Philosophy (1700s–1800s); the Age of Sociology (1800s–1900s); the Age of Psychology (1900s–2000s). Words that reflect absolute truth – revelation, confession, creed, dogma – have slipped through our grid. Now we "feel" our ideas, we "relate" to our beliefs, and we "experience" our religion. Men seem to be able to prevail by the sheer volume of speech and

159

profession of words. The winner of arguments is no longer the one with truth but the best talker. (Don't believe me? When was the last time you watched a Presidential "debate" on TV?)

There is a price to pay for all this. Bishop George Horne captures the "bottom line" of this psalm when he writes, "When men cease to be faithful to their God, he who expects to find them so to each other, will be much disappointed." Gone it seems is any meaning to vows and oaths, promises and pledges, the reliability of a man's word or the ink on the same man's contract. One critic of the media assesses the situation this way, "Words are the currency of ideas, and in a culture where creating word impressions makes presidents and breaks inconvenient promises, words are expendable."

Not so with God. "The words of the LORD are pure words, like silver refined in a furnace on the ground, purified seven times" (v. 6). God's Word is a precious commodity. How precious? It was the Word of the Lord, the promise of God, which Christ made good in His own blood. Peter calls them "his precious and very great promises" (2 Pet. 1:4) and he reminds us that these promises were redeemed – cashed in – by "the precious blood of Christ, like that of a lamb without blemish or spot (1 Pet. 1:19). Postmodern men ought to meditate on Psalm 12 deeply and at length. In the end all our image-building, manipulative speech and empty ideas with glitzy words will be burned to nothing. What remains forever, what endures, is not what we speak but what God says. "The grass withers, the flower fades when the breath of the LORD blows on it; surely the people are grass. The grass withers, the flower fades, but the word of our God will stand forever" (Isa. 40:7-8).

## DAY 90 CALVIN'S DYING PRAYER

### Read Psalm 13

*Consider and answer me, O LORD my God; light up my eyes, lest I sleep the sleep of death*

Psalm 13:3

Some historians relate to us that, as he lay dying, John Calvin uttered the words, "How long, O LORD?" And many believe he was not lamenting his own multiple ailments and sufferings, but rather the calamities of the Huguenots, the French Calvinists who were beginning to suffer persecution in Catholic France. Perhaps Calvin died meditating on Psalm 13 which opens with these same words: "How long, O LORD?" The church has used this psalm in times of persecution, again and again.

David, the psalmist, composes this hymn in three stanzas: a lament about persecution (vv. 1-2); a prayer for deliverance from martyrdom (vv. 3-4); a profession of faith and praise (vv. 5-6). This lament is also full of faith and hope. Calvin himself commented on this spirit of Psalm 13, "And certainly our confidence of life depends on this, that although the world may threaten us with a thousand deaths, yet God is possessed of numberless means of restoring us to life."

Here David, and later John Calvin, faced the pressure of the daily possibility of death. This psalm could have been written at any number of dangerous seasons in King David's life. It certainly fits the turbulent and dangerous era of the Reformation where "changing churches" could cost one his life. And so it serves as a perfect pattern for prayer when living for Christ becomes death defying.

James Luther Mays writes of the unique place Psalm 13 has in the Psalter: "Psalm 13 is the shortest of the prayers for help in the Psalter. In spite of its brevity, the psalm is virtually a paradigm of the essential features of such prayers." Hermann Gunkel called it "a parade example of the laments of an individual." Many of us may still find it difficult to pray Psalm 13, a "Psalm for Times of Persecution," for ourselves.

Here is where John Calvin's example comes into view. As he lay dying Calvin prayed for the success of the Reformation in Geneva, the protection of his spiritual kinsmen in Europe, and the perseverance of his followers, the Huguenots, in his France. Calvin prayed for the persecuted church as he lay dying. As he entered into a common death with those who have Christ in common, he prayed alongside the martyrs. His suffering joined with theirs as a blood offering of intercession for God's people everywhere.

Are you aware that more saints are martyred every year in our twenty-first century, than in any century prior to our own? This year almost 300,000 Christians will die, worldwide, because "they loved not their lives even unto death" (Rev. 12:11) as much as they love Jesus! Are they not worthy of the prayers of their brethren in the Lord who dwell in relative safety? Indeed, God "has dealt bountifully with me" (v. 6). Should I not bountifully praise Him and pray for those not as secure as I, but certainly more tested in faith than I shall probably ever be? "How long, O LORD?" How long will I forsake my suffering brothers and sisters and forget this precious Psalm 13, written for my prayer for them? Lord Jesus, teach us to pray.

## DAY 91 A HEART FOR SOME FOOLISH PEOPLE

### Read Psalm 14

*The LORD looks down from heaven on the children of man, to see if there are any who understand, who seek after God.*

Psalm 14:2

We have already looked at Psalm 53, the almost identical psalm to Psalm 14 here. This psalm speaks of the depravity of the human race: not one man naturally seeks after God, understands spiritual truths, or does good in God's sight. "They have all turned aside; together they have become corrupt" (v. 3).

Our secular, humanistic age has a very difficult time accepting this truth. In reality, I guess, it is fair to say that no age of men have warmed to this truth quickly and easily. Even many Christians still believe there is some innate goodness in man.

Henry Martyn (1781–1812) believed Psalm 14. Inspired by the lives and work of William Carey in India and David Brainard in America, he devoted his life to mission work. A brilliant scholar and fellow of St. John's at Cambridge, Martyn gave up his promising career, the joy of a credentialed life in England and a marriage with Lydia Grenfell in order to sail for India in 1805 as the East India Company's chaplain. We know a great deal of the inner life and struggles of Henry Martyn from his detailed diaries.

An ordained minister in the Church of England, Martyn gave his short life to working for the conversion of the Hindus and Muslims in India. His journals are filled with numerous references to the psalms. Each day he began his daily entries with a reference from the Psalter.

He worked long and hard on a Persian translation of the New Testament. But he also began to translate the psalms into Persian. He would never finish either task. Tuberculosis took its toll on his young life. He died, among the pagan peoples of Hindu darkness, on October 16, 1812.

Toward the end of his life his inability to breathe well, night sweats and fever often kept him awake all night. On September 4, 1812 (six weeks before his death) he wrote in his diary: "I beguiled the hours of the night by thinking of the 14th Psalm." There, dying amidst paganism and a personal yearning to return home to England and Miss Lydia, Henry Martyn meditated all night on Psalm 14 and the deep darkness, depravity and dissolution of the human soul and the human race.

The very thought of the world's second most populace nation plunging into a Christless eternity drove young Rev. Martyn to an early grave at age thirty one. You can almost see his boyish face, tears mixed with the sweat of sickness, running down his face, as he prayed for India, Persia and the hundred millions of the East: "Oh, that salvation for Israel would come out of Zion!" (v. 7). Oh, that the salvation of India would come out of England! And would that the salvation of the nearly ten billion of our day would come from the Church in the West consumed with the idea that human beings have "all turned aside; together they have become corrupt" (v. 3). May God gives us a heart for some foolish people somewhere that we might live and die for, as did Henry Martyn.

## DAY 92 THE PRAYER FOR JUSTICE

### Read Psalm 17

*Hear a just cause, O LORD; attend to my cry! Give ear to my prayer from lips free of deceit.*

Psalm 17:1

Only five psalms bear the inscription: A Prayer. They are Psalms 17, 86 and 142 by David; Psalm 90 by Moses and the anonymous Psalm 102. It has served for hundreds of generations as the prayer for justice for those under persecution and oppression.

David feels horribly attacked by a vicious campaign of slander and a hardened purpose to destroy him. He pleads his case before God and exhorts the Lord to protect him: "Keep me as the apple of your eye" (v. 8). The reason David prays such a way is his complete innocence in the matter of accusation: "You have tried my heart, you have visited me by night, you have tested me, and you will find nothing" (v. 3).

David does not claim sinless perfection or self-righteous goodness; rather, he states that God has seen all that he is accused of doing and all that is plotted against him and knows he is innocent. Franz Delitzsch is correct when he remarks, "In all such assertions of the pious self-consciousness, what is meant is a righteousness that has its basis in the righteousness of faith." How these words have been the prayer of saints throughout the ages.

Alexander Hume of Hume, Scotland was a Presbyterian in sympathies, and attended some of that church's prescribed meetings. He was arrested and convicted of heresy in one of the great miscarriages of Scottish justice. On the morning of his execution in 1682 he ended his life singing this psalm. His wife, Isabella Hume, had appealed to the Lady Perth and begged for her to interpose on behalf of her husband's justice. She was coarsely and callously rebuffed. Hume's estate was taken by others, and his surviving wife and children lived in deprivation until the revolution. Justice is often slow in coming, but come it does.

How this psalm may be sung by all the forty-eight million little souls whose lives were sacrificed on the American altars of pleasure, materialism and shame. I write this devotion after a Right-to-Life prayer meeting at our church. I feel both frustrated, ashamed and a bit discouraged that after hundreds of millions of dollars' investment, a right-wing gain in political power, a November election where pro-life candidates swept the field and decades of Republican promises ... still no law, no justice, no defense for the unborn. Where are all these pro-life men and women – governors, judges, congressmen, senators and even presidents – Americans have put in office over the past twenty years? Where is the legislation? Where is the Constitutional amendment protecting innocent (i.e. defenseless) life?

"Hear a just cause, O Lord; attend to my cry!" the fetus in the womb prays. Oh that God would rise up and protect that little life as "the apple of the eye." May God grant us just a handful of William Wilberforces who will not quit until this prayer is answered by the Judge in heaven through the judges on earth. And may God show our nation mercy and longsuffering until He works in us a soul of compassion and a heart for justice. May this be so, and quickly!

## DAY 93 THE SONG FROM THE CROSS

### Read Psalm 22

*My God, my God, why have you forsaken me?*

Psalm 22:1

This psalm is made famous by the Lord Jesus, who quotes from its first line, while in agony on the cross: "'Eli, Eli, lama sabachthani?' that is, 'My God, my God, why have you forsaken me?'" (Matt. 27:46). This psalm describes, in uncanny detail, the very events and excruciating agony of the crucifixion.

Christ's quote of the first verse is followed by the description of the abject humiliation of the cross ("But I am a worm and not a man") (v. 6), and the mockery of those around Christ's cross (vv. 6-8). David's quote of his enemies is uniquely like that which actually was said, "He trusts in the LORD; let him deliver him; let him rescue him, for he delights in him!" (v. 8). Compare these words to Matthew 27:43: "He trusts in God, let God deliver him now, if he desires him. For he said "I am the Son of God"'.

Verses 14-15 describe the pain, exhaustion and wasting away in death that a man experiences in a Roman crucifixion: "I am poured out like water, and all my bones are out of joint; my heart is like wax; it is melted within my breast; my strength is dried up like a potsherd, and my tongue sticks to my jaws; you lay me in the dust of death." The psalmist describes dehydration, fatigue, muscle spasms, hypervolemic shock and cardiac failure due to crucifixion. David foretells of the casting of lots and division of his garments (v. 18).

In fact, in the book *Christ on the Cross*, Rev. J. Stevenson has a sermon for each and every verse in this psalm: 1, The Cry; 2, The Complaint; 3, The Acknowledgment; 4-6, The Contrast; 6, The Reproach; 7, The Mockery; 8, The Taunt; 9, 10, The Appeal; 11, The Entreaty; 12, The Assault; 13, The Faintness; 14, The Exhaustion; 15, The Piercing; 16, The Emaciation; 17, The Insulting Gaze; 18, The Partition of the Garments and Casting Lots; 19-21, The Importunity; 21, The Deliverance; 22, The Gratitude; 23, The Invitation; 24, The Testimony; 25, The Vow; 26, The Satisfaction of the Meek; the Seekers of the Lord praising Him; the Eternal Life; 27, The Conversion of the World; 28, The Enthronement; 29, The Author of the Faith; 30, The Seed; 31, The Everlasting Theme and Occupation; The Finish of the Faith.

And all this, all this suffering of Christ, because God is holy and hates sin: "Yet you are holy, enthroned on the praises of Israel" (v. 3). God's holiness, which crucifies His Son, is that holiness that justifies us sinners (Rom. 3:21-26). A great sorrow for a holy God becomes the great joy for sinful man. That is why W. Graham Scroggie entitles this Messianic Psalm: "A Sob and a Song" – the weeping of Christ which becomes the joy of His saints!

That is why historically this psalm has always been read on Good Friday, in the various liturgies of the church. It is The Song from the Cross.

## DAY 94 CARRY US FOREVER

# Read Psalm 28

*Oh, save your people and bless your heritage! Be their shepherd and carry them forever.*

Psalm 28:9

Scholars usually locate Psalms 26, 27 and 28 to the time when David fled Jerusalem to escape the rebellion of his son Absalom. This was the darkest period of the king's life. His adultery and murder was judged by God with the promise that the "sword shall never depart from your house" (2 Sam. 12:10-12). Indeed it was so: David's infant son died shortly after birth, his heir-apparent; Amnon committed incest by raping his half-sister, Tamar, David's beautiful daughter; later Absalom murdered Amnon in revenge for his sister's rape and fled to Geshur for three years; then David let Absalom return but spurned him, leading to Absalom's bitterness and rebellion – Absalom would be killed shortly thereafter.

What tragedy and unbelievable consequences due to David's sin - incest, rape, murder, exile, estrangement and rebellion. The Proverbs are correct: "the way of the sinner is hard" (Prov. 13:15, KJV). What is utterly amazing about the psalms (and this period of David's life) is the absence of any sense of bitterness, revenge or violent frustration. David is betrayed by a son who defiles David's wives in public. He is turned on by friends and counselors. He is lied to by the servants of faithful followers. He is cursed by descendants of Saul. And he is disobeyed by generals who take the life of his son, contrary to David's express wishes. Yet in all of this David does not sin with his mouth, let his famous redheaded temper get away from him, or plot some bloody (but "justifiable") revenge. Instead he turns back to his earliest days with God, reverting to his "shepherd motif" in both prayer and trust.

Like the boy-shepherd of Bethlehem that he once was, David sees God as his shepherd, and he calls upon God to carry him through this dark hour. "Oh, save your people and bless your heritage! Be their shepherd and carry them forever" (v. 9). Just

167

as David picked up many a lamb that had stubbornly strayed from the fold and become wounded or broken, so he asks God to do so for him and his flock – Israel. It is for God's people that he prays and not just for himself. And he asks this "forever." Matthew Henry observes, "That He would lift them up forever, lift them up out of their troubles and distresses, and do this, not only for those of that age, but for His people in every age to come, even to the end." David prays like that which he was: a type of Christ.

Oh how differently I pray when I am left to taste the bitter fruit of my sins. I whine, I whimper, I pout and I withdraw in resentment, even accusingly asking God, "Why? Why is this happening to me?" I seem to forget so quickly that the death penalty of my sins has been picked up and carried off into the wilderness by the Lamb of God. I bear some consequences but Christ bears the entire penalty. I so easily forget that I have a Good Shepherd who picks me up from the brink of death and carries me to the next station in life where I dance and play in the fields of sin until the process is repeated all over again: I fall; I cry out; He picks me up and carries me. On and on it goes through all of life, yea, forever! "Blessed be the LORD! for he has heard the voice of my pleas for mercy. The LORD is my strength and my shield; in him my heart trusts, and I am helped; my heart exults, and with my song I give thanks to him" (vv. 6-7).

## DAY 95 THOSE WHO WOULD LIVE GODLY

### Read Psalm 69

*For zeal for your house has consumed me, and the reproaches of those who reproach you have fallen on me. When I wept and humbled my soul with fasting, it became my reproach. When I made sackcloth my clothing, I became a byword to them. I am the talk of those who sit in the gate, and the drunkards make songs about me.*

Psalm 69:9-12

Psalm 69 is the third most frequently quoted psalm in the New Testament; only Psalms 110 and 22, respectively, out-rank it at numbers one and two. David, the author of this Messianic Psalm, is "a typical example of the things that are experienced by all who are truly zealous for the Lord's house" (Leupold). In fact, James Montgomery Boice called this "the most obviously messianic psalm in the Psalter."

Psalm 69 is another of the psalms that cry out to God to "deliver us from evil." It is the cry of a man who is troubled, tried and tormented by his enemies, but this time not for personal or political reasons, but rather because he is zealous for God. He is threatened and beset by opposition because, "... zeal for your house has consumed me, and the reproaches of those who reproach you have fallen on me" (v. 9). Those who disdain God take their anger out on David – that is what David is saying.

Paul reminded young Timothy of this spiritual law of life: "Indeed, all who desire to live a godly life in Christ Jesus will be persecuted" (2 Tim. 3:12). To live for God means you cannot live for men. God and the world will make you choose allegiances; they will allow no neutral bystanders. And, sadly, that is where the majority of evangelical Christians want to be right now – in some spiritual Switzerland, uninvolved in the cosmic conflict of life.

This manifests itself in an obvious number of ways. We see hundreds of Christian pro-family candidates get elected to office by promising a "revolution" in politics, but none step up to the plate to take a swing. We see pastors who have listened to the pundits who say that Fundamentalism has made conservative Christianity mean-spirited. And so our pastors are "nice," but seldom prophetic. We're likely nowadays to hear more about reaffirming a fallen culture and opening our arms indiscriminately to a sinful society than in promoting the kingdom of God. Here is the rule: Be positive; flex a bit; don't be controversial, critical or too committed to absolutes, and people will come to church.

Somewhere along the line it will be our sacred duty to winsomely and clearly say some things that will make us unpopular. Even our own brethren will irritatingly call us "Extremists," or "out of touch"; or worse yet, they'll just shake their heads in disgust and write us off. One of my minister friends here in Jackson said to me recently, as we drank coffee together at a coffee shop, "Down here, when these Southern folks have had enough of you, they never get openly upset. You just discover one day that you're not invited to the 'get-togethers' anymore." And so it goes.

Psalm 69 is about Jesus. He wasn't always popular, and the *Jerusalem Gazette* did not seek out His opinion on current events or moral issues. But He remains the Savior and reminds us that He is Lord ... popular or not. And He also said to us, "Woe to you, when all people speak well of you, for so their fathers did to the false prophets" (Luke 6:26).

Please, don't go looking for trouble or wear it like a garland of honor when it comes. But if you never suffer rejection for your walk with Jesus or witness for His truth, then check again. Popularity may prove the lack of godliness.

## DAY 96 MY TIMES IN GOD'S HANDS

### Read Psalm 31

*But I trust in you, O LORD; I say, "You are my God." My times are in your hand; rescue me from the hand of my enemies and from my persecutors!*
Psalm 31:14-15

To round out our second fifty days of prayer we look at five final psalms that give Thanks for God's Faithfulness. In Psalm 31 David acknowledges one of the greatest, most comforting but often-overlooked doctrines of Christendom: The Providence of God. The Fathers believed this psalm to have been written by David when he fled from Saul into the wilderness of Maon (1 Sam. 23). There in the wilderness he pours out his soul to God.

One commentator muses, "This psalm will always be cherished because it is so human. Most of us rise and fall in our experience; and it will help us if we remember that height implies depth; and depth makes height possible." David reminds himself of the level ground between these heights of joy and the depths of despair. "I say, 'You are my God.' My times are in your hand" (vv. 14-15). How well this truth once came home to me.

I was but a boy of six or seven when, one Christmas I got

an alarm clock – the old wind-up kind. One Sunday the priest preached on the end of the world, and told us that on that horrible day the sky would go black with no sun or moon – pitch black at mid-day. I awoke that Sunday night to find that the clock read 9:00. In the fog of half sleep, my mind jolted, "Nine in the morning and it's pitch black outside! The end of the world has come!" I tried to wake my brother Steve to warn him. He growled and rolled over. I ran down the hallway to tell my sister, Ann. Her door was shut and locked. I then burst into my parents' room, crying almost uncontrollably, "Mom . . .Dad! The end of the world has come!" My poor father, a milkman who got up at 4:00 a.m. everyday for work, came off the bed like a rocket. Minutes later I was tucked again in my bed, soothed by my mom, and informed by my dad that it was 1:30 in the morning. As they left the room my dad said, rather sternly, "When the end comes, Mike, don't worry. It'll be the right time. God knows the best time to end it all." I slept like a rock.

Charles Simeon wrote, "To the ungodly it is satisfaction to deny the providence of God, and to cut Him off, as it were, from any connection with creatures. But the saints find rich consolation that God reigneth ... and however man might be His enemy, God was his God; and that however bitterly his enemies might be enraged against him, his times were not in their hands, but in God's, and consequently, they could do nothing against him but by His permission."

How important it is to realize this when you're thirty-five and still single, when you've put in twenty years and are not yet a colonel, when after seven years you're still not pregnant, when you've worked hard for fifteen years but they ask you to "move one," or when you're six and the end of the world comes! This is the great comfort of the beleaguered saint.

Girolamo Savonarola (1452–1498), the Italian friar who became one of the "morning lights" of the Reformation, wrote in his journal on Psalm 31 the night before his execution for preaching the "heresy" of reform. A cellmate mentioned that Savonarola slept soundly and with a slight smile on his face that evening. He never completed recording his meditations on Psalm 31, but his last entry was this: "My times are in God's hands." And so they were. And so they are.

## DAY 97 THE FOOT OF PRIDE

### Read Psalm 36

*Oh, continue your steadfast love to those who know you, and your righteousness to the upright of heart! Let not the foot of arrogance come upon me, nor the hand of the wicked drive me away.*

Psalm 36:10-11

Of all the great gifts of grace that Christians tend to forget and, therefore, for which they fail to give thanks is the change of heart God gives to the regenerate man. David writes, "Transgression speaks to the wicked deep in his heart" (v. 1). And David tells us five things it does: It tells us there is no God who sees our sins, that we are "basically good" people, that our words and our ideas are O.K., that our wicked plans will succeed and that evil is something to be admired, not despised (vv. 1-4).

But God's lovingkindness – *chesed*, His covenant love and loyalty – overcomes our pride and folly with tender mercy and patient truth. God works in our lives wooing the proud heart to Himself: "For with you is the fountain of life; in your light do we see light." How easy it is to forget this truth. I've seen it reflected on a bumper sticker that said, "I may be a sinner but at least I'm saved." In other words, "I may be sinful but I'm smart enough (good enough) to do something about it." How easily we forget God's mercy and grace.

When I sit sometimes and remember the things I said, the lifestyle that characterized my young manhood, my asinine ideas (I was often wrong but never in doubt) and the pet sins that polluted my soul, I am, quite frankly, ashamed. Oh how terrible it would be if you all could see me as I really was; worse yet, as I really am!

It seems that whenever I get too big for my spiritual britches, the Spirit has a way of letting me hear a foul word, see some perverse act or run into a worldly young man who reminds me of the old Mike Ross. And I am instantly brought back to the truth that is the greatest mystery and marvel of all time: for reasons I will never know and could never imagine, God has chosen to give me a new heart – repentance from sin and faith in Jesus Christ. A new work has begun by His grace (2 Cor. 5:17; Phil. 1:6). I must never stroll too far from that fact.

Derek Kidner remarks, "The psalmist finds himself on the disputed ground between human wickedness (1-4) and divine grace (5-9); so he turns to prayer (10-12)." What a lovely and succinct summary of Psalm 36. He asks God to keep him from the "foot of pride." He probably means the feet of his enemies, the wicked. But perhaps there is also a veiled allusion to the fact that if wicked men prance by too closely and too often, his own sinful heart may say to his own feet, "Let's go with them!" Perhaps when David sees their feet of pride he notices that his own shoes look a lot like theirs!

David Dickson catches the spirit of this psalm with his comments: "It is the Lord only who can divert the proud persecutors, that they hurt not His children and it is the Lord only who can keep His children in the course of faith and obedience, when the wicked employ their power against them." So the next time you meet your old self on the street, stop and give thanks that your feet no longer walk with the feet of the proud. By His grace!

## DAY 98 ONCE SPOKEN, TWICE HEARD

Read Psalm 62

*Once God has spoken; twice have I heard this: that power belongs to God, and that to you, O LORD, belongs steadfast love. For you will render to a man according to his work.*

Psalm 62:11-12

Psalm 62 is one of the most remarkable of all the psalms in the Psalter. So complete and unshakeable is David's confidence in God that not once in the dozen verses of Psalm 62 does the King of Israel utter one petition. Not one! Instead, Psalm 62 is almost "confessional" in tone, testifying to God's complete reliability, consistency and immutability. Divided by the *selahs* (pauses), this little gem in the Psalter divides itself into three equal sections of four verses each: David's rest in God (vv. 1-4), David's summons to others to rest in God (vv. 5-8), and David's reminder that men have a choice (vv. 9-12).

The reason why David possesses this quiet confidence and rest of faith is the certainty of both God and His actions. The one great comfort about God is His predictability. Imagine a deity with infinite power (omnipotence), infinite wisdom (omniscience) and no limits in time or space (omnipresence), and a capricious, even contradictory, nature. A God of such power would be dangerous if He were not "the same yesterday and today and forever" (Heb. 13:8). And this is exactly what David finds comforting.

"Once God has spoken; twice have I heard this: that power belongs to God, and that to you, O Lord, belongs steadfast love. For you will render to a man according to his work." William S. Plummer says that this phrase, "Once God has spoken; twice I have heard this" really "teaches the certainty of the thing." It is an established fact, often repeated that God is omnipotent, loving and loyal in His covenant and the righteous judge of all men.

When Bishop John Hooper of Gloucester, England was sought out for arrest and execution by Bloody Queen Mary, he did not flee to the continent. He said, "I am thoroughly persuaded to tarry, and to live and die with my sheep." In September of 1553 he was confined to the fleet prison. In this foul, stink-hole of a dungeon he wrote an exposition of Psalms 33, 73, 77 and this Psalm 62. In the light of this psalm he wrote, "All men and women have this life and this world appointed unto them for their winter and season of storms. The summer draweth near, and then shall we be fresh, orient, sweet, amiable, pleasant, acceptable, immortal, and blessed forever and ever, and no man shall take us from it." Five months later Hooper passed from his winter prison into his summer reward.

He was able to die with courage and hope because he had read something once about God and heard it repeated again and again: God "will render to a man according to his work." But only after

God first works in him! God's power changes wicked hearts, and His lovingkindness extends to them gracious redemption. He imputes Christ's justification and righteousness to them, on the basis of faith in Christ, after He gives them the gift of that faith. Then – unimaginable grace! He even rewards them for the good He produces in them! And all this for our good and for Christ's sake. "Once God has spoken" the Gospel, "twice have I heard this" repeated: "For by grace you have been saved through faith. And this is not your own doing; it is the gift of God ... There is therefore now no condemnation for those who are in Christ Jesus" (Eph. 2:8; Rom. 8:1). Now that is amazing and worth repeating.

## DAY 99 THE DIVINE REVERSALS

### Read Psalm 75

*But it is God who executes judgment, putting down one and lifting up another.*

Psalm 75:7

Psalm 75 answers the pleas of Psalm 74 (see Day 81, p. 145), and that is why the compilers of the Psalter place them together. This psalm is a Song of Asaph. Many commentators see Psalm 75 in the context of the Assyrian invasion of Israel, the northern kingdom, in the days of Hezekiah. In verse 6 no mention is made of the north, perhaps since the Assyrians were approaching there.

The previous psalm asked God to arise and "defend your cause" (Ps. 74:22). Psalm 75 is an answer to this plea. God is not the Pleading Attorney but the Judge. Verses 6 and 7 reflect the heart of the matter: "For not from the east or from the west and not from the wilderness [i.e. the south] comes lifting up, but it is God who executes judgment, putting down one and lifting up another." Those key words are reflected again and again in the Scripture: "putting down one and lifting up another." We refer to this truth as the divine reversal.

A divine reversal is when God exalts the humble and humbles the proud. Both Joel Green and Michael Wilcock, in their commentaries on the Gospel of Luke note that the evangelist makes much of the divine reversal theme in the Canticles of the nativity narrative: The *Magnificat* of Mary, the *Benedictus* of Zacharias, the *Gloria* of the angels and the *Nunc Dimittis* of Simeon. God, it seems, always favors the humble, poor, oppressed and ignored, but He dislikes and disdains the proud – the social, economic and political elite. James, the brother of Jesus, agrees, and says,

"God opposes the proud, but gives grace to the humble" (James 4:6). Brother James is quoting Psalm 138:6, "For though the Lord is high, he regards the lowly, but the haughty he knows from afar."

This whole "divine reversal thing" is a big deal to God, more so than we could ever imagine. The incarnation proves this beyond pale of doubt. When God chose to visibly enflesh Himself to mankind, He came into a poor, blue-collar, "no-count" family from a town of low reputation. To put this in a modern frame of reference, Jesus did not come to the beautiful people; he was not a yuppie, nor would people say, "Oh, that Nazarene family, now there's a 'sharp' young couple with really 'neat' kids." No, Jesus (and James his younger brother) experienced firsthand what James later brought to the church's attention: "For if a man wearing a gold ring and fine clothing comes into your assembly, and a poor man in shabby clothing also comes in, and if you pay attention to the one who wears the fine clothing and say, 'You sit here in a good place,' while you say to the poor man, 'You stand over there,' or, 'Sit down at my feet,' have you not then made distinctions among yourselves and become judges with evil thoughts?" (Jas 2:2-4). Psalm 75 reminds us that God, not we, is the Judge (v. 2) and we must not forget that the man who had to stand in the back was Joseph of Nazareth, whose son, Jesus, had to sit on the floor by the rich man's feet! Imagine, the Lord of glory, God in the flesh, the Savior and Judge of rich and poor alike, looked down upon by sinners. So be careful, you never know whom you're snubbing when you play the yuppie. It could be the one Christ loves and plans to exalt. Beware! Divine reversal is still God's master plan.

## DAY 100 THE PSALM FOR THURSDAY

# Read Psalm 81

*Those who hate the LORD would cringe toward him, and their fate would last forever. But he would feed you with the finest of the wheat, and with honey from the rock I would satisfy you.*

Psalm 81:15-16

Oftentimes the Lord gives us little bits of encouragement, in order to let us know He is with us in our ventures and approves of our work. The world calls these "coincidences"; I call them providential affirmation. When I originally laid out the 150 psalms, over a three year period – God Our Refuge (Book One), God Our Redeemer (Book Two) and God Our Rejoicing (Book Three) – I did not know upon which day each psalm would fall. How delightful it was to come to the end of fifty days of praying through the psalms in Book Two and discovered that on Thursday, June 19, 2003 we looked at Psalm 81. For this psalm was designated by the Second Temple Levites as "The Psalm for the Fifth Day of the Week" ... Thursday!

This psalm had a rich place in the liturgy of the Old Testament church. Verses 3 and 4 proclaim: "Blow the trumpet at the new moon, at the full moon, on our feast day. For it is a statute for Israel, a rule of the God of Jacob." These two verses have caused scholars to conjecture the following: "This psalm was apparently intended to be sung at one or more of the great national festivals" (J. J. Stewart Perowne). We conjecture that the Feast of Trumpets (the Jewish New Year), known as *Rash Hash-shana*, was the occasion of this psalm. (The Talmud, the Targum, the Midrash and the Book of Zohar all assign Psalm 81 to the Feast of the New Year.) Others assign Psalm 81 to the Feast of Booths or Tabernacles, known as *Sukkoth*, because the Targum assigns Psalm 81 to the month of Tishri. In that month there are three great feasts: Trumpets, the Day of Atonement (*Yom Kippur*) and Tabernacles. But also, some ascribe to Psalm 81 a Passover usage. In any event this was a psalm that celebrated the goodness, graciousness and greatness of our God.

The Levites of restored Israel assigned this precious psalm to the daily prayers of home, synagogue and Temple on Thursday. Every week the people were to thank God because He had determined: "… he would feed you with the finest of the wheat, and with honey from the rock I would satisfy you" (v. 16). This psalm gives a panoramic view of God's great deliverances, His gracious forgiveness and His good works, from the Exodus to the entrance into Canaan's abundance. It celebrates our deliverance from the bondage of sin and the "Pharaoh" Satan, our preservation and provision in this wilderness of the world and our journey through life, and our assurance of entering heaven's glory and good things in the City of God. Every Thursday we are to use Psalm 81 to remind ourselves of these truths. Isaac Watts puts it this way, "Come, we that love the Lord, and let our joys be known. Join in the song with sweet accord, join in the song with sweet accord, and thus surround the throne and thus surround the throne. We're marching to Zion, beautiful, beautiful Zion. We're marching upward to Zion, the beautiful City of God." And so we are, not one by one, but together in the fellowship of God's Pilgrim church. We are passing over from the land of men "Marching through Immanuel's ground" (Watts), home to the City of God. What a joy to be reminded of this each week on Thursday morning – or on Easter, our Passover; or January 1st, our New Year's Day; or even, for Americans, on Thanksgiving, our Feast of Booths. What a happy day to be reminded of the Father's greatness, the Son's grace and the Spirit's goodness. And on what better psalm to end these fifty days of prayer and begin a new stage of worship, work, witness and warfare together!

# Part Three:

## God Our Rejoicing
## Celebrating God the Holy Spirit:
## His Regenerating, Reforming
## and Reviving Work

*Praise the L*ORD*! Sing to the L*ORD *a new song,*
*his praise in the assembly of the godly!*
*Let Israel be glad in his Maker;*
*let the children of Zion rejoice in their King!*

*Psalm 149:1-2*

## DAY 101 BLESSED IS THE NATION

# Read Psalm 33

*Blessed is the nation whose God is the LORD, the people whom he has chosen as his heritage!*

Psalm 33:12

On November 21, 1620, forty-one men of the ship *Mayflower* signed a holy covenant on the day they anchored ship in a "New England," after a sixty-five day journey over turbulent seas. This covenant they called The Mayflower Compact. In it they pledged to form a "body politick" to govern themselves "for the glory of God and the advancement of the Christian Faith." As they began their "errand into the wilderness" these Pilgrim Fathers purposed to build "a city on a hill" as a Gospel light to the heathen nations. They drew much of their inspiration and hope from the Psalms.

In fact, the basic curriculum for the Colonial children of America consisted of three books. The *Hornbook*: a single piece of parchment that included the alphabet, the Lord's Prayer and basic religious doctrines; the *New England Primer*: the Shorter Catechism, the Apostles' Creed, the Lord's Prayer, alphabet lessons, the names of the books of the Bible and other religious resources; and The Psalter, quaintly entitled "The Whole Booke of Psalmes translated into English Metre."

One of the Pilgrims' favorite psalms was Psalm 33: "Blessed is the nation whose God is the LORD." This is indeed a fitting psalm to begin our third instalment of fifty days of prayer together. And what more fitting way to conclude our devotions and prayers in the Psalter than focusing in those last fifty Psalms on the Holy Spirit - the third person of the Trinity ... God our rejoicing!

Psalm 33 comes to us in four stanzas. The first (vv. 1-5) calls us to sing for joy unto the Lord because "His work is done in faithfulness" (v. 4). Stanza two (vv. 6-12) reminds us that God both created the world and controls human history. His counsel stands and His plans succeed from generation to generation. The third stanza (vv. 13-17) paints for us a picture of God who "looks down from heaven" upon the sons of men. He understands them and their ways. He guides them, guards them and governs them. They are not to trust in kings, warriors or war-horses. God is their only hope. The fourth and last stanza (vv. 18-22) is a word of testimony and prayer. We wait upon God to be good to us and bless us. "Let your steadfast love, O LORD, be upon us, even as we hope in you" (v. 22).

The word *chesed* ("steadfast love") found three times in this psalm (vv. 5, 18, 22) is the favorite word of the Psalter. It means more than any one word in English can render accurately: the covenant love and loyalty of God for His people. This was the great longing of Israel, the Puritan hope, and the unfailing prayer of the Christian from age to age. God can and has often in the past chosen to revive His church and restore nations because they hoped in His lovingkindness, His steadfast love. Is that not the great work of God the Spirit, to regenerate dead souls, revive declining churches, reform defective religion and restore decadent nations?

God has sent reformation and revival to the church in the West and other nations many times before. The Holy Spirit is not hindered by postmodernity from doing so again. Blessed are the people who believe this. Blessed is the church that prays this. And "Blessed is the nation whose God is the LORD."

## DAY 102 REMEMBER MY SPAN OF LIFE

### Read Psalm 89

> *Remember how short my time is! For what vanity you have created all the children of man!*
>
> Psalm 89:47

Ethan the Ezrahite was a Levite employed in composing psalms and orchestrating the musical accompaniment to singing the Psalms. He lived after David and Solomon in the time of Judah's spiritual decline, during the days of the divided kingdom. In Psalm 89 he calls upon God to remember His covenant.

In the first section of the psalm (vv. 1-37) he remembers the display of God's faithfulness in the covenant. ("Faithfulness" is

used 7 times; "Steadfast love," 7 times and "covenant," 4 times.)
Ethan praises God's faithfulness to the angels, to Israel, to David
and to the Kingdom of Judah. Then he calls us to pause (*selah*) and
to think. In the second section of the psalm he recounts his dismay
over God's faithfulness (vv. 38-51). God is faithful to discipline,
show His wrath and give reproach for Israel's sins. And so Ethan
laments, "Remember how short my time is! For what vanity you
have created all the children of man! What man can live and never
see death? Who can deliver his soul from the power of Sheol?"
(vv. 47-48). And then, another pause, another selah, a third point
of reflection.

"Lord, where is your steadfast love of old, which by your
faithfulness you swore to David?" (v. 49). What Ethan the Ezrahite
prays here might be paraphrased this way: "Where, O God, is the
covenant love and loyalty that you swore to David, and therefore
to us his people, that we remember from days of old?" What
Ethan had in mind was God's covenant with David recorded in
2 Samuel 7:14-17. There God swore an oath, saying: "I will be
to him a father, and he shall be to me a son. When he commits
iniquity, I will discipline him with the rod of men, with the stripes
of the sons of men, but my steadfast love [there's that word again!]
will not depart from him, as I took it from Saul, whom I put away
from before you. And your house and your kingdom shall be made
sure forever before me. Your throne shall be established forever."
Ethan asks God to remember that promise and to make it good!

This is always the two-fold basis for all our prayers: The
covenant love of God's promises and the union we have by faith
with Jesus Christ, the Son of David – the Messiah. God has sworn
an oath on the basis of "two unchangeable things" (Heb. 6:17-20)
– His covenant and His Christ. And as a result we can plead, with
great boldness, the promise of God and our union with Christ as
reasons why God the Spirit should visit churches with renewing
power and reviving grace. It was C. John ("Jack") Miller who
reminded us that God's promises are the "handles" by which we
lay hold of Christ by faith. That reminder we need to hear again
from brother Ethan and from brother Jack.

These three words shape the heart of our most holy religion: covenant, steadfast love, faithfulness. It is the covenant of grace with God our Father that leads to the steadfast love of Christ in His covenant love and loyalty and provides for us the faithfulness of the Holy Spirit who applies God's promises to us, once we claim them by faith in Christ Jesus! The span of our life is but vanity and sorrow without the promises of God and the love of Christ. Blessed be the Lord, the Spirit, who brings God's Word and God's Christ to us, and gives us the grace-gifts of repentance and faith that we may lay hold of both.

## DAY 103 OLD HUNDREDTH

## Read Psalm 100

*Make a joyful noise to the LORD, all the earth!*

Psalm 100:1

Psalm 100 was known in the medieval church by its Latin name: *Jubilate Deo* (shout joyfully to God). It was sung at the morning service called Lauds; and the Church of England sings it today during the Morning Prayer. It is even more popular in the metrical version of William Kethe, the sixteenth-century Scotsman who was the friend of John Knox.

The psalm has become known as "Old Hundredth" because Louis Bourgeois set Kethe's version to a tune to which he gave that name. The two have been together since 1561, and the tune has become synonymous with the psalm. Henry Wadsworth Longfellow dubbed it "The Puritan Anthem" in his book *The Courtship of Miles Standish*. And due to its popular use at Thanksgiving time, Americans also refer to it as "The Pilgrim Psalm."

James Montgomery Boice describes Psalm 100 with these words: "It is the very quintessence of thanksgiving. Christians have clearly felt that throughout many generations of church history, because numerous poets have rendered it in verse and it has been sung to several well-known tunes." Some of these poets were Isaac Watts and John Wesley, who turned Watts' paraphrase into the hymn "Before Jehovah's Awesome Throne." Charles Haddon

Spurgeon captures the centrality of this psalm in Christian worship: "'Let us sing the Old Hundredth' is one of the everyday expressions of the Christian church, and will be so while men exist whose hearts are loyal to the Great King."

I suggest to you that the reason the "Old Hundredth" is so popular is because its five verses are a mini-course in pure worship. Three things should be noted about the psalm. First, note its seven-fold imperative: (1) Shout joyfully, (2) serve the Lord with gladness, (3) come before Him with joyful singing, (4) know that the Lord Himself is God, (5) enter His gates with thanksgiving, His courts with praise, (6) give thanks to Him, and (7) bless His holy name. The ancients divided the day into seven hours of prayer (based upon Ps. 119:164): *prime, lauds, terce, sext, none, vespers* and *compline*. Here the moderns have seven commands to take them through a day in prayer and praise.

Second, Psalm 100 gives us three reasons why we ought to praise God: He is our Creator (v. 3a), He is our Shepherd-King (v. 3b), He is our Savior (v. 5). When the psalmist says, "Know that the LORD, he is God!," he means simply this: All a man needs in God he will find in the Triune God – a Father Creator, a Son Shepherd-King, a Holy Spirit Savior. We praise God simply because He is GOD!

Third, there is a three-fold reminder of man's chief duty to this God: thanksgiving. In its title and twice in verse 4 we are commanded to give thanks to God. In fact, although there are nine Psalms of Thanksgiving and many others with elements of thankfulness in them, only Psalm 100 bears the inscription "A Psalm for Thanksgiving."

Maybe you and I ought to add to our "morning prayer" this rich and regular call to give thanks to the Lord. After all, "It is he who made us, and we are his" (v. 3). And aren't you glad He did – make us, save us, guard and guide us as His people?

## DAY 104 THE SUNDAY PSALM

### Read Psalm 24

*The earth is the LORD's and the fullness thereof, the world and those who dwell therein*

Psalm 24:1

We now focus on six Psalms of Revelation. These are psalms that reveal from God's Word our purpose and priorities in life. For the immediate result of studying God's Word is to praise and worship God as we ought.

The Levites of the second temple designated seven psalms for daily prayer. The Mishnah (Talmud 7:4) tells us what these daily psalms were: For Sunday, Psalm 24; for Monday, Psalm 48; for Tuesday, Psalm 82; for Wednesday, Psalm 94; for Thursday, Psalm 81; for Friday, Psalm 93; and for Saturday – the Sabbath – Psalm 92. The Mishnah then describes why each of these seven psalms was chosen. For Sunday it is written: "On the first day of the week what psalm did they, the Levites say? The one commencing 'The earth is the Lord's and all it contains,' because He took possession and gave possession and was sole ruler of His universe" (*Mo'ed: Rosh Hashanah*; 31a).

There is something perfectly fitting about praying and singing Psalm 24 on the first day of the week, Sunday, the Lord's Day. Its first two verses remind us that all we have sweated for, worried over, scrambled after and looked to for the previous six days belong to God – and to God alone. "Our stuff" is really His possession. In truth, we own nothing; all we have and those we love are on loan to us from God. Soon we die. And all that "stuff" goes back in the box for someone else to borrow and use for one brief lifetime. All we take with us from the grave and out of this world is ourselves – our souls – and even that "returns to God who gave it" (Eccles. 12:7). In the end we own nothing. All we really have is God.

Second, this psalm warns us that we are not welcome into the sanctuary of God unless we have acted with honesty, integrity and purity in our worldly dealings of the previous week (vv. 3, 4).

185

There is a symbiotic relationship between the Lord's Day and our workweek. We are not invited to come to church on Sunday and sing, "Now I belong to Jesus ... Jesus belongs to me," unless we have lived out from Monday to Saturday that we and all we have belong to God.

Finally we are promised a "blessing" if we seek for God in our weekly life and especially on Sunday (vv. 5, 6). There is a richness that comes from giving everything over to God that only the purposeful and the pious know. "Blessed are the poor in spirit, for theirs is the kingdom of heaven" (Matt. 5:3).

With those three facts in mind we are called to worship as the gates of churches and of the City of God are commanded to open, that King Jesus may once again enthrone Himself on the praises of His people. And so the weekly rhythm begins all over again: praise and piety, production and perspective ... the rhythm of life.

Alfred Edersheim lets us glimpse at the early life of Jesus of Nazareth. Describing the home education of little Jewish children, he writes: "The earliest hymns taught would be the psalms for the days of the week." How precious Psalm 24 becomes when we realize that our Lord Jesus recited it nearly every Sunday of His earthly life. It helped to wean Him off "the desires of the flesh and the desires of the eyes and pride in possessions" (1 John 2:15-17). It honed His vision for the Kingdom of Heaven and the City of God. I believe it will do the same for us if we make it a part of our weekly lives.

## DAY 105 THE VOICE OF THE LORD

### Read Psalm 29

*The voice of the LORD is powerful; the voice of the LORD is full of majesty.*

Psalm 29:4

Years ago Chuck Colson was asked in the context of a socio-ethical debate, "Who speaks for God?" His answer was classic, "God speaks for Himself; and quite nicely, thank you." And so He does. Psalm 29 reminds us of "the voice of the LORD" that is heard throughout the world each and every day. As such, this psalm fits well into the theme of our current sequence: The Psalms of Revelation.

Psalm 29 divides itself into a three-part symmetrical hymn. Its eleven verses form a 2-7-2 structure. The first two verses call us to worship God. The middle seven verses focus on "the voice of the Lord" (repeated seven times in vv. 3, 4, 5, 7, 8 and 9) heard in creation. The final two verses remind us that God also reveals Himself in His dealings with His covenant people, the church.

We are reminded by Psalm 29 of our reformed and evangelical doctrine of revelation. We believe, quite rightly, that God reveals Himself (i.e. He "speaks") in two ways: through general revelation and through special revelation. He reveals Himself generally to all men in the world and specifically to His elect in the church. God uses the "three C's" of general revelation to speak to all men. First, He speaks in *Creation*. He tells forth of His glory and greatness in the world around us by the beauty, intricacy and brilliance of what has been made (Ps. 19:1-6; Rom. 1:18-23; Matt. 6:25-34). He also speaks through the human *Conscience*, placing in every man, woman and child an innate moral compass for discerning right from wrong (Rom. 2:1-16). Finally, God speaks broadly and generally through *Culture*. Corrupted though it is, the culture of various societies, formed by the collective conscience of a people, guides and guards men in God's ways (Rom. 1:24-32; Matt. 11:20- 24; Acts 17:26-29).

In a parallel manner God speaks to His people through the "three C's of special revelation. Most perfectly and most personally God speaks through *Christ* – the Word made flesh, who is God's final word and perfect prophet (John 1:1-14; Heb. 1:1-4). Then He reveals Himself in the *Canon* of Holy Scripture: the sixty six books of the Bible. This is God's perfect and permanent word that continues to speak for God with dynamic power (Heb. 4:12). Lastly, God speaks through His *Church*, the Kingdom of God, Christ's counter-culture, and the Spirit's new society. Guided by Word and Spirit, the church is God's witness in God's world (Acts 1:8).

How wonderful it is to own a God who speaks for Himself. Ours is not a mystery religion, some cult dependent on an unending stream of "mystics" or "guides." We need neither infallible vicars of Christ on earth nor human channels for new age spirits to hear God's voice. God speaks for Himself – generally in a creation He made, in beings formed in His image, and in the peoples He places around the world; specifically through His Son incarnate, through the library He wrote and through the communion of saints He gathers from the nations.

At the end of the classic film, *The Fall of the Roman Empire*, actor Christopher Plummer, playing the role of Emperor Commodus of Rome, says as he is dying, "If you listen you can hear the gods laughing." Not hardly. But the point is well taken: If we listen we can hear the one, true God speaking. "The voice of the LORD" fills the universe, and our little world. The question is really not "who speaks for God" but rather "who is listening when God speaks?"

## DAY 106 THE THREE BOOKS OF GOD

### Read Psalm 19

*Let the words of my mouth and the meditation of my heart be acceptable in your sight, O LORD, my rock and my redeemer.*

Psalm 19:14

Yesterday we looked at Psalm 29 and the two sources of revelation God gives to man: general revelation (creation, conscience, culture) and special revelation (Christ, canon, church). These two sources of revelation are clearly set forth in Psalm 19.

This beautiful wisdom psalm divides itself into three parts. The first six verses speak about general revelation in creation (vv. 1-6). The next four verses speak of special revelation in Scripture (vv. 7-10). The last four verses speak of man as he is impacted by the world and the Word (vv. 11-14) or what we might call personal revelation.

Martin Luther often referred to what he called "the two books of God." The Big Book he called the world. Its vast subject matter of the created universe was written in large script with big pictures, almost like a child's storybook. And so it is intended. For creation, picturesque, vast and colorful as it may be, is an elementary book. Its only purpose is to communicate a basic and elemental message: God exists; He is great; He is to be worshiped, served and obeyed. We can almost hear the world reading aloud its basic message to all mankind: "See God. See God make all things. See God make all things for His own glory. We must love and obey God."

The second book Luther called *God's Little Book: The Holy Scriptures*. Smaller in size and scope than creation, the Bible is for grown-ups. Its print is small. It has no pictures. Its message is full of difficult words, complicated themes and intricate concepts. In fact, this one book is a library of spiritual classics – sixty-six in all – designed to teach "the mind of Christ" (1 Cor. 2:16) to those born-again and growing in grace and knowledge (2 Pet. 3:18).

But the thrust of Psalm 19 focuses on a third book God is in the process of writing – a thin, specialized volume of "limited edition". John R. W. Stott calls it personal revelation. This is a revelation that "needs to be completed by a life that is pleasing to God" (Stott). Paul refers to this third book as a personalized epistle written by the Holy Spirit, not in the stars or on parchments, but on human hearts: "You yourselves are our letter of recommendation, written on our hearts, to be known and read by all. And you show that you are a letter from Christ delivered by us, written not with ink but with the Spirit of the living God, not on tablets of stone but on tablets of human hearts" (2 Cor. 3:2, 3).

We often say of others, "You can read her like a book." The fact is, all of us are read like books by other people. How we live in this world as God's creatures reading His Big Book, and how we live in the church as God's Christians learning His Little Book, will tell all men all they need to know about us. William Graham Scroggie was right: "The skies tell much, the Scripture tells more, but the soul tells most of all, for it is only for the sake of the soul that God has revealed Himself at all."

I wonder what men see when they read me. Is it a tragedy of a melancholy soul? Is it a dime novel of a man bent on pursuing the lesser things of life? Could it be some seamy tabloid? What I hope they read is a true and great romance: The story of a sinner in love with his Savior. Tell me, is your life a good read or not?

## DAY 107 THE WISE MAN'S COURSE OF STUDY

## Read Psalm 111

*Great are the works of the Lord, studied by all who delight in them.*
Psalm 111:2

We who are evangelical and reformed Christians may often fail in a most surprising manner: We may end up being too spiritual. What I simply mean is that we spend more time studying the Word than we do studying the world. Psalm 111 is really the mirror image of Psalm 19. It complements that psalm in this way: Psalm 19 extols the wonders of general and special revelation, while Psalm 111 tells us what to do with these two sources of God's revelation.

But the twist this psalm gives to the wonders of God's revelation is to make us focus on God's revelation in history. In the background of the psalm are the wonders of God's dealings with Israel in the wilderness. History is a great teacher of God's glory.

Even the word "history" beckons us to look to God to understand our world and the men who inhabit it. History is "His story," the story of God moving among the peoples of His creation, and none more so than His church.

Psalm 111 reminds us that "he remembers his covenant forever" (v. 5) because "he has commanded his covenant forever" (v. 9). Regardless of what era of world history one studies, inevitably the people of God are found at the center of the human drama. Indeed, as the church of God moves out to the peoples of the earth (Acts 1:8), the history of mankind is radically changed by the power of the Gospel.

Psalm 111 reminds us, as William Cowper reminds us, no one can understand life and history without the help of God: "Blind unbelief is sure to err and scan His work in vain; God is His own interpreter, and He will make it plain." It is futile to study the workings of the human vascular system, the solar system or systems of politics and economics without knowledge of systematic theology. For God is the designer of all these systems, and to the extent that they follow His design, things work well.

Psalm 111 divides itself into the two books of God. The Big Book of God's works in verses 1-6 and the Little Book of God's Word that interprets His works, in verses 7-10. The genius of the Psalm is found in the two key verses of these two sections. Placed side-by-side, they remind us that a wise man's course of study includes both volumes of God. "Great are the works of the LORD, studied by all who delight in them.... The fear of the LORD is the beginning of wisdom; all those who practice it have a good understanding. His praise endures forever!" (vv. 2, 10).

I find it amazing that doctors who study the human body could be such practical atheists. Equally puzzling is the statement of Carl Sagan, the astronomer, "the universe is all there is." And sad indeed are our lawyers and governors who major in law but are so carnal, so immoral, so lawless. But such is the fate of all of us, if we study only one book of God and neglect the other. Christians who love Bible study but hate to read history will end up just as warped as the makers of history who neglect God's Word. The godless and the godly would draw closer to one another if they made their course of study both God's Word and God's works.

## DAY 108 THE REVIVING POWER OF GOD'S WORD

### Read Psalm 119:1-88

*My soul clings to the dust; give me life according to your word! ... Turn my eyes from looking at worthless things; and give me life in your ways. ... Behold, I long for your precepts; in your righteousness give me life!*

Psalm 119:25, 37, 40

Psalm 119 is the longest, and perhaps the most majestic of all the psalms. Its 176 verses make it the longest chapter in the Bible. An acrostic psalm, it divides itself into twenty-two sections of eight verses each – a section for each letter of the Hebrew alphabet where each verse begins with that same Hebrew letter. This acrostic format was employed for mnemonic purposes. The Hebrew children memorized Psalm 119 to develop a reverence for God's Word.

The men of old devoted a great deal of time and attention to this psalm. Charles H. Spurgeon devoted almost a third of his *Treasury of David* to Psalm 119. Puritan Charles Bridges preached a sermon on each of Psalm 119's twenty-two stanzas. Thomas Menton wrote 190 chapters on this psalm, in excess of one chapter per verse! We moderns find this not only tedious but even ridiculous. We like things "quick 'n' easy" – pre-packaged, microwavable and just add water! But spiritual life is not that way.

In fact, the opposite is true. Paul tells us that the life of a Christian is a walk of faith: "For we walk by faith, not by sight" (2 Cor. 5:7). And he also informs us that faith only grows out of engagement with God's Word: "So faith comes from hearing, and hearing through the word of Christ" (Rom. 10:17). In the fourth and fifth stanzas of this psalm (*Daleth* and *He*), the author reminds us that we are what we look at.

He puts it this way: "Turn my eyes from looking at worthless things; and give me life in your ways" (v. 37). Lutheran Old Testament scholar, Herbert C. Leupold explains this verse to us: "The word of God in its manifold aspects is to be sought rather than certain inferior values that are got to beguile men. One of those values is financial profit, which has been known often to become the object of a man's pursuit... The other objective that could be substituted for these higher values is 'vanity.' The word implies all that is hollow, worthless, and trivial. The cheapest objectives for life may be selected by men and captivate a man's eye or fancy." But all these things do is suck the soul dry, whereas God's Word has power to revive the spirit of a man. This reality hit home with a thud for me this past year.

After a demanding and stressful season of ministry, I took two Saturdays off to go up to my alma mater to watch a couple of football games. I usually enjoy this immensely – the fun of just getting away and joining 105,000 fans in cheering on the Buckeyes. But this year the games I went to left me flat, despite exciting victories over Michigan State and Purdue.

As I gazed out into the fourth quarter haze of the lights and the fading cheers, a Scripture I memorized years ago came to my mind: "Turn away my eyes from looking at vanity, and revive me in Thy ways." Then it dawned on me: a thousand football wins have no more reviving and restoring power than the wind – indeed, they are but "hollow, worthless, and trivial." What my soul needed was a weekend away in God's Word. And so the psalmist prays again and again in Psalm 119, "Give me life … Give me life … Give me life." In other words, "Revive me … revive me … revive me" (NASB). And through the intake of regular and rich doses of God's Word, that is precisely what happens. "This is my comfort in my affliction, that your promise gives me life" (v. 50). And so it will do to us, if we would look on the pages of Scripture rather than staring at vanity.

## DAY 109 THE CUMULATIVE BLESSING OF GOD'S WORD

### Read Psalm 119:89-176

*The sum of your word is truth, and every one of your righteous rules endures forever.*

Psalm 119:160

John Ruskin (1819–1900) was a great English art critic, author and social reformer. He was born in London, the son of a wealthy Scottish wine merchant. His mother was a devout Puritan who immersed John's mind in the Word of God. She made him memorize great portions of the Bible, including much of Psalm 119.

Ruskin's education was closely planned and executed by his doting parents. He always accompanied them on their travels to England, Scotland and Europe. He attended Oxford University where he studied art, literature and culture. He was one of the first art critics to postulate that architectural styles and genres of painting or sculpture reflected the spiritual state of man. He wrote that medieval Gothic cathedrals reflected a culture of faith, virtue and transcendent values, while that of the Renaissance portrayed the moral decay, loss of authority and unbelief of a corrupted humanism. His own writings, even his children's story, *King of the Golden River*, reflected the value of virtues and the bankruptcy and eventual ruin of a life divorced from absolute truth.

During the industrial revolution in England, Ruskin became a benefactor of the poor and slum-dwelling classes. He spent most of his inheritance on philanthropic ventures. In particular, he did much in the way of urban renewal, especially in the area of tenement housing for the sweatshop laborers. His model village, Saint George's Guild, was perhaps the first community renewal work of our times. He founded and financed educational institutions of various kinds, especially those that aided in educating the working classes.

How did the son of a wealthy man, born with a silver spoon in his mouth, come to devote his life to such noble and selfless ventures? Let Ruskin himself tell you: "It is strange that of all the pieces of the Bible which my mother taught me, that which cost me most to learn – the 119th Psalm – has now become of all the most precious to me in its overwhelming and glorious passion of love for the law of God."

It seems that the cumulative effect of God's Word changed Ruskin's life, just as the psalmist of the 119th testified it did to him. For he states that the Law of God changed everything about him. He uses five words to describe the totality of his faculties changed by God's Word: his mind, his eyes, his heart, his feet and his mouth – thoughts, perspective, emotions, direction and communication, all changed for the better by God's Word.

Preachers may often wonder if anyone is listening. Do they remember your outline? Probably not. Can they recite your three main points? Not after an hour past the benediction. Do they daydream or sleep through great portions of your message? They sure do, some of them purposefully. But over time, year after year, the cumulative effect of God's Word changes how they reason, what they see in life, what they want from God, the course of their lives and the words of their mouths. "The sum of your word is truth" – not a sermon or song here and there – but "the sum of God's Word". The cumulative effect of Scripture is powerful.

Over time and a little bit at a time, the living and abiding Word of God makes us better men, weans us off this world, and prepares us for glory forever. And all the while we never know it is happening. But God does, and that's what counts in the end.

## DAY 110 O TASTE AND SEE

### Read Psalm 34

*Oh, taste and see that the LORD is good! Blessed is the man who takes refuge in him!*

Psalm 34:8

In Chapter 21 of 1 Samuel we find the story of David fleeing to the Philistine city of Gath in order to seek protection from the ravages of King Saul. In so doing David finds himself in greater danger than he experienced in Israel. His logic for such an excursion appears sound: Who of Saul's henchmen would look for him in the capital city of Israel's enemy, the headquarters of King Achish of Philistia? Like Merry and Pippin in J. R. R. Tolkien's *The Lord of the Rings*, David no doubt thought, "The closer we are to danger, the safer we are."

That's a great idea if you live in Middle-earth or some other land of make-believe. In the real world to do so is just plain stupid. It sounds so mystically wise when Tolkien writes it, but allegorical tales are severely limited in their ability to help us survive, day to day, in a dangerous world. Ours is not a world of hobbits, orcs and fairies. We live in danger of the world, the flesh and the devil.

For the alcoholic, the safest place is not to sit on a park bench outside the local package store. For a man consumed with lust, there is little safety on the Internet. And a woman who is a glutton should not pray for self-control in the shadow of the food court at the mall. The Scripture tells us to flee from evil, not seek shelter in it. "But as for you, , O man of God, flee these things.... So flee youthful passions" (1 Tim. 6:11; 2 Tim. 2:22).

At the time it seemed like a great idea to hide out in Gath, playing loyalty to one king against loyalty to the other. The problem? It backfired. God intervened, and because He is unimaginably gracious and incredibly patient with us, He "knows that we are but dust" and prone to such stupid schemes. As a postscript to this embarrassingly near miss in his life, David pens Psalm 34.

195

In this thanksgiving hymn, he praises God for His good and tender mercies and invites us to do what he initially failed to do: to "taste and see that the LORD is good" (v. 8). As a refrain in this song David repeatedly states that God "delivered" or "saved" him. And he mentions that four times (vv. 4, 6, 17 and 19). What is it that God delivered him from? David is specific: God saved him from his "fears" (v. 4), his "troubles" (vv. 6, 17), and his "afflictions" (v. 19).

St. Columba experienced fears, troubles and afflictions for over thirty years as a missionary among the Picts and Scots in Ireland, Northumbria and Scotland. He died at age seventy five in the midst of transcribing the Psalter. The last verse he wrote out was Psalm 34:10, "The young lions suffer want and hunger; but those who seek the LORD lack no good thing." With these words Columba said, "Here I make an end; what follows Baithen (another monk) will write." Columba died that night. It is important to connect verse 8 with verse 10 in Psalm 34.

Young lions are known to be foolhardy, brash and prone to placing themselves in danger. Young lions often have to learn about danger the hard way. They tend to attack Cape buffalo alone, run off and hide in the fortress of an enemy, or try their luck in the shadow of the Dark Tower; yet they survive. It is God, their creator and caretaker, who delivers them time and again. So young lions gorge themselves on game God gives them despite their folly. And young princes taste the goodness of the Lord despite their foolishness. Indeed "they shall not be in want of any good thing," in spite of their foolhardy ways, because God is good. And there is only one way to prove this truth. As A. F. Kirkpatrick exhorts: "Make but trial, and you will perceive what His goodness is toward them who fear Him."

And so the saints sing Psalm 34 to this day, as long as silly schemes continue to place us in fear, trouble and affliction. In 1698 Nicholas Brady and Nahum Tate revised the Psalter of the Church of England, used in the Book of Common Prayer. They set to words the paraphrase of this song under the title, "Through all the Changing Scenes of Life." To this day men remind themselves of the goodness of God with these words:

*Fear him, ye saints, and you will then*
*Have nothing else to fear;*
*Make you his service with your delight,*
*Your wants shall be his care.*

## DAY 111 THE PILGRIM'S PERSPECTIVE ON LIFE

### Read Psalm 120

*In my distress I called to the LORD, and he answered me.*

Psalm 120:1

Known as the "Pilgrim Psalms" the *Songs of Ascents* (Pss. 120–134) were used by Jewish pilgrims of the Old Testament era as they made their way, each year, up to Jerusalem for the high holy days of Passover, Pentecost and Tabernacles, or other sacred festivals of Israel. Hence they were known individually, and as a collection, as "the Songs of the Goings-up." They became, we surmise, "a Psalter within a Psalter" (Perowne). Derek Thomas, in his delightful devotional exposition of these psalms entitled *Making the Most of Your Devotional Life* correctly states, "Before the Psalter was compiled in the way we have it now, this collection of psalms might have existed as a special 'hymn book' designed for a 'special occasion.'"

I commend Dr. Thomas' book to you as well as Eugene Peterson's *A Long Obedience in the Same Direction: Discipleship in an Instant Society*. Both books help us rediscover the need to develop a biblically-based and Christ-centered spirituality, and reclaim for ourselves the mind of a pilgrim in the world, passing through life on the way to the City of God.

In these psalms, Zion (Jerusalem) is the joy, hope and final objective of the pilgrim believer. And as we know, Jerusalem in the psalms and poetry of the prophets is a foreshadowing of our home in heaven – the City of God. John Stott notes of these psalms, "They are all brief, and most of them betray a great love of Sion and the temple, and an ardent desire for the peace and prosperity of Jerusalem ... these little psalms all breathe a spirit of quiet, undaunted faith in Israel's God 'who hath made heaven and earth.'"

I happen to believe that they are deliberately arranged by the post-exilic Levites to reflect a progressive view of spiritual maturation all saints must pass through in order to be fit for the kingdom of heaven, the City of God and everlasting life with Christ. And that process begins with *the pilgrim's perspective on life*, what the Puritans called "a holy dissatisfaction," as set forth in Psalm 120.

Notice that Psalm 120's seven verses divide themselves into two parts: A holy dissatisfaction (vv. 1-4) and a holy departure (vv. 5-7). In other words, as Christians grow in grace they realize two things – life is rough and heaven is their real home. They come to see themselves as those who "sojourn in Meshech" and "dwell among the tents of Kedar." This is the language of a nomadic people passing through the world and homeward to heaven. "But our citizenship is in heaven, and from it we await a Savior, the Lord Jesus Christ" (Phil. 3:20). We are just passing through. We are "God's gypsies."

Derek Thomas writes, "It probably goes without saying that Psalm 120 is not a favourite psalm for most Christians. On the surface, it is far too pessimistic and gloomy; it goes against the grain of what we modern Christians are led to expect from our faith." Psalm 120 is too "negative" and "hyper-spiritual." "Why," we ask one another, "if you think like Psalm 120, you'd be so heavenly minded that you'd be no earthly good." My, my, how we moderns cling to platitudes to explain away spiritual truth we find demanding and troublesome to our worldly souls!

The opposite is true. If Christians thought more of heaven and meditated more on the City of God, we would all be better men of this world and better women in the cities in which we live. I love Ohio. Derek Thomas loves Wales. And Eugene Peterson loves Montana. But these lovely places – and all of them are masterpieces of God's creative glory and genius – are not our homes. They are places of deceit (v. 2), danger (v. 4) and death (vv. 6, 7). They are not the home of God.

Our journey toward Jesus begins with the realization that the laying down of this life is the beginning of a pilgrimage to real life! George Beverly Shea came to this realization over seventy years ago, and has sung to two generations of people around this world the truth of Psalm 120:

*I'd rather have Jesus than silver or gold,*
*I'd rather be His than have riches untold.*
*I'd rather have Jesus than houses or land,*
*I'd rather be led by His nail-pierced hand,*
*Than to be the king of a vast domain*
*Or be held in sin's dread sway;*
*I'd rather have Jesus than anything*
*This world affords today.*
    Rhea F. Miller

## DAY 112 LEARNING TO LIVE UNDER PROVIDENCE

## Read Psalm 121

*The LORD is your keeper.*
                              Psalm 121:5

Psalm 121 picks up where Psalm 120 left off, and it serves as the second of the Songs of Ascents that we are reading and praying through this week and next. Many a soul has found Psalm 121 a tremendous comfort because of its opening lines, "I will lift up my eyes to the hills. From where does my help come? My help comes from the LORD.... The LORD is your keeper" (vv. 1, 2, 5).

During the Rebellion in India during the 1840s and 50s, the men of the British Empire found solace in Psalm 121. Captain Arthur Conolly of the British Expeditionary Force was executed in June of 1842 on a mission to negotiate the release of another British officer, a Colonel Stoddart. Years later a Russian purchased a small book in an Indian bazaar in Bokhara. Opening it he found the Book of Common Prayer belonging to Capt. Conolly. In it the Captain had written, "Thank God that this book was left to me.

Stoddart and I did not know before our affliction what was in the psalms, or how beautiful the prayers of our Church."

Later a civil servant, William Edwards, was evacuated through hundreds of miles of enemy territory. He wrote in his diary on August 27, 1857, "Amidst it all, today's Psalms are most consoling, and wonderfully suited to our case, especially the 121st: 'I will lift up my eyes unto the hills, from whence cometh my help.'" The next day he began a three-day, 150-mile journey down the gauntlet of a river. He eventually arrived safely in British custody after three months of suspense, danger and near misses at death.

How could it be that two British men, reading the same psalm, seventeen years apart, yet in the same political upheaval, could find Psalm 121 to be true; especially when one died and the other lived? Did God fail the one and keep the other safe? Not hardly. The Lord proved to be each man's keeper in a different way.

For Captain Arthur Conolly, the Lord answered from the hills of India and visited him in his prison cell, awakening a dead religion into a living faith that brought him home to the City of God once he died. For the magistrate and tax collector, William Edwards, the Lord kept him alive to serve for many more years in British service and as a witness for Christ. The Lord did protect them from evil (v. 7) – for each a different kind of horror. And the Lord did guard their souls (v. 7), in both their "going out" (to India) and their "coming in" (to heaven), in His own timing.

Each man learned, in his own situation, the second lesson that every pilgrim must learn on the way to the heavenly Jerusalem: *learning to live under God's providence*. Each man would learn the struggles of faith (vv. 1, 2), the struggles of fear (vv. 3-5), and the struggles of failure (vv. 6-8). Each would learn to sing John Newton's hymn from the heart, "Through many dangers, toils and snares, I have already come; 'Tis grace hath brought me safe thus far, and grace will lead me home."

When the Jewish pilgrims sang the songs over two millennia ago, the hills that bordered the Jordan caravan route were filled with pagan shrines to Baal, Marduk and other gods. It was sinful nature to look to lesser deities on the hilltops to give them help:

patron gods and goddesses of travel, fertility, success and safety. We see them on our hilltops all the time: health, wealth, popularity and position. But the journey of faith through life teaches us one thing for certain, if nothing else. Help comes from God and not from the imaginations of our mind. Eugene Peterson writes, "Help comes from the creator, not from the creation. The creator is always awake; He will not slumber or sleep. Baal took long naps, and one of the jobs of the priests was to wake him up when someone needed his attention – and they were not always successful." Not so with God; He's always on the job, keeping His watch, in command of His troops, the ministering angels. We don't need "supplementary help from the sun or the moon" (Peterson), or from Mary, the saints and spirit guides. God's providence proves itself in ancient Israel, in nineteenth century India and in postmodern America. "The LORD is your keeper.... The LORD will keep your going out and your coming in from this time forth and forevermore."

Note: Psalm 122 can be found among the Songs of Zion in Part One: God our Refuge, Day 7, page 21. The third step, from that Psalm 122, is *the Celebration of Worship with God's People*, which is not included here.

## DAY 113 THE POWER OF PRAYER

### Read Psalm 123

*So our eyes look to the LORD our God, till he has mercy upon us.*
Psalm 123:2

The Pilgrim Psalms set before us steps of spiritual growth that Eugene Peterson poetically calls *A Long Obedience in the Same Direction*, a phrase he borrowed from German philosopher Friedrich Nietzsche: "The essential thing 'in heaven and in earth' is ... that there should be long obedience in the same direction; there thereby results, and has always resulted, in the long run, something which has made life worth living." I believe Peterson and Nietzsche are giving expression to the idea of Psalm 37:3, "Trust in the LORD and do good; dwell in the land and befriend faithfulness." To do that takes a lifetime of learning.

In this learning process are fifteen steps of growth in grace. Each is poetically set forth in a Pilgrim Psalm, A Song of Ascents, of "going up" to the City of God – Jerusalem on earth, heaven in the future. The first step is developing the pilgrim's perspective on life (Ps. 120); the second step is learning to live under divine providence (Ps. 121); and the third step is the celebration of worship with God's people (Ps. 122). The fourth step may be one of the most difficult: *the Power of Prayer* (Ps. 123).

Two things are extremely difficult for Americans in particular to face: poverty and unpopularity. The last two things we want to be are a beggar and one who is laughed at. The citizen of the United States is known around the world as (often unfairly) "the ugly American" – the loud and gaudy big-spender who desperately wants everyone to like him. But Christians are neither Americans nor ugly. They are the bondslaves of Christ and the friends of God. And that causes both blessings and trouble.

The psalmist has already established the fact, in Psalms 120 and 121, that life in the world is a dangerous and difficult venture, filled with God's enemies who hate us because we love God. They appear here, yet again, in verses 3 and 4, this time full of "scorn" for us (laughing at our beliefs and values) and filling our lives with their "contempt" (their open disdain of what we hold most dear: life with God). And that makes life tough because we are not allowed to walk across the room and punch their faces in! Not even "in the name of Jesus." Nope. What we have to do is pray, and that's it; that's all. And prayer is tough for us because we've got to go begging God while we put up with the nauseating ridicule of a damned humanity. I don't like it, and neither do you. After all, I'm an American for crying out loud!

Recently my wife and I got our youngest child a golden retriever, named Bowley, to fill the void in my son's life when his brother went off to college. Bowley is a shameless beggar. He can sit for hours, big brown eyes sadly fixed on us, until we break down and give him what he wants. Then he just wags his tail and lies down at our feet. I mean the dog has no pride … none!

And that's how Psalm 123 paints us; shameless, pride-less,

needy servants who keep staring at our Master in heaven until He notices us and provides for us, which He always does. For self-sufficient and self-loved Americans to become "poor in spirit" (Matt. 5:3) is really excruciating. And to be laughed at in the process by other proud men is doubly painful. Incidentally, I have, in my travels, found that prideful Englishmen and arrogant Europeans are just as "ugly" as Americans can be when learning this humbling lesson. But, the reality of life with God is this: we either learn to be humble in prayer and before other men or we don't go to heaven when we die. For there's a sign over each of the twelve gates of the City of God, written in all the tongues of the earth, and it reads simply: "Only the penitent and prayerful shall pass. No proud ones allowed." We either learn this lesson now or we learn it later, when it's too late.

Derek Thomas captures the essence of Psalm 123: "Waiting patiently on God's timing can be very difficult, of course. Such delays (and they are delays from our perspective, not from God's) keep us on our toes (or better, on our knees!). They ensure that our faith is nourished rather than lulled to sleep. Abstinence creates appetite. Growing up in grace involves submission to God at every level and lessons learned here will repay dividends."

The last words written by Martin Luther on his deathbed were these: "We are beggars.... That is true." Have you learned that lesson yet? Better get on your knees and get busy!

## DAY 114 THE DANGERS OF DISCIPLESHIP

## Read Psalm 124

*"If it had not been the LORD who was on our side ...*

Psalm 124:2

I admit it. I can get really cranky and irascible. In fact, I can be really, really obnoxious; and especially when I come to disdain someone or something. So I have to watch myself whenever I talk about discipleship. I have become particularly critical in spirit of the para-church paradigm of "discipleship" that puts converts through studies where they fill in the blanks in some study booklet;

that emphasizes four or five disciplines of the Christian life while ignoring those developed and practiced in a local congregation; and that is always asking, "Do you know what's wrong with the church today?" I think these folks need to read, memorize and meditate on Psalm 124.

Discipleship is dangerous. It cannot be programmed, perfected in twelve steps or learned by a "proven process." Psalm 124 proves that beyond a shadow of a doubt. Notice first, that Psalm 124 is the first Pilgrim Psalm that is ostensibly antiphonal. Verses 1 and 2, which open the psalm, are a responsive reading between priest and people. There's a lesson there, as in all the Pilgrim Psalms: They are all, always, in the plural – we, us, our. None of them are about me, myself or mine. True discipleship only happens in the corporate setting of pastors, elders, deacons and the "us" of a congregation.

And true discipleship has a much different curriculum than most Christian book publishers allow. It involves two courses: The Hazards of Life with God and The Help in Life from God. Those are the two parts of Psalm 124. The Christian life is full of spiritual hazards: evil men (2, 3), evil events (4, 5) and the evil one (7). This is the satanic trinity of the world, the flesh, and the devil. Filling in blanks in a booklet won't teach you how to combat them. Eric Routely comments, "God is with us; that is how God is on our side; not to swallow up human enemies, but to enable us to spit in the Devil's eye." I am afraid that all our "short course discipleship" has made us weak and unwilling to fight the good fight of faith.

We also must learn that help comes from God in this life. This is help against men (1, 2), help against the devil (6), and help against our fallen nature (7). We moderns will always turn to three sources of help before we turn to God: other men (therapy), a program of self-help, or legal force. But Psalm 124 says simply, "Our help is in the name of the LORD, who made heaven and earth." God does often use men, methods and the magistrate to help us, but He is our "first stop" in a dangerous world, not our last.

Here, you see, is the fifth step of the Pilgrim's Way: *Learning The*

*Dangers of Discipleship*. For sin, sinful men and Satan are far more dangerous and difficult than we ever imagined. In fact, only one drastic solution breaks their three-cords of power (Eccles. 4:12). That solution is *the Cross*. "The reason the Son of God appeared was to destroy the works of the devil" (1 John 3:8). And Christ's call to discipleship is to pick up our crosses daily and follow Him. The way of the cross is the way of discipleship and it is dangerous. It's serious business, a lot more serious than Bible-study booklets, retreats and catch-phrase solutions. Were it not for Jesus we'd all be ruined. We live on the razor's edge every day. But we live! And we do so because "Our help is in the name of the LORD, who made heaven and earth" (v. 8).

## DAY 115 THE SECURITY OF THE BELIEVER

### Read Psalm 125

*"Those who trust in the LORD are as Mount Zion. Which cannot be moved, but abides forever."*

Psalm 125:1

The Levites who compiled and arranged these Pilgrim Psalms did so with apparent forethought and deliberate order. For after Psalm 124's stark message of the dangers of discipleship, the next psalm reflecting the further step of the pilgrim's life of faith is Psalm 125, which speaks of *the Security of the Believer*.

Derek Kidner paints the picture for us, "The hills and the Holy City, much in view and much in mind to the pilgrims, make their presence felt again; and once more the thoughts they arouse are searching and fundamental, piercing to the realities behind these impressive sights." The pilgrims have now made their climb up the steep slopes from Jericho to the bowl of hills that crests Mount Zion. Those hills that once threatened danger from robbers, lions and false gods now surround the City of God and become a natural citadel (See Ps. 48).

The dangers of the journey are almost over – at least the "going up" part. Soon the caravan will be in the midst of Jerusalem where the Old Testament church was headquartered. Security, if only for a brief time, was felt by all. Discipleship involves security. We live in a dangerous world and travel on a difficult way, but nevertheless we do have security from God. Pilgrims are not fearful people. There is a credit card ad that warns us, "Don't leave home without it." Christians on the way to heaven would smile and answer, "Don't worry; we haven't."

Men look for security in a dozen different places – economics, education, sociology, psychology, politics, military, science and medicine. But the believer finds security in theology – the knowledge of God. Eugene Peterson agrees: "Discipleship is a decision to live by what I know about God and not by what I feel about Him; or myself, or my neighbor." What is it that we know about God that gives us such security? Psalm 125 tells us five things in five verses.

First, God is immutable. He never changes, is always the same and can therefore be relied upon because He is the fixed absolute of life. Second, God is loving and kind. He surrounds His people with covenant love and loyalty and cares for them immeasurably. Third, He is holy. Wickedness He will not tolerate. The closer we get to God the farther we get from evil. Fourth, God is good and His goodness is manifested in the attributes of grace, benevolence, kindness, patience and compassion. When we say, "God is good," we say that God answers in perfection all that God should be. Fifth, God is just and so He will judge the world in righteousness and truth – rewarding the good and punishing the evil. Because God is God there is a moral order to the universe, making it safe for men in Christ to dwell on the earth.

When I was in college there was a rock 'n roll group named The Young Rascals. One of their songs began with this poignant question: "How can I be sure, in a world that's constantly changing; how can I be sure where I stand with you?" Those with good theology and a living faith in Christ can answer that question. When Martin Luther used to be assailed by the devil, and overcome with evil thoughts, he would always say, "Leave me alone, Devil, for I am a baptized man!" Luther's securtity was that he was in Christ and in the church. Christians stand secure in Christ and in the fellowship of Holy Zion, the church. All is well with us for we see on the horizon the beatific vision: The City of God!

Note: Psalm 126 can be found among the Psalms of Revival in Part One: God Our Refuge, Day 48, page 87. The seventh step from Psalm 126 is *Seeking Restoration and Revival*, which is not included here.

## DAY 116 SELF-SUFFICIENCY AND SUCCESS

### Read Psalm 127

*Unless the LORD builds the house, those who build it labor in vain. Unless the LORD watches over the city, the watchman keeps awake in vain.*

Psalm 127:1

The Pilgrim's Way involves multiple steps: holy dissatisfaction (Ps. 120), accepting providence (Ps. 121), corporate worship (Ps. 122), perseverance in prayer (Ps. 123), facing spiritual dangers (Ps. 124), security in Christ (Ps. 125) and restoration and revival (Ps. 126). Step eight on the Journey to Glory involves slaying the Twin Towers of evil in Western life: *Self-Sufficiency and Success*. No one has ever been more qualified to address these two issues than Solomon, the son of David, King of Israel.

This man was the richest man alive in his day; a man of incredible accomplishments and "successes," with cities, chariots, orchards, fleets of ships, houses, temples, farms and slaves beyond parallel, together with a thousand beautiful women who were his wives and concubines (mistresses). And yet, when he writes a psalm he writes about the joys of simple life. I believe Psalms 127 and 128 are placed together as another example of "twin psalms" in the Psalter (like Pss. 3, 4; Pss. 9, 10 and Pss. 42, 43). Solomon puts his name to Psalm 127, and since the Levites placed Psalm 128 parallel to it, we are not exceeding exegetical license to suspect that Psalm 128 was Solomon's work as well.

In Psalm 127 Solomon talks about the three spheres of life each man lives within, holds dear and in which he has great influence: home, city and work. And in each arena of life Solomon says: "God gives success!" God builds the home, guards the city and makes work fruitful – "For he gives to his beloved sleep" (v. 2).

In other words, men can attempt to work themselves to the bone in a self-sufficient effort to build the perfect family, develop the pleasant city and engage in productive work, but it is God who accomplishes those things. He would prefer we work less, sleep more and trust in Him in all these things.

As proof of His sovereign grace in all three of these arenas, God gives us children. Sure, they are a result of our seed and our wife's womb, but we marvel, each of us who are parents, and ask, "Did I make this – that precious boy, this beautiful girl? No. God gave me these little ones!" So He did, and for three reasons. They will build the homes and families of future generations; they will develop and guard the cities we helped begin; and they will carry on and carry to the next level the careers we worked in so diligently.

Then they will come and go, and their children will take up the sacred duties of life: home, city and work. And on, and on it goes. You see, we were never *self-sufficient*, nor was our *success* ever just our own. God was behind it all. People were there alongside us – spouses, neighbors and co-workers. And children were always in the wake, waiting for their turn to work with God in family, community and calling. What a key lesson for life, especially since we are pilgrims, just passing through life and passing on our way to the City of God.

## DAY 117 THE PROSPERITY AND POSTERITY OF FAMILY

### Read Psalm 128

*Your wife will be like a fruitful vine, within your house; your children will be like olive shoots around your table.*

Psalm 128:3

I grew up in a happy and common home. To be sure, there were "dysfunctional" aspects to our family of seven sinners, but my childhood memories are predominantly happy ones. My dad was a blue-collar man. And our home in Columbus, Ohio consisted of very simple things. My mother worked at home; there were three sisters and two brothers. And the joys of life centered around our local church, our parochial school, the neighbors and the latest exploits of the Ohio State Buckeyes, the Cleveland Browns or the Cincinnati Reds. Sunday roasts, Wednesday meatloaves and Friday's fish, interspersed with sausages and sauerkraut made life exceedingly simple, predictable and secure.

Our favorite time of every day was supper. My dad especially seemed to delight in our evening meal, for there he held court, king over his little castle, telling of work as a milkman, listening to mom's comical tales about our eccentric but good neighbors, and giving attention to each of his five kids. They told jokes, asked questions and poked fun at one another.

Solomon seems to sense that his plush life in the palace, his upbringing in courts filled with opulence and intrigue, and the loss of siblings through incest, fratricide and political execution left the world's richest man terribly poor. May I fantasize for a moment? Could it be that the king, while cruising one of his chariots through the streets of Jerusalem, stopped at a corner and at that moment heard the sweetest sound on earth? Through the open window of a workman's home, in the still of evening's dusk, the laughter of parents and the giggles of happy, little "blue-collar" children rose over the din of armored carriages for just enough time to make Solomon realize how much he had missed. The man of a thousand wives would later write, "One man among a thousand I found, but a woman among all these I have not found" (Eccles. 7:28). Lots of people around him but only one male friend? A thousand women to bed down with but not one wife ... no family at all!

On our way through life let us never forget the prosperity family brings us and the posterity family leaves us. That is a spiritual lesson America and the West has forgotten: Family is a priceless treasure, a gift from God. The poor factory worker with a fruitful vine of a wife and little olive shoots of children around his supper table is the richest of all men. That is the ninth step to be learned on the Pilgrim's Way: *The Prosperity and Posterity of Family*.

I will always be grateful for Bob Ross's care and guidance; for the love and prayers of Margie Ann Hillerman Ross, my mom; and for the encouragement and friendship of Ann, Mary Jo and Jane, my sisters; and Steve, my only and dear brother. And I will ever praise God for my godly wife and dearest friend, Jane Virden Ross; and for my four little "round-heads," my Puritan children: Joanna, Abigail, Nathan and Aaron. No man has ever traveled through life's journey in better company. If this is what earth is like, I can't wait for heaven!

## DAY 118 THE NECESSITY OF PREVAILING PERSEVERANCE

### Read Psalm 129

*Greatly have they afflicted me from my youth, yet they have not prevailed against me.*

Psalm 129:2

As we travel on in the Pilgrim's Way we will inevitably come to difficult stages of faith's journey through life. Steep, rugged and dangerous terrain; foul weather and blistering sun and heat; dangers from brigands and bad situations confront every pilgrim. Likewise, the life of faith has seasons where little forward progress is made and all one does is simply survive: *Prevailing Perseverance* is the tenth step of the Songs of Ascents.

C. H. Spurgeon acknowledges that perseverance is precisely what Psalm 129 is advocating. He comments, "I fail to see how this is a step beyond the previous psalm; and yet it is clearly the song of an older and more tried individual, who looks back upon a life of affliction in which he suffered all along, even from his youth. Inasmuch as patience is a higher, or at least more difficult, grace than domestic love, the ascent or progress may perhaps be seen in that direction." And so it is. That is why Psalm 129 follows Psalm 128 – from happy home to dangerous world.

I can remember yet how this reality first came crushing in on me. I was only eight years old, and as a young Roman Catholic boy I walked home from the Immaculate Conception Catholic School past the public school known as Crestview Elementary. It was on Ash Wednesday, the beginning of Lent, and I had a black smudge on my forehead. Earlier that day, the parish priest had taken ashes from the burned fronds of the previous year's Palm Sunday, mixed them with holy water, and made the sign of the cross on my forehead with them, saying, "Remember, son, that you are dust and to dust thou shalt return."

As I passed by their school on the way home, three boys began to make fun of me, my ashened forehead and my Catholic beliefs. Never one to back down, I returned fire. Soon the fire became fists, and I got the shorter end of that stick. I found out in our exchange that they were Lutherans. Bloodied nose, soiled white shirt and tie, and my disheveled uniform betrayed to my mom what had happened. What I did not tell her was that between Crestview and East Kelso Road, where I lived, I sat down in an alley and wept – from pain, from shame, from frustration. But in the end, God used it for good.

Later, my theology, my rubrics and my church would change. I would also discover that those boys might have been Lutheran, but they sure weren't Christian – and neither was I. Still, this persecution "from my youth" just drove deeper and deeper a life-shaping belief: God, Christ and the church were worth fighting for, even dying for; nothing is more important in life than the Kingdom of God.

The fight of faith continues; not with fists but with the Word, prayer, the sacraments and the fellowship of the believers. And the goal is no longer to beat up the Lutherans, but to win the spiritually dead to a new life in Christ.

Somewhere along the line we all must leave our safe and happy homes to engage in the fight of faith. We will either sue for peace and give up what little faith we have, or we'll fight the good fight and grow in faith and love for Jesus Christ. God's grace will be the difference. Paul's charge to Timothy remains the Pilgrim's call to arms: "Fight the good fight of the faith. Take hold of the eternal life to which you were called and about which you made the good confession in the presence of many witnesses" (1 Tim. 6:12). Prevailing perseverance – you can't reach heaven without it!

Note: Psalm 130's devotion can be found in the Penitential

Psalms in Part One: God our Refuge, Day 41, page 75. The eleventh step from Psalm 130 is *Waiting for Forgiveness*, which is not included here.

## DAY 119 THE WONDER OF A SIMPLE LIFE

### Read Psalm 131

*But I have calmed and quieted my soul.*

Psalm 131:2

To move through life on the road to the City of God, we must be unencumbered with junk. We have got to "travel lightly." A book entitled *Journeys of Simplicity* by Philip Harnden advocates just that: a simple lifestyle. Henry David Thoreau, who wrote *Walden*, a journal about his two years of hermit-like living near Walden Pond on Ralph Waldo Emerson's estate, advocated a simple lifestyle. Thoreau may well be considered the first "hippie." But, in reality, Thoreau did not practice what he preached. On a twelve-day canoe trip into the Maine woods, the list of junk Thoreau took with him filled three pages. Harnden writes, "The man who preached 'simplify, simplify' assembled 166 pounds of baggage, enough to nearly swamp the canoe when they launched it."

A simple life is not attained by living in a hut you build for $28, raising your own vegetables, catching your own fish and game, or doing odd jobs to make ends meet. Simplicity is a spiritual discipline gained, not through external methods but by a change of heart. According to Psalm 131, simplicity is achieved through humility, resting in Christ, and spiritual naiveté. And simplicity of life is a grace needed for the Pilgrim's Way; step twelve on our journey: *The Wonder of a Simple Life*.

First, humility before the Lord makes us face a certain truth (v. 1). We are not "big" enough to handle the "great matters" of God, "things too difficult" for you and me. As Moses said, "The secret things belong to the LORD our God, but the things revealed belong to us and to our children forever, that we may do all the words of this law" (Deut. 29:29). Our lives give us enough to deal with just applying God's Word to us and our families. We need not

212

worry ourselves in affairs God reserves for Himself. Ours should be a life of humble aspirations, humble involvements and humble limits.

Second, resting in Christ helps us live in contentment and calm that creates an inner environment for simplicity of soul (v. 2). Quiet composure in faith, quiet contentment in hope, and quiet rest in love cause the soul of a Christian to run quietly but deeply, like an old river that has flowed along age after age.

Third, simplicity calls for what some call "spiritual naiveté" as seen in verse 3: "O Israel, hope in the LORD from this time forth and forevermore." It's just that simple: We hope in the Lord and that gives us strength of soul. The less cluttered our lives are with "stuff," and the less busy we are, the more room there is for hope in Christ.

Americans really believe that "Busyness is next to godliness." Or so they act. But Isaiah reminds us of the message of Psalm 131 and its appeal to the simple life: "In returning and rest you shall be saved; in quietness and in trust shall be your strength" (Isa. 30:15). If we're going to make it on the Pilgrim's Way we've got to "center down" on God and travel lightly. Years ago I was in the mall during Christmas season. I sat on a bench waiting for my wife, when I saw a dog-tired mother pushing a carriage seat with a girl toddler in it. Around the stroller danced an impish little boy, who was taunting his little sister with this teasing mantra, "I've got candy! I've got candy! And you don't!" Over and over he said that, "I've got candy! And you don't!" The mother was obviously too worn out to tell him to shut up. But finally his little sister took her thumb out of her mouth and quietly said, "So what? I've got mama." The words surprised and devastated the boy. He shut up and the family walked quietly on toward home. I think little sister had read Psalm 131. All around us the world dances and taunts: "I've got a big house, I've got a nice car, I've got luxuries and much, much more! And you don't!" We have only one thing to say to them. "So what? We've got the Father and His Son Jesus. And we're on our way home; home to the City of God." And that is simply the truth.

## DAY 120 A PASSION FOR THE CHURCH

### Read Psalm 132

*Let us go to his dwelling place; let us worship at his footstool.*
                                                        Psalm 132:7

Somewhere along the line a man or woman has got to get passionate about someone or something. Men made in God's image are made for "a cause" — something larger than life, greater than self and lasting forever. Most of the passionate people we find have lost their souls in something unworthy of their lives: the workaholic consumed by his career; the woman at *Fitness Lady* who worships her own body; the mother who lives for her children to the neglect of even her husband's love; the fellow out in the woods, in a canoe or on a hiking trail fifty weekends out of the year.

For the believer who is on the Pilgrimage to the City of God there can only be one consuming passion: The church. That is the message of Psalm 132 and the thirteenth step of the Pilgrim's Way: *A Passion for the church*. The church has fallen on hard times. Fewer and fewer who confess Christ are interested in the church. Kent Hughes in his book *Disciplines of the Godly Man* gives seven reasons why the church is so neglected: lone-ranger Christians, evangelical theology that emphasizes the "invisible church," lack of commitment to relationships and service to others, a distrust and disdain for traditional institutions, rebellion against authority, and selfishness. Postmodernity does not treat the church well.

But Psalm 132 reminds us that if we don't like the church on earth very much, we won't like heaven at all. For the City of God is simply the church triumphant assembled forever. The church on the corner near your home, and the one in which you worship, is a type of heaven to come; a dress rehearsal for the life in the New Jerusalem. Psalm 132 tells us that the church is God's dwelling place (vv. 1-5), God's house of worship (vv. 6-9), God's covenant people (vv. 10-12) and God's chosen possession (vv. 13-18). All these things are true of the church on earth and the church in heaven. "But you have come to Mount Zion and to the city of the living God, the heavenly Jerusalem, and to innumerable angels in festal gathering, to the assembly of the first-born who are enrolled in heaven" (Heb. 12:22, 23). That should excite the Christian even if nothing else does. This may be the primary difference between the theistic mind of the medieval man and the humanistic mind of the postmodern man. For at the heart of life in the middle ages was the church – they called it "Christendom." At the heart of postmodern society are the individual and his recreations – bodybuilding, sports, hunting and the accumulation of stuff. We call that an empty life.

Martin Luther wrote several hymns. One of them is about the church. It is entitled "The Worthy Maid." Its meter is odd, even awkward, but its words are wonderful. Its first stanza reads like this:

> To me she's dear, the worthy maid,
> And I cannot forget her.
> Praise, honor, virtue of her are said
> Then all I love her better.
> I seek her good
> And if I should
> Right evil fare
> I do not care.
> She'll make up for it to me
> With love and truth that will not tire
> Which she will ever show me
> And do all my desire.

I sure hope someone, someday puts that hymn to music. What a beautiful song to sing as we're "Marching to Zion, beautiful, beautiful Zion, the beautiful city of God" (Isaac Watts).

Note: Psalm 133 is found on Day 50, page 90, the last devotion of Part One: God Our Refuge. It is the psalm The Presbyterian Church in America sings together at the end of each General Assembly. The fourteenth step from Psalm 133 is *The Preciousness of Church Unity*, which is not included here.

## DAY 121 LOVE FOR THE MINISTERS OF GOD

# Read Psalm 134

*Come, bless the LORD, all you servants of the LORD, who stand by night in the house of the LORD!"*

Psalm 134:1

Psalm 134 is the last of the Songs of Ascents, the fifteenth and final Pilgrim Psalm. It is my favorite of the group because of the image it paints in my mind. It speaks of the final step on the Pilgrim's Journey of Faith: *A Love for the Ministers of God.*

There is a progressive message in the Songs of Ascents, from the beginning of the journey, to the arrival in Jerusalem, to the beginning of the journey back home. These fifteen psalms break themselves down into three groups of five psalms each, reflecting the three phases of the pilgrim's journey. Psalms 120–124 speak of fear, trouble, fatigue, danger and toilsome travel on the way up to Jerusalem. The middle group, Psalms 125–129, focuses on the joy and excitement of entering the holy city: hope, victory, security, family life and renewal. The last group, Psalms 130–134, tells of the joys and duties of entering the holy Temple: confession of sin, the wonder of simple faith, a passion for the church, fellowship, and love for the servants of God.

Now the high holy days are over. Special services and sacred rituals surrounding the festivals are over. It's back to the routine of normal life. And for the pilgrims it's a journey back home, and one that will seem twice as long as the journey to the holy city. And one that may also be a bit melancholy and anticlimactic, sort of like the quietness in the family van when vacation is over and it's back to life in the grind.

But as the pilgrims leave the holy city a most wonderful sight catches their eyes. Psalm 134 describes it. There, on the towers of the wall, by the gates into the Temple, stand watch the Levites. They man the guard over the eight gates flowing out of the Temple, out of the city, and onward toward home in every direction. And in the early morning the sunrise catches the glory of these young priests: golden helmets gleaming in the sun, white

216

ephods bleached brighter by the morning light, bronze shields and spears reflecting the dawn's glorious hue. These tall, stately young Levites guard the house of the Lord and the city of Jerusalem.

As the "tourists," look back for one more look at the holy city before they head home, like vacationers always do, the sight of the City of God is overwhelming. These pilgrims have said goodbye to parents, grandparents, aunts and uncles, cousins and friends whom they won't see perhaps for another year or more. The tears in their eyes are tears of both joy and sorrow. And now as they look upon the house of God one last time, they do what is almost unintentional, and perhaps surprises even themselves. They raise their hands to say goodbye to the men who serve in the house of the Lord, day and night. And, to their thrill and joy, the Levites raise their hands in return, in order to give the blessing that sends them home in safety. A silent interchange ... a sacred moment ... a spiritual salute. It is the exchange of blessings: "I love you, Pastor. ... And I love you, too. Go in peace!"

This Sunday, when you shake hands with your pastor at the back door remember this psalm. For your pastor is to you the one who serves "by night in the house of the LORD," keeping watch over your soul and guarding the flock of God. What a blessing to have such men. Why not bless them in return? Why not tell them how much you appreciate them because they shepherd your soul homeward to the City of God? It will mean a lot to them to hear you say that. And it will make your trip home from church this Sunday a lot more joyful.

## DAY 122 THE GOD TO WHOM ALL MEN COME

### Read Psalm 65

*O you who hears prayer, to you shall all flesh come.*

Psalm 65:2

There is a mini-collection of four psalms (Pss. 65–68) each of which is called "A Song." They comprise a group of four psalms apparently used by Israel during Israel's main feasts of Passover, Pentecost, and Tabernacles. These were hymns sung by Jewish

217

pilgrims after they reached the Temple in Jerusalem. Michael Wilcock comments about them: "The next four psalms are also called songs. Though we can only guess at the precise meaning of this double title (i.e. *psalm/song*), it does at least serve to mark off 65-68 as a group. Certainly we are here breathing a different air from that of 51-64, a sequence of psalms so readily identifiable with many of the conflicts that harassed David." Psalm 65 begins this collection.

A. F. Kirkpatrick explains, "It is clear from the allusions to the gathering of the people to the Temple that it was composed for use at one of the great festivals." Most probably, that festival was the Feast of Tabernacles (Ingathering), the longest and one of the happiest festivals of Israel. The eight days of the feast were a celebration of bringing in the fall harvest. It followed but five days after Yom Kippur (the Day of Atonement); hence the beginning of Psalm 65 that references atonement and forgiveness of sins (vv. 3, 4).

This psalm primarily celebrates the goodness of God through nature, although it also celebrates God's mercy and creative power. Derek Kidner states, "Whatever event or season it first celebrated, its grateful delight in God as Redeemer, Creator and Provider makes it a rich and many-sided act of praise, not merely a psalm for a harvest festival." Thus the psalm presents God as the Gracious Redeemer (1-4), the Mighty Creator (5-8) and the Benevolent Provider (9-13).

Recently, a ruling elder at our church dragged me out of my house at 4:30 a.m. and drove me out to a dark woods. He set me, rifle in hand, on the edge of a pasture, in 35-degree temperature, to wait for the sun to come up and the deer to come out. As the sun slowly peaked up over the horizon (and as I began to thaw out in the morning sunlight), I could not help but worship God for all His wonders and beauty. The fall colors in the woods, the pink morning sky, and the sounds of creature-life awakening in the forest all reminded me how good God is to us.

As I sat there the prayers and praise began to flow: for my salvation, for my wife and four children, for their souls gripped by grace, for family and friends, for my nation, America, for the privilege of pastoring and the glories of the church, for Ohio, for Mississippi, for all the wonderful experiences I've had and the beauty of each place I have lived. And then ...

As I placed the sight upon the second of two does with two yearlings I hesitated. Such grace! Such mysterious wonder! Such a lovely creature, living, breeding and moving about by the hand of her Creator! And in this world there are numberless creatures of such rare beauty and billions upon billions of men made in God's image. And all of them – every single one – dependent upon God for life, provision and grace. David was right, "O you who hears prayer, to you shall all flesh come," and all the beasts of the field as well.

Moments later, as I stood over the fallen doe in the woods, I felt a tinge of sadness. I had taken this beautiful creature's life. And yet, I knew that there were many more like her in the wild, placed there for God's glory and our enjoyment. "The pastures of the wilderness overflow, the hills gird themselves with joy" (v. 12). Men are still in-gathering the harvest of God's good gifts, and still praising Him in prayer for such bounty.

## DAY 123 THE RIGHT KIND OF OBEDIENCE

### Read Psalm 66

*Come and see what God has done: he is awesome in His deeds toward the children of man.*

Psalm 66:5

When I wrote the first installment of these devotions in the Psalms for the PCA's Fifty Days of Prayer (now Part One: God our Refuge: Celebrating God the Father – Jehovah), we were living in the wake of a terrible terrorist attack upon the Twin Towers of New York. When the original booklet was published and these devotions were read, America and England were basking in the wake of a God-given victory in the war with Iraq. Psalm 66 is a song-psalm written to celebrate some wonderful victory given to Israel by Jehovah. H. C. Leupold comments, "Some deliverance had apparently come to the children of Israel, the magnitude of which made them feel that they alone could not offer sufficient praise to the Lord for His goodness.... Israel was not oblivious of the fact that the things that were done to her were to be made known among the peoples."

This psalm was used at Passover because it references deliverance from Egypt in verses 5-7. Yet, unlike American post-war celebrations there is no note of triumphalism; no talk of "Israel's might and right"; no politicians saying to the nations of the world, "Israel will triumph because Israel is good!" Quite the contrary.

Psalm 66 acknowledges God's gracious actions toward the sons of Abraham: the display of His power (1-4), the marvel of His deliverance (5-7), the graciousness of His discipline (8-15), the compassion of His answered prayers (16-20). The psalmist does not boast in the nation's "most favored status" with God, but testifies to a fact people and nations do not want to face: "If I had cherished iniquity in my heart, the Lord would not have listened. But truly God has listened; he has attended to the voice of my prayer" (vv. 18, 19). His syllogism is his testimony to God's forgiveness and faithfulness: God does not hear unrepentant sinner's prayers; God has heard our prayers; God is therefore gracious to us (because we have repented). These exact words are not spoken but surely implied.

In the heat and dust of 9-11, we all debated the issue: "Could the Twin Towers disaster be a judgment of God on America?" I noticed an amazing thing: Muslims, many African Americans, and others who felt disenfranchised thought that it was discipline from God. The consensus of middle class, white, suburban preachers was "these things just happen." Perhaps Psalm 66 is the answer. "For you, O God, have tested us,; you have tried us as silver is tried." If that is the case – God "purging" the American soul – then we give praise, as the psalmist did, for the difficulty, for the deliverance, and for the difference it made in our lives.

The focus, you see, is not on us and our enemies; it is on God and His enemies: "So great is your power that your enemies come cringing to you" (v. 3). God's friends will yield true obedience

to Him. Who is God's enemy? Surely the worshippers of another
god are – at least now, until the Gospel reaches them and turns
them into the friends of the true God. But so are "Christians" in
America or England who "come cringing" to Jesus every day.

When God attacks that evil of false worship, in either form of
idolatry, He causes a reaction in us. Either we give Him lip service
of some sort or another – "God bless America!" or "God Save the
Queen!" – or we repent and turn in true faith and obedience. Either
way, the call of the psalm is appropriate: "Come and see what God
has done: he is awesome in His deeds toward the children of man"
(v. 5). May the nations see in us, and in our land and people, true
obedience born out of penitent hearts and lives.

## DAY 124 THE REASON FOR OUR BLESSEDNESS

Read Psalm 67

*God shall bless us; let all the ends of the earth fear him!*

Psalm 67:7

Psalm 67 is the third psalm in the mini-collection of songs for use
at the holy festivals of ancient Israel. A. F. Kirkpatrick describes
it as, "Another bright and joyous song, evidently intended for use
in the Temple worship, perhaps, like the two last, at the Passover,
but more probably, as the harvest seems to have been gathered in,
at the Feast of Pentecost (Harvest), or Feast of Tabernacles (In-
gathering)."

It has a rich legacy in the Christian church. Although not as
popular as other psalms, as James M. Boice noted, it nevertheless
has been a part of the daily prayers of the saints for ages. Years ago
I came across a little book in a London used bookstore, by John
R. W. Stott, entitled *The Canticles and Selected Psalms*. It was one of
nine books in a little series entitled *The Prayer Book Commentaries*,
edited by Frank Colquhoun. In that book (that later was released
in a much abridged form entitled *Favorite Psalms*) Stott informs us
that Psalm 67 has made up part of the Evening Prayer service of
the Anglican Church for over 450 years.

Michael Wilcock speaks of Psalm 67's two themes – both

having to do with harvests. "All four psalms in this group touch on the theme of harvest… What the psalmist is looking forward to is something infinitely greater than that. Abundant crops are his starting point, not his goal. 'The earth has yielded its increase' (NRSV), and that is a metaphor for his other, grander, theme. In New Testament terms this is the spread of the gospel…. The gathering of the nations – now that is a harvest." Jesus Himself, in His parables and His preaching, spoke of a great harvest of souls that He sought for His Father in heaven.

For this reason many commentators call this "The Missionary Psalm." Alexander Maclaren says, "This psalm is a truly missionary psalm, in its clear anticipation of the universal spread of the knowledge of God, in its firm grasp of the thought that the Church has its blessings in order to the evangelization of the world." I see a definite connection between the beginning and the end of this psalm.

In verse one God is gracious to His church and causes "his face to shine upon us." That is, God looks with favor on us; He smiles upon His church. The Hebrew idiom, "to cause the face to shine," means simply to smile. What is it that makes God smile? It is to see His grace-gifts returned to Him in a harvest of souls because of the witness and work of the church. This again is parabolic truth from Christ: God is a master who gives His gifts to men and who expects a return on His investment.

Often we take smug pleasure in the theological strength, the ecclesiastical order and the popularity of our denominations. I am certain God is pleased with these things to a point. But what makes God's face gleam, what makes Him smile, is to see His house full and His banquet table with no empty seats. He delights in the salvation of lost souls.

Our Anglican cousins are dead on: The best way to end the workday is to sing Psalm 67, the last psalm of the Evening Prayer. We go home from work and home to bed, asking ourselves: "Is God smiling on us tonight? How many more to the harvest did we add today?"

## DAY 125 A PSALM FOR PENTECOST

# Read Psalm 68

*You ascended on high, leading a host of captives in your train and receiving gifts among men, even among the rebellious, that the LORD God may dwell there.*

Psalm 68:18

In the *Book of Common Prayer* the Church of England assigns Psalm 68 to be read on Pentecost Sunday. Michael Wilcock comments on that, saying, "This is the fourth and last of the great poems of Book II that share the heading 'song-psalm,' and deal, even if only briefly, with the theme of harvest. Psalm 68 has been used traditionally in Jewish synagogue worship at the feast of Weeks, or Pentecost. For Christians too it is a Pentecost psalm ..."

What informs us of the true intent and meaning of this psalm is the Holy Spirit's use of it in Paul's letter to the Ephesians: "But grace was given to each one of us according to the measure of Christ's gift. Therefore it says, 'When he ascended on high he led captive a host of captives, and he gave gifts to men'" (4:7-8). Then Paul goes on to speak of apostles, prophets, evangelists and pastor-teachers in the church; men with spiritual gifts for ministry. These verses in Psalm 68:18 and Ephesians 4:7-8 have in view the Ascension of Christ into heaven, the outpouring of the Spirit on Pentecost, and the spiritual gifts the Lord gives to every believer He regenerates and indwells.

For some strange reason Paul was not led by the Spirit to quote the last part of Psalm 68:18 – " even among the rebellious, that the LORD God may dwell there." And yet this is the most astounding and heart-touching part of the verse. Referencing verse 18 of Psalm 68, John Bunyan wrote, in *Grace Abounding*, "That saying would sometimes come into my mind, 'He hath received gifts for the rebellious.' The 'rebellious,' thought I! Why, surely they are such as once were under subjection to their Prince; even those who after they have sworn obedience to his government have taken up arms against Him; and this, thought I, is my very condition. I once loved Him, feared Him, served Him; but now I am a rebel; I have sold Him. I have said, 'Let Him go; if He will'; but yet He has gifts for rebels; and then, why not for me?"

Such is the wonder of grace. Not only covenant children, who grow up in the faith and never know the wanderings of a rebel, receive gifts of grace. Yea! Even the once grossly corrupted and greatly compromised are called to faith and then gifted for service for Christ. For every C. H. Spurgeon there is a John Bunyan. For every Billy Graham there is a Chuck Colson. For every Mary of Nazareth there is a Mary Magdalene. God often chooses the chief of sinners in order that in "the foremost, Jesus Christ might display his perfect patience as an example to those who were to believe in him for eternal life" (1 Tim. 1:16).

In this way God's victory (Ps. 68:1-4), God's compassion (Ps. 68:5-6), God's goodness (Ps. 68:7-10), God's spoils of victory (Ps. 68:11-14), God's gifts to men (Ps. 68:15-18), God's saving mercy (Ps. 68:19-23), God's songs of praise (Ps. 68:24-27), God's strength (Ps. 68:28-31) and God's worship (Ps. 68:32-35) might be known to both kinds of men: to the Covenant people and their consecrated children, and to the unclean and uncircumcised of heart and their sons of rebellion. God is glorified in both harvests of souls – in one for His faithfulness, in the other for His mercy. The end result is the same in both harvests of souls. The people of God sing, "Blessed be God!" (v. 35). And the people who were once not the people of God but who by grace now are, sing the same, "Blessed be God! The God of the rebels!"

## DAY 126 THE EGYPTIAN HALLEL

### Read Psalm 113

*Praise the LORD!*

Psalm 113:1, 9

The Hebrew word for "praise" is *hallel*. Hence the Hebrew word, transliterated into English "Hallelujah," means literally "Praise (*hallel*) to (*lu*) Jehovah (*Jah*)." Within the Psalter, in Book V, there is a collection of six psalms known as "The Egyptian Hallel" (the Egyptian Praises). These hymns are Psalms 113–118, and they derive their name from Psalm 114:1 ("When Israel went out from Egypt") and from the fact that they are the six psalms sung, to this day, at the Jewish Passover meal.

The first two (Pss. 113 and 114) are sung before the Passover meal. The last four (Pss. 115–118) are sung after the Passover meal. When Matthew and Mark record the Last Supper, "And when they had sung a hymn, they went out to the Mount of Olives" (Matt. 26:30; Mark 14:26), they made reference to the singing of Psalm 118, the last hymn of the Egyptian Hallel, after the fourth Passover cup had been filled.

The Anglican Church sings Psalms 113, 114 and 118 at Evensong on Easter Sunday, connecting Christian Resurrection Day with Jewish Passover Day. For this reason J. J. Stewart Perowne sees "a connecting link between the Song of Hannah and the Magnificat of the Virgin." Both women seem to borrow from this psalm, although in reality Hannah's song gives idea to Psalm 113, which gives substance to Mary's Canticle.

The psalm recounts the one thing above all other glories for which men praise God the most: God is always the Champion of the little guy. Always! This has both blessed the saints and angered the world.

The Roman Empire accused the early church of ten notorious crimes: Incest (they called each other "brethren" and loved one another), cannibalism (they ate and drank Christ's body and blood), novelty (they were not part of an official religion), sectarianism (they were selective and secretive), economic disruption (they did not work on Sundays), sedition (they would not worship Caesar), atheism (they would not worship the gods), causing natural disasters (because the gods were angry at Christians), lack of patriotism (because they were loyal to the kingdom of God, not Rome), and undermining the social order (because they welcomed slaves, the poor and foreigners into their fellowship). Even in pagan Rome, the prevalent idea was that the gods only welcomed "respectable" people. This idea still bothers some, the idea that God loves the little guy. Friedrich Nietzsche referred to God as "god of the weak, god of the stupid, god of the spider." This is the same mentality of the Pharisees who said to Jesus, "Why do you eat and drink with tax gatherers and sinners?" I ask you, "Who else would God eat and drink with?" Certainly not His "equals" for there are none. Whenever God socializes He has to condescend.

The real question is, "What kind of people need God?" Well, certainly not the "divine" Caesar, or philosophers who have all the answers, or people with dozens of gods and goddesses to choose from, or the suburbanite whose prosperity numbs the aching for God in his soul. But to the poor, the needy, the barren woman, the slave, the soldier of fortune, the prostitute and the "loser," God seems just wonderful, so lovely!

And so a people once slaves – in Egypt, in Rome, in sin – but now freed by Christ, will always love to sing The Hallel. For when Christ sets them free, they are free indeed (John 8:36). And their spontaneous, unashamed and unbridled response will always be, "Praise the LORD! Praise, O servants of the LORD, praise the name of the LORD" (113:1). And if that bothers people, if they're "embarrassed" for God, too bad. God prefers praise to pride.

## DAY 127 THE GREAT ESCAPE

Read Psalm 114

*When Israel went out from Egypt ...*

Psalm 114:1

The second psalm of the Egyptian Hallel is truly the heart of the Hallel, and from whence it derives its name. This little psalm is a masterpiece. It is a victory song of praise concerning the exodus from Egypt and God's redemptive victory over bondage – physical and spiritual – and the liberation of His people. Derek Kidner writes, "A fierce delight and pride in the great march of God gleams through every line of this little poem – a masterpiece whose flights of verbal fancy would have excluded it from any hymn book but this."

Like most of the psalms in Book V, these Hallel Psalms may well have a post-exilic date. That enables the authors of them to look back on the exodus with the clear vision of a thousand years of history and reflection. H. C. Leupold notes, "If this date for the psalm is assumed, it is quite likely that the immediate purpose of the psalm was to encourage the downhearted people in those gloomy days that followed for quite a while after the captives had come back home and were encountering nothing but difficulties and disappointments." And so the Psalter was written; to remind us that God in the past has been "good to Israel" (Ps. 73:1), and God will be good to the church, again and again.

This lovely little psalm divides itself into three "stanzas" in the New American Standard Bible. We might outline the psalm this way: Israel Freed From Egypt (1, 2); Israel Fled Through the Sea (3-6); Israel Fed in the Wilderness (7, 8). In eight poetic verses of outrageous praise, the psalmist condenses the four books of Exodus, Leviticus, Numbers and Deuteronomy!

We Christians are correct to see Christ and the church in the types of Moses and Israel. Paul himself tells us as much: "I want you to know, brothers, that our fathers were all under the cloud, and all passed through the sea, and all were baptized into Moses in the cloud and in the sea, and all ate the same spiritual food, and all drank the same spiritual drink. For they drank from the spiritual Rock that followed them, and the Rock was Christ.... Now these things happened to them as an example, and they were written down for our instruction, on whom the end of the ages has come" (1 Cor. 10:1-4, 11). Psalm 114 is, therefore, also the "Christian Hallel."

Bishop George Horne reminds us of the spiritual message of Psalm 114. "This world and the prince of this world, are to us, what Egypt and the Pharaoh were to Israel. The redemption of our nature, by the resurrection of Christ, answereth to their redemption by the hand of Moses. .. In the passage of Israel through the Red Sea, we may contemplate our passage from a death of sin to a life of righteousness, through the waters of baptism; as our translation from death temporal to life eternal is figured by their entrance into the promised land, through the river Jordan." We are still freed from bondage by Christ, flee through sin by the Spirit, and are fed with grace-gifts by God. Nothing has changed, nor will change as long as men in this world travel the wilderness of a fallen creation, led by the Redeemer Christ and chased by the Prince of this world, the Devil. The God of Jacob still delivers us in the person of the God Jesus. The preachers of this world continue to say to us, "Fear not, stand firm, and see the salvation of the LORD, which he will work for you today.... The LORD will fight for you, and you have only to be silent" (Exod. 14:13-14). What else can our response be but to tell the story of our salvation in beautiful hymns; then teach them to our children?

## DAY 128 NON NOBIS, DOMINE

Read Psalm 115

*Not to us, O LORD, not to us, but to your name give glory, for the sake of your steadfast love and your faithfulness!.*

Psalm 115:1

Years ago Kenneth Branagh produced and starred in a cinematic rendition of Shakespeare's *The Life of King Henry V*. In that movie, after the English victory over the French in the Battle of Agincourt, the soldiers break into a hauntingly beautiful melody, singing "Non nobis Domine." These are the Latin words that form the first line of Psalm 115. "Not to us, O LORD," not to men the glory, but only to God!

What few moviegoers know is that the words and melody come from the Gregorian chant of the middle age monasteries where Psalm 115 was sung regularly. John Stott comments on this psalm, "The six psalms from 113 to 118 constitute the Jewish 'Hallel' or 'Hymn of Praise'. It was sung at the major festivals, and probably by our Lord and His apostles in the upper room at the Passover-time. Its form certainly suggests liturgical use, and parts of it were no doubt sung antiphonally between priest and people or choir and congregation."

The reason for praise is straightforward: God's covenant love and loyalty (His steadfast love, or *chesed* in Hebrew) had delivered Israel from some great danger and the truth of His promises had stood firm yet again. Why should the pagan peoples around Israel doubt the reality of Jehovah? "Our God is in the heavens; he does all that he pleases" (v. 3).

For most men in the world the thought of God doing whatever He pleases is not comforting. In ancient Canaan, Egypt, Assyria and Babylon, the gods were to be appeased and preoccupied with pleasures and gifts: sexual orgies, gifts of food and drink, the sacrifice of a young virgin or even a baby. If the gods were preoccupied with sex, food and drink or blood lust, then they would have no time to meddle in men's affairs. Idle idols doing whatever they felt like doing, on the spur of the moment, was a dangerous state of affairs.

The psalmist of Israel laughs at the pagan idols (vv. 4-8) and he celebrates the real and personal goodness of His God to His people: "The LORD has remembered us; he will bless us" (v. 12). What simple and yet profound faith in a simple but profound truth. God is good. And God's goodness is reflected to His creation and His creatures in that He fulfills all their longings and fills all their needs. Theologian Louis Berkhof defines the goodness of God in just such terms: God answering in Himself the idea and ideal of the word "God," because of His perfection. In other words, when men say the word "God" and think of the Divine One, all the idols fall miserably short of the ideal they have in mind. Men want a God who is a "Spirit, infinite, eternal and unchangeable in His being, wisdom, power, holiness, justice, goodness and truth" (Westminster Shorter Catechism). And that is exactly what Israel's God is!

Therefore, it stands to reason that no other god, no other being and no other thing can, or does, deserve "glory" – the Hebrew word that means heavy with substance, significance and singular worth. Oh! How you and I seek daily to "share" God's glory; to take a lot of it for ourselves and to give a little of it to others. Surprisingly, our good and generous God is stingy about only one thing: "I am the LORD; that is My name; My glory I give to no other, nor my praise to carved idols" (Isa. 42:8). God's glory is God's, and God's alone.

And so, when we sing, "Not to us, O LORD, ... but to your

name give glory," we are not doing God any favors. We are just saying this: "Lord God, we have looked around us to see whom we might praise, give thanks to and express affection for the goodness of providence and the glory of redemption, and we have found none other to whom all this rightly belongs but You. Receive the glory, Lord; after all, it's all Yours anyway!

## DAY 129 PRECIOUS IN GOD'S SIGHT

### Read Psalm 116

*Precious in the sight of the LORD is the death of his saints.*

Psalm 116:15

As I write this devotion I have just returned from the hospital where an elderly member of my congregation found out he has a malignant tumor in his stomach the size of a softball. Tears flowed and prayers were lifted up. The fellowship of the saints is precious at such times. Whether or not this aged brother in Christ will die at this time waits to be seen, but there is preciousness about that as well. "Precious in the sight of the LORD is the death of his saints" (v. 15).

H. C. Leupold comments upon this truth, when he says, "That seems to involve at least two things. One is that He is manifestly watching over what takes place even when His saints are not rescued but seemingly perish. His saints can have assurance either way." Why this psalm is included in the Egyptian Hallel is uncertain.

Some Jewish tradition holds that Psalm 116 was composed in 516 BC when the captives returned from the Babylonian exile. Its simple message is the heart and soul of a living faith in Christ, a saving relationship with God. We love God (v. 1) for three reasons: because He answers prayer (1-4), because He can be trusted (5-11), and because He cares for us (12-19). Michael Wilcock defines a "saint" in just such terms of mutual love, "Those upon whom the Lord sets His 'covenant love' are His 'saints,' because being loved by Him, they respond in kind."

This is a tell-tale mark of a true believer: He sees every day as a day of deliverance from evil and death, by the sovereign and saving hand of the God who loves him and whom he loves in return. "We love because he first loved us" (1 John 4:19). Whether it is deliverance from Egyptian slavery or Babylonian exile, or perhaps deliverance from personal sources of evil or pain, this fact remains: We live today because God loves us every day of our lives. So whether in birth, life or death the saints of God are "precious in the sight of the LORD."

The Book of Common Prayer uses this psalm for liturgy of "The Churching of Women." This ancient service is a thanksgiving for women who survived childbirth. At first this may seem odd to pray a psalm that speaks of death (v. 15) at an occasion that celebrates the life of newborn children. But we miss the point. Even to this day, the majority of women who give birth to children do so at great peril of their own lives. The curse remains in full force: "I will surely multiply your pain in childbearing; in pain you shall bring forth children" (Gen. 3:16). But Isaac Watts is correct, "He comes to make His blessings flow far as the curse is found." So it is right for "godly ones" who give birth and survive to say, "I love the LORD, because he has heard my voice and my pleas for mercy.... Precious in the sight of the LORD is the death of his saints."

So for the young mother who lives through childbirth and for the old man who faces death by cancer, the prayer of the Anglican Church follows the spirit of Psalm 116. "O Almighty God, we give Thee humble thanks for that Thou hast been graciously pleased to preserve, through the great pain and peril of childbirth, this woman, Thy servant, who desireth now to offer her praises and thanksgivings unto Thee. Grant, we beseech Thee, most merciful Father, that she, through Thy help, may faithfully live according to Thy will in this life, and also may be partaker of everlasting glory in the life to come; through Jesus Christ our Lord. Amen."

## DAY 130 THE CENTERPIECE OF SCRIPTURE

# Read Psalm 117

*Praise the LORD, all nations! Extol him, all peoples!*

Psalm 117:1

Psalm 117 has a two-fold distinction. First, it is the shortest psalm in the Psalter and hence, the shortest chapter in the Bible. Second, Psalm 117 is the middle chapter of the Scriptures. There are as many chapters before Psalm 117 as following it. It is very close to the middle verse of the Bible: Psalm 118:8. The Authorized Version of the Bible contains 3,566,480 letters; 733,746 words; 31,163 verses and 1,189 chapters in 66 books. The centerpiece of it all is Psalm 117.

And so it should be. Psalm 117 encases in its two verses of twenty seven words the entire theme of the Scriptures. All the peoples of the earth are called to praise God and worship Him because of His steadfast love and because of His truth. God has kept His covenant of grace and been faithful to His promises of redemption. Now the peoples of the world should feel free to come to God, believe in Him, make Him their God and worship and serve Him everywhere and evermore. His steadfast love (there's the favorite word of the Psalter again: *chesed*) and His truth (*emet*, from where we get our root word for "Amen") are repeatedly the two reasons given why people should love, thank and serve God (cf. Ps. 115:1).

Martin Luther caught the significance of these two words and this small psalm, "This is a prophecy concerning Christ; that all peoples, out of all kingdoms and islands, shall know Christ in His kingdom; that is, in His Church." And so it is. The psalm promises the nations that if they believe the truth of God's Word and receive the steadfast love of God's grace, found in the Christ, they would have reason to praise God forever. Matthew Henry postulates correctly when he writes, "This psalm is short and sweet; I doubt the reason why we sing it so often as we do, is for the shortness of it; but, if we rightly understood and considered it, we should sing it oftener for the sweetness of it; especially to us sinners of the Gentiles, on whom it casts a favorable eye." This little psalm is indeed the "Great Commission Psalm!"

This centerpiece of the Bible reminds us of the heart of God, and exhorts us to the same heart for the world. James Luther Mays reminds us of this. "When Christians say and sing this psalm they remind themselves that the praise of God is complete only when they intend to praise in concert with all people.... It is a psalm for any Lord's day, but it is especially appropriate for the celebration of Worldwide Communion Sunday."

Although we conservative and Reformed types are not very ecumenical, the celebration of Worldwide Communion Sunday is not such a bad idea. Always on the first Sunday of October, this Worldwide Communion reminds us of Christ's final prayer and hope, "that they may all be one" (John 17:20-23). That is still Christ's prayer and therefore our duty: to take the steadfast love of God's true gospel and the truth of God's Scriptural promises, and to preach the gospel in such a way as will lead to the unity of the church in Christ, in grace and the word, throughout the world. And the hope of our unity and unified praise is that the peoples of the earth might say, "If their God is so full of steadfast love and truth that He has brought the people of the churches together, then I will make their God my God, and join them in their praises – everywhere and evermore! I will worship the One God together with His one people."

Note: Psalm 118, Luther's favorite psalm, may be found in Part One: God Our Refuge, Day 1, page 14.

## DAY 131 THE GREAT HALLEL

### Read Psalm 136

*For his steadfast love endures forever.*

Psalm 136:1

Psalm 136 is known as The Great Hallel (The Great Praise). Most commentators believe this psalm was used antiphonally in Temple worship, and was recited after the Passover meal along with the

Egyptian Hallel (Pss. 113–118). James M. Boice informs us, "It does not use the words 'hallelu-jah,' but it is called the Great Hallel for the way it rehearses God's goodness in regard to his people and encourages them to praise him for his merciful and steadfast love." Instead the words *hodu le Yahweh* ("give thanks to the Lord") replace the standard hallelu-jah.

We are reminded by Psalm 136 that gratitude, or thanksgiving, is the highest form of praise. Remember when Jesus healed ten lepers? Only one returned to give Him thanks. He asked that one leper, "Was no one found to return and give praise to God except this foreigner?" (Luke 17:18). To give thanks to Christ is to give glory to God. This psalm gives thanks and praise to God for His great works.

Like Psalm 135 that precedes it, this psalm praises God for His work in creation, redemption and providence. In fact, Psalm 136 is a rendition of much of Psalm 135, only written in the form of a *litany*. Bishop J. J. Stewart Perowne acknowledges this, "The first line of each verse pursues the theme of the psalm, the second line, 'For His lovingkindness endures forever,' being a kind of refrain or response, like the response, for instance, in our Litany, breaking in upon and yet sustaining the theme of the Psalm: the first would be sung by the Levites, the second by the choir as a body, or by the whole congregation together with the Levites." Presbyterians like myself historically don't use litanies very often, leaving them to the more liturgical churches, like Roman Catholic or Anglican.

This may seem awkward or even too "high church" for most folks in a denomination like mine. But there is a purpose to a litany. As in the case of the ten lepers, gratitude does not come easy for sinners. How often do we stop and thank parents, pastors or magistrates for what they do for us? So a litany allows the pastor to list the great works of God, and the people to say, in effect, "Yes! We thank You for that, too! Praise the Lord!"

Theologians speak of the "works" of God the Father in three categories: Creation, Providence and Redemption. This psalm divides itself into a three-part litany. After the introduction (1-3), the people are led to thank God for His work of creation (4-9), His work of redemptive history (10-22), and His work of providence (23-25) – a repeat of the opening verse serves as the conclusion to the whole (26).

This sacred litany, inspired by God the Spirit, is perfect for family worship and congregations on the Lord's Day. James M. Boice remarks, "A disaster such as the one that has overtaken the evangelical church in regard to its worship is not going to be cured overnight, but we ought to make a beginning, and one way to begin is by studying what the psalms teach about worship." Obviously, litanies are not "an invention of man," but rather a design for praise that comes from God Himself. Why not begin at home and at church, to use the Great Hallel more often? After all, when Jesus asks, "Was no one found to return and give praise to God except this foreigner?" our answer should be, "No, Lord, just us 'foreigners,' us Gentiles; but we will glorify You for creating us, sustaining us and redeeming us. We give thanks to You, O Christ, for Your steadfast love endures forever!"

## DAY 132 PROTECTION FROM GOD

### Read Psalm 141

*Set a guard, O LORD, over my mouth; keep watch over the door of my lips!*

Psalm 141:3

We turn to a sequence of seven psalms that may well be entitled "Psalms for Times of Trouble." They all call upon God and praise God for a deliverance from one sort of evil or another. We moderns live with a false sense of security. We are like the foolish men Peter foretells of who say, "For ever since the fathers fell asleep, all things are continuing as they were from the beginning of creation" (2 Pet. 3:4). So we say? Do we really believe that "life goes on" unthreatened by forces of evil? Have we forgotten the vulnerability of life, even in America, so soon after September 11, 2001? I fear we have. What a delusion!

But perhaps our greatest myth is that evil always comes from "out there": those Muslims, those liberals, those homosexuals, those Yankees, (or, Southerners, depending on your side of the Mason-Dixon Line). Well, true, they may all be a threat to us – even those Yankees! But the greatest threat of evil is always from within; it comes from inside us. Christ said, "For out of the heart come evil thoughts, murder, adultery, sexual immorality, theft, false witness, slander" (Matt. 15:19). As hard as that may be to believe, the fact remains, "The heart is deceitful above all things, and desperately sick; who can understand it?" (Jer. 17:9).

So David prays for protection from himself and for himself. He asks God to guard his mouth (1-4), guard his mind (5-7), and guard his steps (8-10). And he is wise to do so. For he believes that Jesus knows our spiritual anatomy well: the mind is connected to the tongue, which is connected to the feet. In other words, our thoughts form our words that give our bodies permission to act.

Jesus put it this way: "You brood of vipers! How can you speak good, when you are evil? For out of the abundance of the heart the mouth speaks.... But what comes out of the mouth proceeds from the heart, and this defiles a person" (Matt. 12:34; 15:18). So David prays for God to guard his mouth from justifying evil things; guard his head from forming bad ideas and wicked prayers; guard his eyes from losing sight of God; and guard his steps from falling into the snare of the devil.

Why does the shepherd of Israel do this? He does not trust himself apart from God's grace; and neither should we. One thing I must consistently remind myself, every morning in prayer, is that I am not a "basically good guy." Quite the contrary; I am radically a wicked fellow. I am, indeed, far worse than I ever imagined, but I know that God's grace is more wonderful than I ever dreamed! The same must be true of you.

To acknowledge and live in the light of this truth is what keeps you and me from becoming Pharisees. The root problem of those self-righteous men, who spurned gospel and grace, was their belief that they were "basically good people" unlike the "tax-gatherers and sinners" Jesus hung around with, and seemed to like. Because these men could not face the truth about themselves they could not embrace the truth about Christ. God deliver us, by His grace, from such sorrowful folly.

J. Ker tells us, "This psalm was the Evening Song of the early Christian Church. The calm floating of the fragrant cloud upward, the hands outreached to God when the day's work is done, are a contrast to the morning prayer, full of purpose and aim like an archer that fits the arrow to the bow and follows it to the mark (Ps. 5:3)." What a fitting way to end the day, praising God for the answer to the morning's prayer. For when we prayed the Lord's Prayer in the dawn, God heard us and answered. When we prayed "deliver us from evil," He did. He saved us from the greatest evil of all ... ourselves!

## DAY 133 THE PRAYER OF A LONELY MAN

## Read Psalm 142

*When my spirit faints within me, You know my way.*

Psalm 142:3

I am a person who doesn't cry a lot. In fact, I wish I wept more. I think it is spiritually healthy to cry now and then. But two of the times I wept the hardest were when I felt terribly alone. I can remember those two occasions even today, though they happened decades ago.

The first time was when I was fourteen years old, back in 1963. My family had just left me at the Divine Word Seminary in Perrysburg, Ohio, a Catholic monastery. As they drove off in the family station wagon – father, mother, three sisters and a brother – I felt this crushing, dark, and even fearful, spirit come over me. And I felt so alone. I walked off to the gym, sat down and wept.

Eight years later, in 1971, I found myself going through the whirlwind of events that process you into the United States Army. I was at Fort Sam Houston in San Antonio, Texas. I had arrived and had no lodging, no car and very little money. I was on my own until the next day. And as I walked off post in my new Second Lieutenant's uniform, it dawned on me: I was two thousand miles from home, knew no one, had nothing, and was staring the Vietnam

War in the face. As I walked to find some place to eat I said to myself, "I'm all alone. So alone." And, yep, at the age of twenty-two I walked along the sidewalk and wept. I have experienced my share of pain and spilled my share of tears in my fifty-seven years, but, I mean this, those two moments of loneliness were the worst I've ever felt.

David felt like that, quite often. The job of being king is a lonely job. Everybody likes the king. Few people love him. And, by nature of his position, the king is often alone, the odd man out. I remember reading, years ago, that President John F. Kennedy often looked out the window of the Oval Office and fought back the tears of feeling so alone. But he was never alone; neither was David, nor was I.

God is always with us – even if we are an unconverted seminarian, an unconverted lieutenant or an unconverted commander-in-chief. We are never alone in God's world. His common grace sustains and refreshes us, until His saving grace leads us to "fellowship divine." Once God deals bountifully with us and brings us to Christ, we are surrounded by the righteous in the church and full of the Spirit within (v. 7). David was "in the cave," according to the inscription of this psalm, and feeling "the strain of being hated and hunted" (Kidner), the dark night of loneliness in the soul. In the end, it was his fellowship with God and, no doubt, the fellowship of his six hundred mighty men that uplifted his soul. Thank God for the indwelling Spirit and the fellowship of the church!

As I write this devotion it dawned on me, that since being converted in 1976, I have never felt alone – not once. In fact, as a busy pastor, I now treasure moments to be off someplace where nobody knows who I am – just to be alone for a day or two! But I am mindful that I cannot last for long alone. I was made for fellowship with God, with family, with the church. And therein lies the utter horror of dying in the unconverted state, for hell is nothing more or less horrific than this: an eternity in the darkness of being alone! There, Jesus said, the gnashing of teeth and the shedding of tears never ceases. And why not? Because hell is the

---

only place in the creation where God is not. And that, my friend, is the ultimate horror: eternity alone without God! It is almost too much for the mind to take in. I can hardly imagine – I don't want to think about – being in darkness, in pain, surrounded by countless, screaming souls in utter agony, and then calling out to God, only to be reminded that God is not with me and never will be! For if in this life I wanted a life free from the fellowship of God, in hell I will have an eternity to spend without Him ... all alone! May God save us all from that lonely fate!

## DAY 134 GOD IS NOT A SCROOGE

### Read Psalm 30

*For His anger is but for a moment, and his favor is for a lifetime. Weeping may tarry for the night, but joy comes with the morning.*

Psalm 30:5

The saddest of all creatures is the crotchety old man whose inner misery makes him angry at the world, cantankerous toward all and easy to offend. I have a tendency to be crotchety. It scares me to death to think of myself as the Scrooge of wherever I live. What makes the Scrooge such a sad character is that his life is so contrary to God's.

Although made in the image of God, and living under God's grace, the Scrooge's life may be described as follows: "His anger went on for a lifetime, his favor was seen for but moments. He wept forever and knew little joy in his day." Contrast that with what David says of God, "For His anger is but for a moment, and his favor is for a lifetime. Weeping may tarry for the night, but joy comes with the morning" (v. 5).

What marvelous truth. We live with a God who is "slow to anger and abounding in steadfast love" (Pss. 103:8; 145:8). It takes a lot to tick off God. This is not a truth to toy with, nor some grace upon which to presume. But it is a great comfort. Those preachers who paint a picture of a God irritated at humanity and crotchety over the fallenness of creation put before us an idol, a false god. William S. Plummer reminds us, "Great is the mercy to us that God is slow to anger and that His anger endureth but a moment. If He delighted in punishing, who could stand before Him? While the Scriptures assure us that God's anger is short, they as clearly teach us, that His mercy endureth forever. Oh that the saints would study God's character. Wonderful love, mercy and purity shine in all. His name is the glory of the universe."

Who is this god who wants us to stone to death the homosexual, rather than lead him to the transforming mercy of God? Who is this god who would reject forever those who love Jesus but whose theology is seriously defective elsewhere? Who is this god who would tolerate our refusal to forgive others for sins He forgave long ago? I know not, but I know this is not David's God, the God of Psalm 30.

The gospel has a marvelous way of humbling a man. Look at Psalm 30:6, "As for me, I said in my prosperity, 'I shall never be moved.'" It is easy to feel smugly religious when we think we're doing well. But once we grasp the longsuffering love of God, then verse 7 follows verse 6: "By your favor [grace], O LORD, you made my mountain stand strong."

In other words, it was God's slow anger and quick grace that showed forbearance when I returned to pet sins again and again, like a dog to its vomit. It was God's lifetime of favor that forgave me of my unforgiveness of others. It was God's delight in me, in Christ, that tolerated so much that was wrong in me because of what was right in Jesus!

In these "Psalms for Times of Trouble" there is a place in Psalm 30 to celebrate the fact that God has delivered us from the worst of all evils: life under a god who is crotchety. Aren't you glad that when you invoke God in prayer and tell Him that you love Him and need His forgiveness yet again, you never hear, "Bah! Humbug!" You find only a listening ear, an understanding heart and a smiling face. And you hear only this: "Come to me, all who labor and are heavy laden" (Matt. 11:28-30).

## DAY 135 THE ROCK WHO IS OUR GOD

# Read Psalm 18

*For who is God, but the LORD? And who is a rock, except our God?*

Psalm 18:31

During this sequence of "Psalms for Times of Trouble" we have looked at the different ways God delivers us from evil. He saves us from ourselves (Ps. 141), from loneliness (Ps. 142), and from a god who is crotchety and unkind (Ps. 30). God also delivers us from evil and dangerous men. Even though our humanistic culture wants to say, "There is no such thing as a bad person," and even when the church echoes this false idea, "Men are not our enemies; the devil is," the fact remains: There are evil men in this world who will harm us, especially if we love and serve God.

This reality has become evident in the war with and capture of Saddam Hussein. Contrary to the media's spin that Saddam is just another Muslim leader who happened to be the victim of a personal vendetta by an American president, the facts tell a different story. Hussein was a despot who attempted to assassinate other world leaders, who supported terrorists and took joy in their destructive ways, who used chemical weapons on his own people, raped and tortured many Iraqis, abused women sexually, stole billions from his own people, and even murdered his own sons-in-law. The man is evil.

And this world is full of those men: drug lords, pornographers, pimps and gangsters. But they also dress up in respectable garb to do the evening news, run for elected office, teach our sons at college and entice our daughters with fashion and cosmetics. They are men whose goal in life is to design a world completely devoid of God, His Word and His church.

David faces such men, head on, in Psalm 18. And his note of praise is that God has consistently delivered him from such evil men, and will continue to do so. Psalm 18 is one of the longer psalms in the Psalter (only Pss. 119, 78 and 89 are longer, and

241

in that order). Yet, Derek Kidner writes, "For all its length, its structure is coherent and clear, and its energy unflagging."

It is one of the few psalms whose historical context is known with certainty. The entire psalm first occurs in 2 Samuel 22. It is introduced by these words, "And David spoke to the LORD the words of this song when the LORD delivered him from the hand of all his enemies, and from the hand of Saul" (2 Sam. 22:1). David sings of God's rescue, refuge, reward and rout of his enemies. The psalm is summarized in the last verse: "Great salvation he brings to his king, and shows steadfast love to his anointed, to David and his offspring forever" (v. 50).

The same can be said of Christians. God is their rock, refuge and redeemer. He delivers His saints, in age after age, from the Pharaohs, emperors, dictators and despots who seek their blood. He is faithful in His Covenant of Grace – first to Christ and then to those in Christ. So we might well apply the last verse of this psalm to Jesus and the church: "Great salvation he brings to his king, [Jesus (Ps. 2:6)] and shows steadfast love to his anointed, [(i. e. Messiah), to Christ and His brethren, the church] forever."

William Graham Scroggie calls Psalm 18 "The Hebrew *Te Deum*," a long confession of faith in God expressing its beliefs in words of praise. Over the millennia, the beleaguered and oppressed church has sung this victory song, both in times of persecution and in times of deliverance. Again and again the vicious men and vicissitudes of this life have driven the church to pray this psalm. And each time they have done so, the saints have discovered, once again, this marvelous truth: "For who is God but the LORD? And who is a rock, except our God?"

## DAY 136 THE HEART OF A GODLY KING

Read Psalm 101

*I will walk with integrity of my heart within my house.*

Psalm 101:2

Psalms are like siblings in a large family. Inevitably some girls will seem less attractive next to a more beautiful sister, and some boys will seem less intelligent next to a brilliant brother. So it is with Psalm 101. It follows one of the most popular of all psalms – and the one most sung by the church – Psalm 100. Yet, in its own right, it carries a beauty of its own which one only sees when the psalm is examined on its own.

Why have we chosen this psalm in this sequence of readings, "Psalms for Times of Trouble"? What has this psalm got to do with the deliverances God gives us? It does seem more like a personal testimony than a hymn of praise. But as we think deeply about the psalm, the message becomes clearer. David says, "I will know nothing of evil" (v. 4). He wants to make certain that he and his administration are a source of godliness, not a fountain of evil.

They say that power corrupts. I'm sure it does. But so does financial prosperity, popularity or fame, beauty, brilliance, or success in business, profession or ministry. Before long, the sinful heart ruins what was a gift of God and a good reward for godly labors. The rich become greedy. The pretty become vain. The powerful become manipulative. The athletic become sensuous. The popular become people-pleasers. And the man blessed in ministry soon serves only himself and his inflated sense of importance.

David fears all this: a gallant warrior, a handsome man, a gifted musician and poet, a ladies' man and a king with power – he fears corruption. And so he takes a stand: he will guard his integrity, purge his administration and keep his city clean of such corrupting influences. He will work hard at it; and God will bless his efforts and deliver him from evil. And what evil is it that threatens the king and us all? It is the evil of pride. For pride is the cause of Lucifer's fall, the source of Adam and Eve's sin, and the only thing that can keep a man or woman from saving grace and eternal life with Christ. Pride is a horrible monster and a very present evil, deep down inside all of us.

Pride will eventually cause us to compromise all we are and contradict all we stand for just to gain an advantage. Pride is ultimately the source of fear, for pride and fear are the opposite of faith. Integrity – what David speaks of in verse 2 – is the courage, honesty and humility to be the same person when we are alone with God as when we are in a crowd of men.

When Henry Ward Beecher was a child in school, his teacher once asked him to stand and recite. As he answered the question, the teacher suddenly grew angry and said, "Sit down!" Beecher did so, embarrassed and confused. Going through the entire class of young boys the teacher repeatedly did the same thing: to the apparent right answer, given by every boy, the teacher barked back, "Sit down!" Coming again to Beecher, the same question was asked, the same answer given and the same response came back, "Sit down!" But this time Beecher did not. He stood his ground and said, "No, Sir, I will not. My answer is the correct answer, please." The teacher then smiled and said, "And so it is, but you were the only boy sure of it enough to stand your ground and answer with courage and integrity." May God deliver us from the corruptions of pride and fear, and help us to "walk with integrity."

## DAY 137 A CONFESSION OF FAITH, A CALL TO PRAISE

### Read Psalm 135

*For I know that the LORD is great, and that our LORD is above all gods.*
Psalm 135:5

A. F. Kirkpatrick says of this psalm, almost dismissively, "Though the Psalm is a little more than a mosaic of fragments and reminiscences from the Law, Prophets, and other Psalms, it possesses real vigour of rhythm and spirit." H. C. Leupold adds, "On closer investigation it becomes apparent that the psalm quotes frequently from earlier psalms and should, therefore, be called a mosaic." But the reason the psalmist writes as he does has been explained by Alexander Maclaren: "The flowers are arranged in a new bouquet, because the poet had long delighted in their fragrance." This is not a bad thing.

Religion, by its very nature should never be novel. That, I fear, is the danger of our present age and our post-modern way of "doing church." We are, more and more, doing away with professions of faith and creeds, prayers of confession, litanies, responsive readings, the Lord's Prayer and the reading of portions of Scripture. The time once devoted to them is now filled by music and more music. "Young people love music," we are told, "and so our worship must be high-impact, high emotions, 'authentic' and relevant. Young people don't relate to sixteenth century hymns and seventh century creeds." Or do they?

I suspect that the shelf life of the jazz service will be relatively short lived. It's a baby-buster thing, like Maranatha music was with the baby boomers. And the Willow Creek model is a young dinosaur walking toward extinction already. We are seeing the beginning of a return to "traditional" worship. Young people are returning to liturgical services, and they want to recite the Apostles' Creed, pray the Lord's Prayer, and sing *Amazing Grace,* and to the old tune. Why is this so?

Trendsetters, pollsters and sociologists never factored in one key ingredient of Christianity in an age of postmodernism. When a culture abandons absolute truth, deconstructs language, walks away from the structures of family, community and church, then the soul reacts. People look for four things in their religion: transcendence, permanence, authority and tradition. They come to realize that God is ever the same, that mankind's fundamental nature and problems don't change, and that what men need most are roots in the past that give hope for the future. The last thing people want is a "trendy" God. And how we worship goes a long way in communicating Whom we worship.

Psalm 135 finds its place in the Psalter and its strength by reminding us of key redemptive events and great works of God. They are borrowed from other places: Deuteronomy, Numbers, Jeremiah, Exodus, and more than a dozen previous psalms. But that is the point of the psalm: "For I know that the LORD is great, and that our LORD is above all gods" (v. 5). And the psalmist "knows" this from what he learned as a child in Torah school, what psalms he has recited in the Temple for decades, and what truths now return to his aging mind, again and again. God is greater than our generational shifts, our fads and fashions in music, and our constant craving for something new – the sure mark of a rootless and restless soul. Tradition is not a bad word to everyone. (In fact it seems only boomers and busters hate the word.) Tradition that is biblical, and has served the church for over four millennia, has the power to ground us in God's track record in the past so that we move with hope and confidence into the future. Since God and Christ are "the same yesterday and today and forever" (Heb. 13:8) we might do well to recite our creeds, sing our old hymns, and read the "old, old stories" a bit more. We just might be surprised to find the children of the church returning home to the great and good God they knew as a child.

## DAY 138 A SONG FOR THE SABBATH DAY

## Read Psalm 92

> It is good to give thanks to the LORD, to sing praises to your name, O Most High.
>
> Psalm 92:1

We mentioned earlier that post-exilic Jews recited a special song, designated for each day of the week. From Sunday to Saturday these psalms were, in order: Psalms 24, 48, 82, 94, 81, 93 and 92. The psalm appointed for Saturday was entitled "A Psalm. A Song for the Sabbath Day." Never was a hymn written that captured the essence of true religion and balanced worship like God's Psalm for the Sabbath. Its three stanzas give us the substance and ethos of Biblical worship.

First, it calls us to the *Melody of God's Goodness*. Verses 1-4 remind us to sing and rejoice because God has made us, and then made us glad. Every good hymnal fills its first section with hymns of praise for God's creation blessings. How often we take for granted that God chooses to give us life and then to fill that life full of the joys of common grace – a family and friends, favorite foods and drink, seasons of bounty and beauty, sports and recreation, and good health with a sound mind. The first stanza of every hymn of praise should be a celebration of this truth: It is better to be than not to be; better to be alive than to be dead. How precious is each day. (Remember Ps. 90?) And how glad we are that when God said, "Let there be..." we were!

In the second stanza (vv. 5-9) we are called to the *Mystery of God's Greatness*. God's "thoughts are very deep" and that's the way it should be. After all, who wants to worship a God who can be scientifically explained, psychologically analyzed, always predicted and never surprises us? For God to be, in great measure, a mystery to us is for God to be God. In His providence God is mysterious. He does not explain Himself to us in all things, but does provide for us in everything. God's greatness is tied to His mysteriousness; something post-modern men may not like but desperately need. Our modern search for transcendence is our compulsion to find a God of mystery, and worship Him for such hidden glory. This truth fills up the middle of our hymnals with songs of trust.

Finally, verses 10-15 form the third stanza. It calls us to the *Marvel of God's Grace*. The words of these final verses speak of God's redemptive work: anointing (v. 10), triumph over sin and Satan (v. 11), sanctification (vv. 12-13), perseverance (v. 14) and eternal praise (v. 15). The wonder of His marvelous, saving work is always the third and final section of a good hymnal – the hymns of testimony and salvation. What a wonderful outline for worship: rejoicing over creation's goodness; reverence, awe and adoration for God's greatness; testimony to saving and sanctifying grace. This is a "Song for Saturday," a psalm to prepare us to use our hymnals well on Sunday and sing to God our melodies, our mysteries and our marvels; to remind ourselves that God is God and we are not. We open our worship with our lips but we close it with our lives. What we sing on Sunday sends us gladly and strongly into Monday and beyond, to be to the praise of His glory.

## DAY 139 PRAISE, MY SOUL, THE KING OF HEAVEN

## Read Psalm 103

*Bless the LORD, O my soul, and all that is within me, bless his holy name.*
Psalm 103:1

Henry Francis Lyte's superb hymn, "Praise, My Soul, the King of Heaven," is one of the most beloved and oft sung hymns of the faith. That beautiful and uplifting hymn – none better for opening a service of worship – is Lyte's free paraphrase of Psalm 103. This magnificent psalm begins our new sequence of devotions in "Seven Songs of Wonderment."

A wonderful way to enjoy the comforting truth of Psalm 103 is to see Lyte's four stanzas as summaries of the psalm's four stanzas (or parts). The psalm begins with the truth of God's blessing of each of us (vv. 1-5). "Ransomed, healed, restored, forgiven" is a marvelous way to summarize these verses. We should indeed "forget not all his benefits" (v. 2) for God indeed pardons sins, heals diseases, redeems souls, crowns with grace and satisfies with good things those who trust in Christ. But God does more than that. He is also the God of our Fathers.

The second stanza (vv. 6-14) celebrates the truth of God's "grace and favor to our fathers in distress." Time and again God has remembered the frailty, folly and failures of our fathers before us. He does not stay angry for long (v. 9). His way is more gracious; He separates us from our sins "as far as the east is from the west" (v. 12) so that we do not keep recycling through the same sorrows. He proves indeed that He is "slow to chide and swift to bless." And He is ever so because He "knows our frame; he remembers that we are but dust" (v. 14). He realizes we are human and accommodates His dealings to our state of being.

This third stanza (vv. 15-18) recognizes that God is sensitive to the difference between Creator and creature: "Frail as summer's flow'r we flourish; blows the wind and it is gone. But, while mortals rise and perish, God endures unchanging on." Here God tells us that He will bless our descendants as He has blessed each of us and our fathers. His goodness and righteousness will be seen by our "children's children" (v. 17). They, too, will be ransomed, healed, restored and forgiven – like their fathers before them.

Finally, the fourth stanza (vv. 19-22) reminds us that God blesses all of His creation: angels, saints in heaven and the church on earth. "Angels in the height, adore Him; ye behold Him face to face; saints triumphant, bow before Him; gathered in from every race." On and on, through all of life's existence, God will bless those He has made in His image – the sons of God and the sons of men. And we are called to praise Him: "Praise the everlasting King, glorious in His faithfulness; Praise the high Eternal One; Praise with us the God of grace."

There are many things about which we stand in awe and worship in wonder, but none is more awesome and wonderful than the truth that God is eternally good to us and will, ever and always, bless us. Never was there such a great God like our God. And rare is the psalm that touches Psalm 103 in the height of its praise. And seldom has there been a hymn like Henry Lyte's to lift our souls in purest praise. Why not find a hymnal, right now, and sing with the angels and saints in glory, "Praise, My Soul, the King of Heaven"?

## DAY 140 ALL CREATURES OF OUR GOD AND KING

### Read Psalm 104

*O LORD, how manifold are your works! In wisdom have you made them all; the earth is full of your creatures.*

Psalm 104:24

Last spring I sat on our back deck as the sun rose in the early morning. It was one of those pristine spring mornings that only the deep South knows. I had a cup of coffee, a rocking chair, my Bible, a hymnal and the dog – all a man needs for a quiet time! As I got ready to read I heard a scamper off to my left. Two little squirrels chased each other in childlike bliss. They tumbled onto the railing of the deck only to realize that Bowley and I were eyeing them – and probably for two different reasons! Off like a shot they were, once they were discovered.

Then I caught the eye of a cardinal, bright red and drinking from a puddle in our backyard, left by the previous night's rain. Soon there were other birds chirping, pecking, drinking and chasing one another. It seemed that all of God's creation was awakening to say, "Good morning, Lord!" And so it was.

I turned to the hymnal and sang, in my mind, the words of Francis of Assisi's medieval hymn: "All creatures of our God and King, lift up your voice and with us sing Alleluia, Alleluia!" There in the brother's hymn were burning sun, silver moon, rising morn and fading lights of evening, wind, clouds, water and men of tender heart all awakening from another night under providence to sing their creator's praise.

Psalm 104 is believed to be the inspiration for Francis's hymn. Michael Wilcock notes of this song and the others in Book IV of the Psalter, "It says something about the psalms of Book IV that they should have given rise to so many of our most enduring English Hymns." Robert Grant's famous hymn, "O Worship the King," is a loosely constructed hymn derived from Psalm 104.

This psalm celebrates the majesty and mastery of God's creative genius. Its structure is unique and a literary masterpiece. Its presentation of God's glory parallels Genesis 1. Beginning in heaven is the glorious splendor of God hovering over the primordial darkness and deep of Genesis 1:1 (vv. 1-4). But then God goes to work: He establishes the earth upon its foundations (vv. 5-9); He sends forth the waters (vv. 10-13); He grows the good food for man and beast (vv. 14-17); He sets in order the cycles of life and the abode of every creature (vv. 18-23); He covers the earth and fills the seas with living things – swarms of them (vv. 24-26); He then sustains, governs and guides them in His providence (vv. 27-30); and finally, He receives unending praise from "all creatures of our God and King" (vv. 31-35).

We evangelicals often overlook the importance of creation. As such we have not yet made our lasting, Christ-centered mark in music, art, conservation, architecture, agricultural or animal husbandry. Our singular concern for justification tends to make us neglect the glory and goodness of God's creation. Jonathan Edwards reminds us that God receives great pleasure from His creation because creation serves the chief end of all that God has made: His glory! As the squirrels played, the birds sang, the dog slept at his master's feet and as that master worshipped his maker, all creatures of our God and King did precisely what they should do – give glory to the God of all creation.

## Day 141 Remember the God of History

### Read Psalm 105

*O give thanks to the Lord; call upon his name; make known his deeds among the peoples!*

Psalm 105:1

Psalms 105 and 106 are two more "twin psalms" that belong side by side. They both tell the same story but from a different perspective. Psalm 105 is positive and focuses on remembering the God of History. Psalm 106 is more negative and focuses on remembering the sins of our fathers in history. But first, the positive side of the story.

There is a geographical progression in the psalm from Canaan to Egypt, then from Egypt to Canaan, just as in the Genesis and Exodus accounts. Psalm 105 has five stanzas: The introduction calling us to remember God's wondrous acts in the history of Israel (vv. 1-7); God's covenant with Abraham, Isaac and Jacob (vv. 8-15); God's sovereignty through Joseph (vv. 16-24); God's judgment on Pharaoh (vv. 25-36) and God's deliverance through Moses (vv. 37-45). The inclusio at the end ties the psalm together, closing the psalm by connecting it to verse one: "That they might keep his statutes and observe his laws. Praise the Lord!" (v. 45).

As I write this psalm devotion I have playing in the background Johan De Meij's Symphony No. 1 (inspired by *The Lord of the Rings*), and performed by David Warble and the London Symphony Orchestra. The composer describes the fifth and final movement entitled "Hobbits": "The fifth movement expresses the carefree and optimistic character of the Hobbits in a happy folk dance; the hymn that follows emanates the determination and noblesse of the hobbit folk. The symphony does not end on an exuberant note, but is concluded peacefully and resigned, in keeping with the symbolic mood of the chapter 'The Grey Havens' in which Frodo and Gandalf sail away in a white ship and disappear slowly beyond the horizon." This final movement is the most majestic of all and yet it is written about Hobbits! How strange. But then, as I listened to the music it dawned on me, the people of God are but Hobbits!

251

In Psalm 105 there is an old man desperate for a son; an only child who leads a simple life, sandwiched between two greater men – his father and his son; and a conniving, manipulative boy who becomes the father of a people. His son is an ex-con who rises to become prime minister of Egypt. He is followed in the history of God's covenant people by a stuttering man, exiled for murder and with forty years of shepherding as his only qualification for leading over three million people out of Egypt in a massive exodus.

These are little people made heroic in character and large in history by the Spirit of Christ who dwelt in them. And that is the nature of spiritual Hobbits: little people with Christ in them, sent on a great and dangerous errand throughout the earth; little folks given "determination and noblesse" by the Spirit of God. There, you see, is God's glory in history – that He uses such comical, little, insignificant and common creatures as Bilbo, Frodo, Sam, Merry and Pippin; and the likes of Abraham, Isaac, Jacob, Joseph and Moses.

But that is the drama of history and its glory: God is guiding and guarding His little people through time and space as He uses them on their dangerous journey. The story of man ends like the symphony does, "peacefully and resigned," as the people of God sail beyond the horizon, across the crystal sea, toward the City of God. In the end, the world will discover that it was the little people of God, led by Christ, who were the real heroes of the story called "Life."

## DAY 142 REMEMBER FOR THY NAME'S SAKE

### Read Psalm 106

*Yet he saved them for his name sake, that He might make known his mighty power."*

Psalm 106:8

Psalm 106 is the most humbling and convicting of all the psalms in the Psalter. It covers the same span of history as Psalm 105 (the exodus and the time of the judges), but from the perspective of Israel's sins against God. As noble as Psalm 105 makes the people of God look and feel, Psalm 106 does the reverse. Scroggie writes, "We have said that this Psalm and the preceding one are a pair; that one telling of how God treated Israel, and this one telling of how Israel treated God; that one revealing God's faithfulness, and this one revealing Israel's faithlessness; that one showing Divine favour, and this one showing human failure. Both Psalms are historical, and belong to the same period, presumably toward the end of the exile." This psalm details the dark side of the church in the annals of history.

The contrast between the gracious works of God and the sinful responses of His people is, candidly, embarrassing. The psalmist chronicles the ingratitude, tempting of God, insubordination, idolatry, rejection of God's word, murmuring, worldliness, infant sacrifices, rejection of discipline and spiritual declension of God's people. "Nevertheless, he looked upon their distress, when he heard their cry. For their sake he remembered his covenant" (vv. 44, 45). God's mercy and our sin; these are the two sides of history we can never forget.

Although Psalm 106 is a most embarrassing psalm, it is also a most encouraging one. It reminds us that God is gracious to His church, and delivers her from her own evil, "for his name's sake." In today's newspaper there is a photograph of Sheik Ahmed Yassin, the "spiritual leader" of the militant Muslim terrorist group known as Hamas. He sits, head covered, during prayers in a mosque in Gaza City. He has just let the Israeli government know that, despite Israeli threats on his life, the Hamas will continue to attack and kill both Israeli soldiers and citizens. I thought to myself, "If I were a Muslim I would be ashamed. Here is one of Islam's 'spiritual leaders' who does not seem to be able to discern the difference between murder and prayer. He thinks they are both acts that honor Allah!"

Then it dawned on me how often the church in the West has plundered the life of a nation by the way we mix worship and worldliness, never realizing how shameful it is to God. That is why God "for their sake ... remembered his covenant" (v. 45), and "saved them for his name's sake" (v. 8). God redeems, revives, reforms and restores His people in order to clear His own name, the name of Christ.

When God reaches down into the heart of His worldly church and brings them to repentance, renewal and the obedience of faith, He clears His name. The "Christ-ians" begin again to live holy lives for God's sake and God is no longer shamed but glorified in what they do, how they live, why they worship. We, like Israel, often pass on with embellishment the sins of our fathers. The prayer Bishop George Horne offers at the end of his commentary of Psalm 106 may well serve as a prayer for us and our Western churches. "Nevertheless, O Lord, regard their affliction, when Thou hearest their cry. Grant them repentance first, and then pardon. Remember for them Thy covenant; let them change their mind, and do Thou change Thy purpose, according to the multitude of Thy mercies. Make them also to be pitied of all those that have carried them captives. Cause them, upon their conversion, to find favour in the eyes of the nations. And do Thou, who hast so long been 'a light to lighten the Gentiles,' become once more the 'glory of Thy people Israel.'"

## DAY 143 OUR WONDERFUL WONDER-WORKING GOD
## (THE PILGRIM PSALM)

### Read Psalm 107

> Let them thank the LORD for his steadfast love, for his wondrous works to the children of men!"
>
> Psalm 107:8, 15, 21, 31

Book V of the Psalter continues the theme that closed Book IV: the "Seven Songs of Wonderment." We have seen in the current sequence of devotions the wonders of God in creation (Pss. 103 and 104), the wonders of God in the history of Israel (Pss. 105 and 106) and now a continuation of that theme: *Our Wonderful Wonder-working God*.

America's Pilgrim Fathers adopted Psalm 107 as "their" psalm. When they sailed to America and began their "errand in the wilderness," they saw Psalm 107 as a summation of all their physical sufferings and spiritual struggles. Governor William Bradford wrote of the arduous sixty-five-day journey across the North Atlantic in the fall of 1620. Of the original small band of 102 passengers, four died at sea – one as the ship put into Plymouth Bay. After their first cruel and cold winter, half of the remaining ninety-eight people died. All but a few women died, and only twelve of the original twenty-six fathers of families and four of the original dozen single men survived. And those forty-some souls were very sick and beleaguered once spring arrived in New England. When Bradford wrote in his diary he referenced this psalm in his comments: "May not and ought not the children of these fathers rightly say, 'Our fathers were Englishmen which came over this great ocean, and were ready to perish in the wilderness; but they cried unto the Lord and He heard their voice and looked on their adversity.' Let them therefore praise the Lord, because He is good, and His mercies endure forever."

Governor Bradford's words make reference to the four-fold double refrain of Psalm 107: "Then they cried to the Lord in their trouble, and he saved them out of their distress.... Let them thank the Lord for his steadfast love, for his wondrous works to the children of men!" (Ps. 107:6, 8; 13, 15; 19, 21; 28, 31). The Psalm presents four striking word pictures of calamity and divine deliverance.

First God saves them from wandering (vv. 4-9); then from imprisonment (vv. 10-16); then from sickness (vv. 17-22); and finally from dangers at sea (vv. 23-32). In each case the imagery is two-fold. These were actual situations that also point to deeper spiritual realities. In the last section of the psalm (vv. 33-43) God reverses their fortunes. Their "errand into the wilderness" becomes a City on a Hill!

It is interesting that none of the English commentators on the psalms connected Psalm 107 to the American Pilgrims. Only American preaches and pastors do so. But in his marvelous little book *The Psalms in Human Life*, Rowland E. Prothero chronicles the hundreds of ways the psalms have enriched and empowered the people of God, and spoken specifically to saints in various circumstances.

Alexander Duff became the first Presbyterian missionary sent out from the Church of Scotland. He and his wife sailed to India on October 14, 1829. On February 13, 1830 the *Lady Holland* ran aground and broke apart in Table Bay at the Cape of Good Hope, South Africa. All lives were saved but all cargo was lost! A sailor searching for food and fuel for the survivors, found awash on the beach two books, both belonging to Rev. Duff: a Bible and a Psalter. The little group took this find as a word from God assuring them of the care of divine providence. They knelt together on the beach as Alexander Duff read from Psalm 107, the last verse: "Whoever is wise, let him attend to these things; let them consider the steadfast love of the LORD." Once again, Psalm 107 had become a "Pilgrim Psalm" to weary, endangered and forlorn travelers. And so it remains for us pilgrims on the way to our home in heaven.

## DAY 144 THE COMBINATION PSALM

### Read Psalm 108

*With God we shall do valiantly; it is he who will tread down our foes.*
Psalm 108:13

Psalm 108 is a combination of two portions from other psalms: verses 1-5 are from Psalm 57:7-11; and verses 6-13 are from Psalm 60:5-12. In this short psalm are the three prayers commonly prayed by Christians.

First there is a prayer for God's salvation in verses 1-6. Then there is a prayer of confidence in God's sovereignty in verses 7-9. Finally there is a prayer for God's strength in verses 10-13. These are the common concerns of godly people: for God to redeem, for God to superintend and for God to empower His beloved and their lives.

When we look into the background of these three psalms (Pss. 57, 60 and 108), there is a distinct difference in them. Psalm 57 was written when David was under duress and fled

256

from Saul to hide in the cave of Adullam (See 1 Sam. 22:1ff.). Psalm 60 was written when David was at war with the Arameans, and the Edomites struck him as well, causing a defeat that Joab later reversed with a great victory in the Valley of Salt in Edom (See 2 Sam. 8).

Psalm 108 however is much more positive and hopeful than the first parts of Psalms 57 and 60. Only the parts of thanksgiving and praise from those two psalms are repeated in Psalm 108. Derek Kidner writes, "The new psalm starts at this more positive point in each of them, and so provides for a situation which is certainly chastening, but whose challenge is that of an inheritance not yet seized, rather than a defeat not yet avenged. For our use, the earlier psalms may well provide for times of personal or corporate peril, but the present one for times which call for new initiatives and ventures of faith." And that, I think, is the purpose of Psalm 108 in the Psalter.

When life is not going well we tend to pray these three classic prayers of the Christian. When our relatives and friends live reprobate lives, we pray for God's salvation. When difficult and dangerous situations threaten us, we pray for God's sovereignty. When we feel worn down or defeated by life, we pray for God's strength. But we usually stop praying when things are going well.

Yet we know that children can often grow up in the church, be active in campus ministries and marry a nice Christian spouse, but still not be saved. And we know that when life is going so well that we think we can manage it ourselves, we are only sowing the seeds of future problems and guaranteed troubles. And when we feel spiritually strong we may be most vulnerable to the snares of the devil. Psalm 108 reminds us that one of the wonders of life is that God is ever ready to save, superintend and strengthen His saints, even when they say, "No thanks, Lord; I think I'm doing fine. I'll call You when I need You." Here is the wonder of life: We always need the Lord to redeem us from sin, govern our lives and strengthen our souls.

C. H. Spurgeon reminds us, "The Holy Spirit is not so short of expressions that He needs to repeat Himself ... there must be some intention in the arrangement of two former Divine utterances in a new connection." And the intention of God is to remind us that we must always pray about salvation, sovereignty and strength – when we feel desperate and when we feel safe. In either case "with God we shall do valiantly." We should never forget that ... never.

## DAY 145 THE PRAISE PSALM

## Read Psalm 145

*The LORD is good to all, and his mercy is over all that he has made.*

Psalm 145:9

This psalm is unique. It is the only psalm to bear the title *Tehillim* (Praises). This psalm has a rich history. It was sung twice in the morning prayer and once in the evening prayer of ancient Israel. The Talmud said, "Whoever speaks it three times a day may be sure that he is a child of the world to come." This was also the psalm of the mid-day meal of the ancient church. St. John Chrysostom speaks of its use in the early church's communion services, especially due to verse 15. English colleges have used its verses 15 and 16 for centuries as a prayer before meals. It finds its way into the liturgy of Pentecost Sunday because it celebrates the universal and eternal kingdom of God.

A. F. Kirkpatrick writes of this psalm: "This noble doxology worthily heads the series of Psalms of praise with which the 'Book of Praises' ends. 'Thine is the kingdom, the power, and the glory, for ever and ever,' is the thought which it expands."

It is the last psalm bearing David's name, and we have no reason to doubt the authenticity of David's authorship. It is also the final acrostic in the Psalter. Walter Brueggemann states that Psalm 145 "may be regarded as a not very interesting collection of clichés." So it seems to some, but only to postmodern men.

We have become a grossly negative and frankly ugly people. We trash our heroes after their deaths. We love trash-talk television and shock-jocks on radio. If someone expresses faith, joy, optimism, patriotism, vision and values or a spirit of hope, we ridicule them. I really believe that the majority of Americans are eaten up inside by three spiritual cancers: unforgiveness, the angry root of bitterness and the self-pitying mindset of victimization. I believe the physician who recently told me that he estimates that one in five Americans is on some mood-changing, chemical-altering drug. We have become a people of the sneer, rather than a people of the smile. America is one unhappy place. And this grieves my soul for my people.

That is why I love Psalm 145. Its optimistic, grand and sweeping vision of life and its simple – almost blunt – professions of faith in God are a tonic for the American soul. Is David "naïve"; is he a type of the Pollyanna we so despise today? I think not. David writes truth from God; inspired truth from the Holy Spirit. God is speaking Psalm 145 through David.

Michael Wilcock hits the nail on the head when he observes this about Psalm 145, "It is not inexperience, but experience that enables him to write as he does. He has long since been reoriented, and has discovered on the far side of trial and suffering and mystification that in the end this is how things are. Yes, there is much evil in the world; but taking the long view, a single half verse – 'the wicked He will destroy' (20b) – is all that it will amount to in the end."

What makes Psalm 145 one of my favorite psalms is simply this: In a world full of self-focus, self-seeking and self-sufficiency, we are reminded that God is good and God gives to all. Our life of faith in God is one of receiving, trusting, resting. And such a life brings joy and causes praise. And I believe that my nation's one crying need is the joy of being alive and under the daily graces of God. Oh! What a treasure to be alive! What a blessing to belong to God! What a reason to praise heaven: to call upon God and be saved! (v. 19).

## DAY 146 PRAISE THE LORD!

### Read Psalm 146

*Praise the LORD! Praise the LORD, O my soul!*

Psalm 146:1

Psalm 146 begins the last collection of psalms in the Psalter, the final block of psalms in our prayers for the church. We will have read, prayed through and reflected upon all 150 psalms in the Psalter. We have divided them into three parts: God Our Refuge, God Our Redeemer, and God Our Rejoicing. And what more fitting way to end our journey through the Psalter than the "Psalms of Pure Praise."

Psalms 146–150 all begin with the Hebrew words *Hallelu Jah*. "Praise to the LORD!" Derek Kidner writes, "Five joyous psalms of praise, each of them beginning and ending with Hallelujah, bring the Psalter to a close. So in this respect as in many others, the Psalms are a miniature of our story as a whole, which will end in unbroken blessing and delight." The Levites who arranged the Psalter placed the psalms in a deliberate manner.

William Graham Scroggie writes, "As we look forward from this Psalm we must allow ourselves a sigh of relief. So many Psalms in this Song Book have been sad, have been the expression of doubt or disappointment, have been darkened by the wicked, have been cries of distress, have been calls for judgment, that to find at last a group of Psalms so full of sunshine, so overflowing with joy, so trustful and hopeful, so restful and confident, is like moving into a new world." And so it is. As Spurgeon puts it, "The rest of the journey lies through the delectable mountains." So there follows a pentad of praise – pure, unadulterated celebration of the goodness of the Good God. Perhaps five make up the group because there are five books in the Psalter – one for each book.

One thing that holds literary evidence is that these five psalms were doxologies for each of the five books of the Pentateuch: Psalm 146 for Genesis, Psalm 147 for Exodus, Psalm 148 for Leviticus, Psalm 149 for Numbers and Psalm 150 for Deuteronomy. Words and phrases connect these psalms to those books, so that the Law (*Torah*) is always ended in praise (*Tehillah*).

And this is how it should be. Life should have a happy ending, and so it does in God's world. The cities of men give way to the City of God; death dies and eternal life begins; and "He will wipe away every tear from their eyes, and death shall be no more, neither shall there be mourning nor crying nor pain anymore, for the former things have passed away. And he who was seated on the throne said, 'Behold, I am making all things new'" (Rev. 21:4, 5). And that is as it should be.

Years ago my second son-in-law was dating my second daughter. One weekend they came from Mississippi State University with a video for us to watch. It was entitled *Arlington Road*. It was a frustrating and frightful tale of terrorists who move into a community, posing as model citizens and neighbors, only to use others to blow up federal buildings. The hero of the story discovers the plot and seeks to save Washington, D.C. from a terrorist strike. In the end, he is duped and used inadvertently to blow up a federal building. He dies. His wife is killed. The terrorists move off to another plot, this time with his son whom they've adopted and made one of their terrorist group. The movie had such an abysmal ending, that I almost broke the engagement of my daughter to that young man!

Life is not that way. In God's world, all ends well as it should. And the people of God really do "live happily ever after." So now, in this life, they begin their rehearsal of praise, because forever and ever they will be glorifying God for the happy ending to life – "The LORD will reign forever, your God, O Zion, to all generations. Praise the LORD!" (v. 10).

## DAY 147 PRAISE IS BECOMING

### Read Psalm 147

> *Praise the LORD! For it is good to sing praises to our God; for it is pleasant, and a song of praise is fitting.*
>
> Psalm 147:1

Psalm 147 is the longest in a group of "Psalms of Pure Praise" (Pss. 146–150) that are characteristically quite short. The Septuagint divides Psalm 147 into two psalms (vv. 1-11 are Ps. 146 and vv. 12-20 are Ps. 147). Its opening line makes a rather understated point that should not be passed over by readers: "praise ... is pleasant, and ... praise is fitting" (v. 1). This line is also translated "for it is good and praise is delightful" (NRSV).

James Luther Mays explains the first verse in this way: "The Lord is so much the content of praise that praise begins to reflect his attributes. In it his goodness is apparent. Through it the singers experience pleasure over the delightfulness of the Lord. The psalm can be read as a verbal portrait of that delightfulness." In a culture, like ours, that is becoming increasingly vulgar, mean-spirited and impious, the idea of praise bringing pleasure and delight to men is important. This propensity to praise God and show forth a delight in Him is called "piety."

Years ago, back in 1988 while I was at the General Assembly of my denomination in Knoxville, I was riding down an escalator after lunch on the way back to the general sessions. My friend, Rev. Jim Barnes, and I were chit-chatting when all of a sudden Jim said – rather out of context to our discussion – "You know what the PCA is lacking, Ross? ... Piety." I've never forgotten that statement, and Jim was (and is) right!

Here is a psalm that calls us to honor and praise God for being, as Mays puts it, "God of Cosmos, Congregation and City." For that is how the psalmist divides the three parts (stanzas) of this hymn of praise. First, we should praise God for His restoration of the congregation of Israel after the Babylonian captivity (vv. 1-6). God is forever it seems, reviving, reforming and restoring His church. Second, we should sing to the Lord because He orders the cosmos (vv. 7-11). And in that world of heavens and clouds, rain and grasses, beast and birds, there are men who "fear him" and "hope in his steadfast love." These are the people of His covenant; this is the church in whom He takes pleasure (v. 10). Finally, we are to praise God because He prospers the City of Zion, a type of the City of God, the worldwide church (vv. 12-20). Through that city in which are many congregations throughout God's cosmos, the Lord sends forth His word on a great mission to bring other peoples into this church.

What ties the congregation, city and cosmos together is the praise of God. Timothy Dudley Smith has captured that idea in his modern hymn-rendition of Psalm 147: "Fill Your Hearts with Joy and Gladness." The hymn puts forth what the psalm communicates as a central idea: The piety of God's people – their humble honoring of God in praise – is what will draw the nations into the church of

Christ. What an infectious force of goodness and light in a crude, rude and repulsive culture! Although piety may sound a little "pietistic," let not the reader be mistaken. Piety is what the New Testament calls "godliness" (the Greek word *eusebeia*). And piety is simply that religious devotion to God that leads to worship. Piety is the antidote to an impious society. It tells the world around us, "Come with us to church and learn to praise God. It is a pleasant thing to do. It brings great delight – both to God and to us. Come; join us in devotion to Christ. It will be good for you and me." And, you know … it will!

## DAY 148 THE ETERNAL DECREE

### Read Psalm 148

*He gave a decree, and it shall not pass away. … for the people of Israel who are near to him.*

Psalm 148:6, 14

As I write these final few devotions, our state of Mississippi has just inaugurated a new governor. The newspapers have been filled the last few weeks with information about new appointments to office, removal of old party faithfuls and last minute pardons of criminals by the outgoing governor. Now there follows news of orders and decrees being repealed by the new governor. I have read recently that George W. Bush spent the first week in office repealing last minute executive orders that Bill Clinton issued, concerning issues he could not get through Congress by regular means. The world of politics is a huge seesaw; a law passed one day, repealed the next.

But this is not the case with God. Psalm 148 celebrates the eternal decree of God: "He gave a decree, and it shall not pass away" (v. 6). That idea sits at the center of this psalm, and on either side of it are repeated calls for "all creatures of our God and King" to praise the Lord for His decree.

One of the several hymns written around the words, ideas and theme of Psalm 148 is the anonymous hymn, "Praise the Lord! Ye Heavens, Adore Him." In that hymn the poet celebrates this truth: "Laws which never shall be broken for their guidance He hath made." Then the writer explains what those laws are: "Praise the Lord! For He is glorious; never shall His promise fail; God hath made His saints victorious; sin and death shall not prevail." What a marvelous truth to celebrate in praise!

The Westminster Shorter Catechism gives us the classic definition of this eternal decree: "The decrees of God are, his eternal purpose, according to the counsel of his will, whereby, for His own glory, he hath foreordained whatsoever comes to pass" (WSC #7). That wonderful truth becomes the basis for a summons to universal praise. The summons touches the three "regions" of creation: the heavens (vv. 1-6), the earth (vv. 7-12), and Israel, the church (vv. 13, 14).

In the apocryphal literature, the "Song of the Three Holy Children," Shadrach, Meshach and Abed-nego, is sung while they are preserved in the fiery furnace. In reality, this non-inspired, non-canonical hymn known as the Benedicite is modeled after Psalm 148. John Stott comments: "Indeed, there is no doubt that the Benedicite is a poetical elaboration of Psalm 148, which has the same three divisions.... So we may say that, although the Benedicite is quite apocryphal in the setting it has been given, it is thoroughly biblical in its thought and language." For that reason the Anglicans include this Benedicite as an optional canticle in their Morning Prayer. (John Milton put Psalm 148 in the mouth of Adam and Eve, as a morning prayer, before the fall.) Psalm 148 is indeed a wonderful way to begin the day.

Life would be a terrible and frightening adventure in which to step out each morning, were it not for the decree of God. But knowing that "He gave a decree, and it shall not pass away" gives us not only the courage to face each day, but it even lets us leave for work, school or the church office, every day, with a song in our hearts and praise on our lips.

So in the morning why not join Shadrach, Meshach and Abed-nego, Adam and Eve, the psalmist, the Anglicans, the angels in heaven, the creatures on earth, and the saints in the church in praising God for His eternal decree? After all, by God's decree, we are "a people ... who are near to him." So, praise the Lord!

## DAY 149 THE VICTORY SONG

## Read Psalm 149

*This is honor for all his godly ones. Praise the LORD!"*

Psalm 149:9

I find it interesting that the first two psalms recorded in the Bible are found in Exodus 15. They are the Song of Moses, "God is a Warrior" (Exod. 15:1-18) and the Song of Miriam, "The Horse and the Rider" (Exod. 15:21). Now we come upon the last two psalms of the Psalter, both again warrior psalms; psalms of victory for God the Warrior King.

Songs and warfare have a long history together. Soldiers used to sing songs as they marched to battle and as they marched home. Four of America's favorite march-songs are their military's songs: *"The Halls of Montezuma"* (marines), *"Anchors Away!"* (navy), *"Off We Go into the Wild Blue Yonder!"* (air force) and *"As the Caissons Go Rolling Along"* (the army). As I listen to them played and sung they give me goose bumps. James Montgomery Boice comments on this phenomenon of "Songs and Soldiers": "Someone has pointed out the possibility of tracing the changing mood of our century by remembering that the soldiers of the First World War sang as they marched into battle. The singing soldier was a heroic figure. The GI of the Second World War was not a heroic figure but a wisecracking joker. He had nicknames for his officers and poked fun at them. By the time the Vietnam War came around, the typical fighting man neither sang nor joked. He took drugs instead."

The late Dr. Boice, good and godly man that he was, was never a soldier. I was. And I served in the Army during the Vietnam era. Dr. Boice was wrong on one count. The GIs of the 60s and 70s did sing and joke. But their songs were crude and immoral, and their jokes weren't funny but cynical. Nevertheless, Dr. Boice's point is well taken. What caused such a shift in soldiers and singing?

It has to do with pride. My grandfathers in World War I (army and navy) had a gentleman's view of women, a pious view of church and a patriotic view of nation. Therefore their love songs, hymns and marches were full of concepts of love, devotion and duty. They were honorable songs for honorable men in honorable times. My dad's generation was sassy. Zoot suits, jitterbugs and smart-aleck one-liners from B-grade movies took the edge off the reality of the Depression, Nazism and a world at war yet again. Those were fearful times. By the time I came around with 28 million other baby boomers the threat of communism, nuclear holocaust and the assassination of presidents and civil leaders left us all cynical, especially about a war in Indochina that would not end and could not be won. Those were frustrating times.

The watering down of the pulpit, the loss of moral vision and authority of Christendom and the rising tide of worldliness in the church left us without victory songs. People focused purely on self have no heart to sing about love of wife, duty to country and devotion to God. Their ballads about women are rock songs about sex. Their odes to a nation are folk songs of protest. And their hymns to God are mantras about self.

That's why Psalm 149 is so important. It reminds us that God is at war for us, that God has never lost a battle with the devil, that God is conquering the world for Christ and that God's victory is certain. There is no doubt about the final outcome. When the psalmist writes, "This is honor for all his godly ones" it makes reference to the pride the soldiers of Christ have in their Captain and King. They march through life, Bibles "at arms" by their side … and they sing! They sing of love for family, of duty to the church and of devotion to Jesus. And they are proud to do so!

## DAY 150 THE FESTIVAL PSALM

### Read Psalm 150

*Let everything that has breath praise the LORD!*

Psalm 150:6

Bishop J. J. Stewart Perowne describes Psalm 150 as "The great closing Hallelujah, or Doxology of the Psalter, in which every kind of musical instrument is to bear its part as well as the voice of man, in which not one nation only, but 'everything that hath breath' is invited to join." Just as each book of the Psalter had its own doxology (see 41:13; 72:18-20; 89:52; 106:48), so Book V ends with a doxology; only it is the entire psalm that serves as a doxology for the entire Psalter. Derek Kidner is correct, "Its brevity is stimulating." In its brief six verses, its thirteen calls to praise bring the entire Psalter to a magnificent close and a fitting climax. It finishes, as well as summarizes, the one hundred forty-nine psalms before it. Michael Wilcock astutely observes, "This psalm with which the Psalter ends is as brief and as deceptively simple as the one with which it began."

Psalm 150 answers Psalm 1. The good will prosper, the wicked will be destroyed, and God will be glorified in both outcomes. Everything will work out just fine, just as your mother used to tell you it would. In the end God will make everything all right. Psalm 150 celebrates that truth with unabashed exuberance.

This psalm does not call people to worship God in the Temple. H. C. Leupold is right, "We feel strongly that the sanctuary referred to in v. 1 is the heavenly one. The phrase 'in His sanctuary' does not modify the noun 'God' but the verb 'praise.'" In other words, in the heavens as well as on earth God is to be praised. The "mighty heavens" is the "sanctuary" in reference.

Ancient Israel did not use orchestration, as included in this Psalter, in Sabbath or festival worship, in either Temple or synagogue. Nor did they dance during Levitical services (v. 4). What is in view here is some cosmic and future festival celebration: a parade with angels and men praising, dancing, playing and singing in concert to the Victory of God. David danced before the ark when he brought it into the holy city, leading a great parade of worshipers: "And David and all the house of Israel were making merry before the LORD, with songs and lyres and harps and tambourines and castanets and cymbals.... And David danced before the LORD with all his might. And David was wearing a linen ephod" (2 Sam. 6:5, 14).

In the Book of Revelation Jesus appears as a glorified priest garbed in a glowing white ephod (Rev. 1:13). That same ephod is worn by all the saints, resurrected and glorified (Rev. 7:9). They form a great parade and a mighty chorus, carrying palm branches and singing along with the angels the praises of God (Rev. 7:9-17). Is this a picture of Jesus "dancing" before the people of God as He marches His army home, in victory, to the New Jerusalem? Are you embarrassed by such an "undignified" picture of Jesus? Well, Michal was embarrassed for David; but God was not.

Where I went to school the great tradition that begins each football game is the entrance down the ramp, by the largest all-brass band in the world. Each Saturday in the fall the Buckeye Band struts onto the field as 105,000 fans clap, sing, yes, and dance along with them. We don't feel foolish at all in doing so. Quite the contrary, we're so proud of the Buckeyes that we can't imagine how visitors can cross their arms, lock their jaws and not celebrate with us! And leading them out onto the field is a young man, dressed in the uniform of a drum major. He struts, he prances, he dances before the multitude. We call him "the Pride of the Buckeyes."

In Psalm 150, after all the sorrows and struggles of life, Jesus leads His people home to heaven, with great fanfare. Alexander Maclaren has it right: "This noble close of the Psalter rings out one clear note of praise, as the end of all the many moods and experiences recorded in its wonderful sighs and songs. Tears, groans, wailing for sin, meditations on the dark depths of Providence, fainting faith and foiled aspirations, all lead up to this. The psalm is more than an artistic close of the Psalter; it is a prophecy of the last result of the devout life, and, in its unclouded sunniness, as well as in its universality, it proclaims the certain end of the weary years for the individual and for the world."

The warfare is over. The Victory of God has come. And now "the Pride of the Nations" leads His people home ... home to the City of God. And what celebration awaits us there! God our rejoicing!

*Rejoice, the Lord is King!*
*Your Lord and King adore;*
*Mortals, give thanks and sing,*
*And triumph evermore:*
*Lift up your heart, lift up your voice;*
*Rejoice, again I say, rejoice.*
    Charles Wesley

## Toward a Recovery of Genuine Biblical Piety:
## A Commendation of the Psalms

Having now come to the end of a season of devotional exercises, aided by Pastor Ross's rich meditations in God our Refuge, God our Redeemer, and God our Rejoicing, perhaps a little more reflection is in order. Having worked these truths down into our own hearts, and having prayed them up to God, how might we encourage the appropriation of these blessed truths about God among His flock?

What can we do to foster a grasp of the distinctive doctrine, experience and practice of biblical Christianity today? Surely, the starting point is in the recovery of the knowledge of the God of the Bible, a knowledge that was not lost on the Reformers. Healthy Christian spirituality cannot flourish without the true knowledge of God. Biblical piety is inextricably related to biblical theology and especially what theologians call "theology proper" – what the Bible teaches about God Himself, or, to put it correctly, what God reveals about Himself in His inspired Word, the Bible. False doctrine cannot lead to fellowship with the living God. And without fellowship with the living God, true doctrine cannot be maintained. Real godliness, anchored in the truth of who God is, keeps us from following after the imaginations of our heart in our thinking about God.

So how do we foster the true knowledge of God in relation to Christian experience? Well, at least a part of the answer, I would propose, is found in the theology of the Psalms. Today's church has lost the Psalms. We rarely sing them (the choruses and praise songs of today only feature snippets dislocated from their rich

269

contexts, and many churches in which psalms used to be sung sing them no more). We are confounded by their robust and realistic spirituality. We are uncomfortable with their sharp denunciations and imprecations. Our theology is effeminate by comparison. But we need to recover the Psalms. The early church (and indeed the church in almost all ages) saw the Psalms as not only the church's main hymnbook but also as the definitive, inspired guide to Christian experience. The great Thomas Scott once said: "There is nothing in true religion – doctrinal, experimental, and practical – but will present itself to our attention whilst we meditate upon the Psalms. The Christian's use of them in the closet, and the minister's in the pulpit, will generally increase with the growing experience of the power of true religion in their own hearts."

The recovery of the Psalms for the Church today can help in at least three ways. First, the God of the Psalms is pronouncedly politically incorrect, but He is also a God worth living and dying for. Second, the spiritual experience or piety of the Psalms is far superior to the silliness and superstition that often characterizes modern evangelical spirituality. Indeed the piety of the Psalter is paradigmatic of the very best of Christian experience. Third, the New Testament writers and early Christians saw the Psalms as essentially about Christ. They explicitly asserted that the Psalms revealed His person and work, His divinity and ministry, His incarnation and resurrection, His humiliation and glorification. That being so, to become acquainted with the Psalms is to become acquainted with the Christ of the Psalms. My friend and fellow servant of the Word, Mike Ross, has helpfully drawn our attention to these things in *God Our Rejoicing*, and in its sister volumes in *God Our Refuge* and *God Our Redeemer*.

## The God of the Psalms is a God worth living and dying for

The God of the Psalms is incomparably great, and thus worth knowing, glorifying and enjoying. "Postmoderns" (so our contemporaries like to designate themselves, whether they are or not) care far more about their opinions about God and their own spiritual experiences than they do the testimony of religious authorities. They disdain the didactic and prefer the poetic. They distrust propositions but warm to story. How do we get to them? Where can we take them to hear what God says about Himself and what His messengers have said about their own spiritual experience of Him? What better place for this could there be than to take a person to the Psalms, which are simultaneously a revelation of God by God, and an inspired expression of human experience of God? The Psalms approach the objective from the subjective. They confirm propositional truth, in the heat of trial and experience, in the language of song and of tears. They affirm a sovereign God amidst the vicissitudes of life.

People today need desperately to become reacquainted with the God of the Scriptures, and a particularly suitable gateway to this reacquaintance in our time is the Psalter. J. I. Packer is surely right when he says that the greatest need of this generation is a recovery of a sense of the greatness of God. Well, the Psalms are all about the greatness of God and we need to learn of God through them.

The Psalms can help us break the spell of defining God by the standards and expectations of our age, as we listen to him define Himself as He speaks to us through the inspired songs of the people of God. Here we meet a God who is His people's greatest desire, whose plans and purposes are bigger than all the problems of life. Here we meet a God who is His people's priority – not a means to an end, nor an instrument for accomplishing their own purposes, nor a tool for achieving their goals, but a God whose favor and fellowship are dearer to them than life itself and of greater significance to them than the sum total of everything else. This was a key to the spirituality of the Reformers, and the Psalms can help us reintroduce it to the church today.

## The spiritual experience of the Psalms is paradigmatic of the very best of Christian piety

We, in our own day, have a rootless, imbalanced and superficial spirituality. Look all around and the piety reflected in the church is shallow – it penetrates no deeper than the surface. Some expect Christians to go through life with no struggle, no pain, no weakness, no difficulty, and no sense of absolute tragedy – and are utterly dismayed when they meet it. Some preach health and wealth – and counter the trials of life with positive thinking and denial. Some think that God exists for their personal benefit – and so want the world and use God to get it (instead of, as the wise old Puritans used to say: "loving the Lord and using the world). Some give us a scaled-down God who is supposedly more empathetic with the intractable problems of our lives than is the transcendent God of historic Christian belief, but who is also less capable of doing anything about them.

What is the way out of such a morass? Read the Psalms (and sing them too!). Read the anguish of the Psalmist's heart and there you will find the resources for spirituality deeper than the surface, a piety that equals the exigencies of our experience. The Psalmist deals with the realities of life and he pours his soul out to the living God, his complaints, his heartaches, his emptiness–all of these things he pours out to God. And yet alongside these, he acknowledges a God who is incomparably great, whose plans and purposes are far above our agendas and understandings, but who also loves us with an everlasting covenant love.

Thus, we see in the Psalms, conjoined, a perfect biblical balance of objective and subjective in spiritual experience. Here, God and His word are clearly dominant in the believer's experience without any diminution whatsoever of the wounds and quandaries and questions of life in a fallen world. Until we recover that kind of godliness, we are ignoring all the wealth of the riches of spirituality deposited in the Psalms. The Reformers not only thought we ought to sing the Psalms, they thought the Psalms ought to be at the very core of a well-rounded Christian experience. Given the present neglect of the Psalms, it is not too much to say that until we recover them, we will be experientially imbalanced and malnourished.

# The Psalms are about Christ and we meet Christ everywhere in the Psalms

Psalm quotations are ubiquitous in the New Testament, and not surprisingly, most of those quotations are applied to Jesus, because the New Testament writers and early Christians saw the Psalms as essentially about Christ. This is partly because early Christians in the apostolic and post-apostolic eras saw the Old Testament as an essentially Christian book and partly because they believed that the Psalms were uniquely Christological amongst the inscripturated revelation of the old covenant era. They believed that there was more of Christ in the Psalter than just that which is found in what we call the "Messianic Psalms." Jonathan Edwards catches their spirit perfectly when he says: "The main subjects of these songs were the glorious things of the Gospel, as is evident by the interpretation that is often put upon them, and the use that is made of them, in the New Testament. For, there is no one book of the Old Testament that is so often quoted in the New as the Book of Psalms. Here Christ is spoken of in multitudes of songs."

This is precisely the kind of assertion that liberal Old Testament scholars love to parody as a gross interpretive abuse of the Psalter. They argue that authorial intent as well as contextual relevance are savaged by such a "Christianized" reading of the Psalms. Jesus can be read into the Psalter, they say, but He wasn't there in the first place. Christians may "apply" portions of the Psalter to Christ, but the original meaning and references of the Psalms are to be found elsewhere. In contrast, the earliest Christians viewed the New Testament Scriptures as the definitive inspired hermeneutical manual for the Old Testament, and they saw the Psalms as fundamentally Christological. That this is no exaggeration can be easily shown by a review of the New Testament's Christological deployment of the lion's share of Psalm quotations.

## A Call to the Psalms

So now that you have benefited from Pastor Ross's faithful exposition of just these sorts of themes, export the revolution!

Share this truth with your family and friends. Introduce them to the God of the Psalms, through the Psalms.

J. Ligon Duncan III
Senior Minister, First Presbyterian Church, Jackson, Mississippi

## BIBLIOGRAPHY

Adams, James E. *War Psalms of the Prince of Peace: Lessons from the Imprecatory Psalms.* Phillipsburg, NJ: Presbyterian and Reformed Publishing, 1991.

Alexander, Joseph A. *Commentary on Psalms.* Grand Rapids: Kregal, 1991.

Allen, Leslie C. *Psalms 101-150.* Word Biblical Commentary, vol. 21. Waco, Texas: Word Books, 1983.

Augustine, Aurelius. *Expositions on the Book of Psalms.* A Select Library of the Nicene and Post-Nicene Fathers of the Christian Church, vol. 8. Edited by Philip Schaff. Grand Rapids: Eerdmans, 1989.

Bellinger, W. H., Jr. *Psalms: Reading and Studying the Book of Praises.* Peabody, MA: Hendriksen, 1990.

Boice, James Montgomery. *An Expositional Commentary on Psalms*, 3 volumes. Grand Rapids: Baker Books; 1994, 1996, 1998.

Bonhoeffer, Dietrich. *Prayerbook of the Bible.* Dietrich Bonhoeffer Works, vol. 5. Minneapolis: Fortress Press, 1996.

Brown, John. *The Psalms of David in Metre.* Edmonton, AB, Canada: Still Waters Revival Books, 1844 (reprint).

Calvin, John. *Commentary Upon the Book of Psalms.* Calvin's Commentaries, volumes 4-6. Grand Rapids: Baker Book House, 1989.

Clarke, Adam. *Commentary on the Psalms.* Clarke's Commentaries: vol. 3, Job-Song of Solomon. New York: Abingdon-Cokesbury Press, n.d.

Craigie, Peter C. *Psalms 1-50.* Word Biblical Commentary, vol. 19. Waco, Texas: Word Books, 1983.

Dahood, Mitchell. *Psalms.* The Anchor Bible, 3 volumes: 16, 17 and 17a. Garden City, NY: Doubleday; 1965, 1968, 1970.

Dickson, David. *A Commentary on the Psalms.* 2 volumes in one. Edinburgh: Banner of Truth; 1653-1655; 1959.

Exell, Joseph S. *The Psalms.* 5 volumes. The Biblical Illustrator. Grand Rapids: Baker Book House, 1954.

Henry, Matthew. *The Book of Psalms.* Matthew Henry's Commentary on the Whole Bible, vol. 3. Peabody, MA: Hendricksen, 1991.

Holladay, William L. *The Psalms through Three Thousand Years: Prayerbook of a Cloud of Witnesses.* Minneapolis: Fortress Press, 1996.

Horne, George. *A Commentary on the Book of Psalms.* Audubon, NJ: Old Paths Publications; 1771, 1997.

Kidner, Derek. *Psalms 1-72: An Introduction and Commentary on Books I and II of the Psalms.* Tyndale Old Testament Commentaries, vol. 14a. Downers Grove, IL: Inter-Varsity Press, 1973.

------*Psalms 73-150: A Commentary on Books III-V of the Psalms.* Tyndale Old Testament Commentaries, vol. 14b. Downers Grove, IL: Inter-Varsity Press, 1973.

Kirkpatrick, A. F. *The Book of Psalms.* Scripture Truth, n.d.

Kraus, Hans-Joachim. *Psalms*. A Continental Commentary, 2 volumes. Translated by Hilton C. Oswald. Minneapolis: Fortress Press. 1993.

Law, Henry. *Daily Praise and Prayer: The Book of Psalms Arranged for Private and Family Use*, 2 volumes. Edinburgh: Banner of Truth; 1878, 2000.

Leupold, H. C. *Exposition of the Psalms*. Grand Rapids: Baker Book House, 1969.

Lewis, C. S. *Reflections on the Psalms*. San Diego: Harcourt; 1956, 1986.

Lloyd-Jones, D. Martyn. *Spiritual Depression: Its Causes and Its Cure*. Grand Rapids: Eerdmans, 1965.

Longman, Tremper, III. *How to Read the Psalms*. Downers Grove, IL: Inter-Varsity Press, 1988.

Luther, Martin. *First Lectures on the Psalms*. Luther's Works, volumes 10-11. Edited by Jaroslav Pelikan. St. Louis: Concordia, 1975.

------*Selected Psalms*. Luther's Works, volumes 12-14. Edited by Jaroslav Pelikan. St. Louis: Concordia, 1955.

Mays, James Luther. *Psalms*. Interpretation Commentaries. Louisville: John Knox Press, 1994.

Maclaren, Alexander. *Expositions of Holy Scripture*, vol. 3: The Psalms and Isaiah 1-48. Grand Rapids: Eerdmans, 1952.

------*The Life of David as Reflected in His Psalms*. Grand Rapids: Baker Book House, 1955.

------*The Psalms* in 3 volumes. The Expositor's Bible. Edited by Robertson Nicoll. London: Hodder and Stoughton, 1901.

Perowne, J. J. Stewart. *The Book of Psalms: A New Translation with Introduction and Notes, Explanatory and Critical*, 2 volumes. Grand Rapids: Zondervan; 1878, 1966.

Plummer, William S. *Psalms: A Critical and Expository Commentary with Doctrine and Practical Remarks*. Edinburgh: Banner of Truth; 1867, 1975.

Prevost, Jean-Pierre. *A Short Dictionary of the Psalms*. Collegeville, MN: Liturgical Press, 1997.

Prothero, Rowland E. *The Psalms in Human Life*. London: Thomas Nelson and Sons, 1903.

Scroggie, W. Graham. *The Psalms*. London: Pickering and Inglis, 1948.

Seybold, Klaus. *Introducing the Psalms*. Edinburgh: T and T Clark, LTD, 1990.

Simeon, Charles. *Psalms*. Expository Outlines on the Whole Bible, volumes 5-6. Grand Rapids: Baker Book House; 1847, 1988.

Spurgeon, Charles Haddon. *The Treasury of David*, 3 volumes. McLean, VA: MacDonald Publishing, n.d.

Stott, John R. W. *The Canticles and Selected Psalms*. The Prayer Book Commentaries. London: Hodden and Stoughton, 1966.

Tate, Marvin E. *Psalms 51-100*. Word Biblical Commentary, vol. 20. Waco, Texas: Word Books, 1990.

Terrein, Samuel. *The Psalms and Their Meaning for Today: Their Original Purpose, Contents, Religious Truth, Poetic Beauty and Significance*. Indianapolis: the Bobbs-Merrill Co., 1952.

Weiser, Arthur. *The Psalms: A Commentary*. The Old Testament Library. Philadelphia: Westminster Press, 1962.

Westermann, Claus. *The Living Psalms*. Grand Rapids: William P. Eerdmans, 1984.

Wilcock, Michael. *The Message of the Psalms*. The Bible Speaks Today, 2 volumes. Edited by J. Alec Motyer. Downers Grove, IL: Inter-Varsity Press, 2001.

## INDEX

| Psalm | Part | Day | Psalm | Part | Day |
|-------|------|-----|-------|------|-----|
| 59 | Redeemer | 67 | 93 | Refuge | 9 |
| 60 | Refuge | 43 | 94 | Redeemer | 85 |
| 61 | Redeemer | 84 | 95 | Refuge | 10 |
| 62 | Redeemer | 98 | 96 | Refuge | 11 |
| 63 | Redeemer | 72 | 97 | Refuge | 12 |
| 64 | Redeemer | 38 | 98 | Refuge | 13 |
| 65 | Rejoicing | 122 | 99 | Refuge | 14 |
| 66 | Rejoicing | 123 | 100 | Rejoicing | 103 |
| 67 | Rejoicing | 124 | 101 | Rejoicing | 136 |
| 68 | Rejoicing | 125 | 102 | Refuge | 40 |
| 69 | Redeemer | 95 | 103 | Rejoicing | 139 |
| 70 | Redeemer | 86 | 104 | Rejoicing | 140 |
| 71 | Refuge | 44 | 105 | Rejoicing | 141 |
| 72 | Refuge | 33 | 106 | Rejoicing | 142 |
| 73 | Redeemer | 73 | 107 | Rejoicing | 143 |
| 74 | Redeemer | 81 | 108 | Rejoicing | 144 |
| 75 | Redeemer | 99 | 109 | Refuge | 20 |
| 76 | Refuge | 4 | 110 | Refuge | 34 |
| 77 | Redeemer | 75 | 111 | Rejoicing | 107 |
| 78 | Redeemer | 76 | 112 | Refuge | 27 |
| 79 | Refuge | 17 | 113 | Rejoicing | 126 |
| 80 | Refuge | 45 | 114 | Rejoicing | 127 |
| 81 | Redeemer | 100 | 115 | Rejoicing | 128 |
| 82 | Refuge | 18 | 116 | Rejoicing | 129 |
| 83 | Refuge | 19 | 117 | Rejoicing | 130 |
| 84 | Refuge | 5 | 118 | Refuge | 1 |
| 85 | Refuge | 46 | 119 | Rejoicing | 108,109 |
| 86 | Redeemer | 37 | 120 | Rejoicing | 111 |
| 87 | Refuge | 6 | 121 | Rejoicing | 112 |
| 88 | Redeemer | 77 | 122 | Refuge | 7 |
| 89 | Rejoicing | 102 | 123 | Rejoicing | 113 |
| 90 | Refuge | 26 | 124 | Rejoicing | 114 |
| 91 | Redeemer | 74 | 125 | Rejoicing | 115 |
| 92 | Rejoicing | 138 | 126 | Refuge | 48 |

| **Psalm** | **Part** | **Day** | **Psalm** | **Part** | **Day** |
|-----------|----------|---------|-----------|----------|---------|
| 127 | Rejoicing | 116 | 139 | Refuge | 28 |
| 128 | Rejoicing | 117 | 140 | Refuge | 21 |
| 129 | Rejoicing | 118 | 141 | Rejoicing | 132 |
| 130 | Refuge | 41 | 142 | Rejoicing | 133 |
| 131 | Rejoicing | 119 | 143 | Refuge | 42 |
| 132 | Rejoicing | 120 | 144 | Refuge | 35 |
| 133 | Refuge | 50 | 145 | Rejoicing | 145 |
| 134 | Rejoicing | 121 | 146 | Rejoicing | 146 |
| 135 | Rejoicing | 137 | 147 | Rejoicing | 147 |
| 136 | Rejoicing | 131 | 148 | Rejoicing | 148 |
| 137 | Refuge | 47 | 149 | Rejoicing | 149 |
| 138 | Refuge | 49 | 150 | Rejoicing | 150 |

# DETAILED TABLE OF CONTENTS

## PART TWO: GOD OUR REDEEMER
### Celebrating God the Son: Jesus

## PSALMS FOR THE DAYS OF THE WEEK

The Second Temple Levites, who arranged the Psalter as we now have it, ministered to Israel after the return from the Babylonian exile in 539 BC. They selected seven Psalms to be prayed and sung on a weekly basis: one Psalm for each day of the week.

The Greek version of the Old Testament, known as the *Septuagint*, and the rabbinical writings compiled in the *Mishnah* and the *Talmud* indicate what the seven "Songs of the Day" were.

Sunday: Psalm 24
Monday: Psalm 48
Tuesday: Psalm 82
Wednesday: Psalm 94
Thursday: Psalm 81
Friday: Psalm 93
Saturday: Psalm 92, The Song for the Sabbath

## THROUGH THE PSALMS IN 30 DAYS

The Anglican Church, in forming its *Book of Common Prayer*, devised a way for church members to read through the Psalms in 30 days (one month). Rather than read five Psalms per day – not practical with the length of some of the longer Psalms – the Prayer book divided the Psalter into thirty equal portions. This reading plan, using the old *Coverdale Bible* originally used at this time of the English Reformation, is still published by the Church of England and made available in all her cathedrals and churches. The monthly reading plan includes both Psalms to the *Morning Prayer* and Psalms for the *Evening Prayer*.

| Day | Morning Prayer (Psalm) | Evening Prayer (Psalm) |
|---|---|---|
| 1 | 1–5 | 6–8 |
| 2 | 9–11 | 12–14 |
| 3 | 15–17 | 18 |
| 4 | 19–21 | 22–23 |
| 5 | 24–26 | 27–29 |
| 6 | 30–31 | 32–34 |
| 7 | 35–36 | 37 |
| 8 | 38–40 | 41–43 |
| 9 | 44–46 | 47–49 |
| 10 | 50–52 | 53–55 |
| 11 | 56–58 | 59–61 |
| 12 | 62–64 | 65–67 |
| 13 | 68 | 69–70 |
| 14 | 71–72 | 73–74 |
| 15 | 75–77 | 78 |
| 16 | 79–81 | 82–85 |
| 17 | 86–88 | 89 |
| 18 | 90–92 | 93–94 |
| 19 | 95–97 | 98–101 |
| 20 | 102–103 | 104 |
| 21 | 105 | 106 |
| 22 | 107 | 108–109 |
| 23 | 110–113 | 114–115 |
| 24 | 116–118 | 119:1-32 |
| 25 | 119:33-72 | 119:73-104 |
| 26 | 119:105-144 | 119:145-176 |
| 27 | 120–125 | 126–131 |
| 28 | 132–135 | 136–138 |
| 29 | 139–140 | 141–143 |
| 30 | 144–146 | 147–150 |

## Christian Focus Publications
### publishes books for all ages

Our mission statement –

### *STAYING FAITHFUL*

In dependence upon God we seek to help make His infallible Word, the Bible, relevant. Our aim is to ensure that the Lord Jesus Christ is presented as the only hope to obtain forgiveness of sin, live a useful life and look forward to heaven with Him.

### *REACHING OUT*

Christ's last command requires us to reach out to our world with His gospel. We seek to help fulfill that by publishing books that point people towards Jesus and help them develop a Christ-like maturity. We aim to equip all levels of readers for life, work, ministry and mission.

Books in our adult range are published in three imprints.

*Christian Focus* contains popular works including biographies, commentaries, basic doctrine and Christian living. Our children's books are also published in this imprint.

*Mentor* focuses on books written at a level suitable for Bible College and seminary students, pastors, and other serious readers. The imprint includes commentaries, doctrinal studies, examination of current issues and church history.

*Christian Heritage* contains classic writings from the past.

Christian Focus Publications, Ltd
Geanies House, Fearn, Ross-shire,
IV20 1TW, Scotland, United Kingdom
info@christianfocus.com

For details of our titles visit us on our website
www.christianfocus.com